The Better Angels of Our Nature

The Better Angels of Our Nature

Freemasonry in the American Civil War

MICHAEL A. HALLERAN

THE UNIVERSITY OF ALABAMA PRESS
Tuscaloosa

The University of Alabama Press
Tuscaloosa, Alabama 35487-0380
All rights reserved
Manufactured in the United States of America

Typeface: Perpetua

∞

The paper on which this book is printed meets the minimum requirements of American
National Standard for Information Sciences-Permanence of Paper for Printed Library
Materials, ANSI Z39.48-1984.

Library of Congress Cataloging-in-Publication Data

Halleran, Michael A. (Michael Anthony), 1963–
The better angels of our nature : freemasonry in the American Civil War /
Michael A. Halleran.
p.   cm.
Includes bibliographical references and index.
ISBN 978-0-8173-1695-2 (cloth : alk. paper) 1. Freemasonry—United States—
History—19th century. 2. Freemasons—United States—History—19th century.
3. United States—History—Civil War, 1861–1865. I. Title.
HS529.H357 2010
973.7'1—dc22

2009026108

Optimus Parentibus

Contents

Preface   ix

Acknowledgments   xiii

Introduction   1

Prologue   8

1. Masters and Fellows   31

2. *Plures Ex Uno*   49

3. "If That Is Masonry I Will Take Some of It Myself"   61

4. Saving the Life of the Enemy   78

5. Gentlemen of the White Apron   98

6. A More Decent Interment   128

7. All Passions Laid Aside?: Freemasonry in the Army   140

Afterword   159

Notes   167

Glossary of Masonic Terms   193

Bibliography   203

Index   223

Photographs follow page   122

Preface

The Better Angels of Our Nature: Freemasonry in the American Civil War is a myopic view of the American Civil War. No battles are dissected here, nor are grand strategies explained; rather, this study examines the intersection of Freemasonry and warfare. I have striven, to the extent possible, to rely primarily upon two types of original sources: narrations by individual soldiers and civilians, nearly all of whom witnessed the events firsthand, and Masonic and other fraternal books and circulars that were in print during the nineteenth century.

In most cases I have reproduced the statements and assertions of the witnesses verbatim, without altering the text or correcting grammar, spelling, punctuation, or usage. Fraternal sources have been accorded the same respect, generally being reproduced in full to illustrate a particular point, with any abbreviations or omissions noted by the use of ellipses. In some cases, for the sake of clarity, I have included editorial corrections (of proper names or identifications of regimental affiliation, fraternal titles, place names or dates), indicated by the use of brackets, but my object has been to interfere with the quoted passages as little as possible. The decision to reproduce original source material has resulted in some quoted passages that are lengthy; my intent has not been to overwhelm the reader with tedious inclusions, rather to present the material unfiltered, allowing the original author the opportunity of addressing the reader in a more intimate fashion.

It should be noted that upon joining, Freemasons take an oath to never reveal the secrets of the Order, and I may fairly comment upon this fact, for I am a Freemason. This oath, which has been in place since at least the seventeenth century and probably much longer, is the subject of considerable popular fascination that is outside the scope of our subject, but which complicates the role of the historian. Soldiers and civilians who witnessed the events and who were members of the fraternity do not report any details that would violate this oath. Thus period accounts will refer, for example, to a soldier giving "the Masonic distress signal," but will omit stating what exactly that signal is. Critics may find that a Masonic author, such as myself, cannot objectively write an academic history about the fraternity. Perhaps this is so, but that argument can be countered by the assertion that *only a Mason* can write a history of this nature where the allusions to Masonry are couched in terms that only a member of the fraternity can recognize. An example illustrates this: while conducting research at a university library for this book, I was privileged to examine the personal papers of an officer who served in the Union Navy. Among the many boxes of material was a small leatherette memorandum book, about the size of a pack of playing cards, described in the catalog as a military codebook. Upon examination, I found that it was not a military cipher. Rather it was a Masonic aide-mémoire—encoded simply by using the first letter of each word for Masonic ritual. When I read some of the more innocuous words to the research librarian, the astonishment was palpable. None of the library staff were Masons, had they been, the contents of the memorandum book would have easily been discovered.

While there exists certain advantages in my Masonic experiences, there are also corresponding disadvantages. I have omitted descriptions of Masonic ritual that conflict with my fraternal obligation, not because they are too important to reveal, but simply because I took an oath and I intend to keep it. The purpose of this monograph is not to be an exposé of fraternal secrets. Discussion of ritualistic events that occurred during the war and the inclusion of ritualistic information from various fraternal exposés here are done to provide the reader with some perspective on Masonry itself. This perspective necessarily includes commentary on fraternal ceremonies, and where Masonic ritual can be explained by references to other fraternal orders' customs and traditions, I have included them to illustrate the concepts. Fortunately for the non-Mason, Masonic secrets, far from being impenetrable, are widely available to the general public in any of a number of books and on the Internet for anyone willing to take the time or trouble to seek them out. And while the secret history of the Freemasons has been a subject of endless, and sometimes breathless, fascination by the popular press since the 1700s (and more recently by television and Hollywood) these secrets are largely irrelevant to this story. The object of this study is a simple one: to illustrate how the fraternal bonds of Freemasonry influenced men in the midst of America's greatest calamity, and in that context, whether or not the secret handshake is given with two fingers or three is entirely unimportant.

Acknowledgments

No book is entirely the product of an author, and without the contributions of many learned and generous people, this narrative would have not have been possible. For assistance in various archives, I am particularly beholden to Candy Johnson and the superlative staff at the William Allen White Library at Emporia State University; they were ever ready to accommodate any request for documents with alacrity. Also deserving of special thanks is Glenys Waldeman of the Masonic Library and Museum of Pennsylvania for assisting me with the details of Pennsylvania Masons as they related to the Battle of Gettysburg, and to Connie Connor and the Ohio Historical Society for timely and gracious help. Bruce Mercer, assistant librarian, Grand Lodge of Texas, Marie Barnett, librarian, Grand Lodge of Virginia, and Alicia Darr of the Grand Lodge of Wisconsin, also provided me with substantial assistance, and demonstrated extraordinary skill in locating old fraternal records.

I would also like to thank historian and author Wayne E. Motts of Gettysburg, Pennsylvania, for his patience in answering many elementary questions. I am also obliged to to David L. Canaday of the Orient of Georgia, for his meticulous scholarship on the Masonic affiliation of Gen. John B. Gordon and for his good and timely counsel on matters of Masonic research. Dawn Hall has also aided me greatly with her insight and valuable editing, and a simple thank you seems somehow insufficient.

Closer to home, I am very grateful to the Grand Lodge of Kansas, and in particular Robert Pfuetze and Joesphe Stiles, for the unfettered access they afforded me to the Grand Lodge library. They and Don Anderson, Kim Crofoot, Dave Hendricks, Blaine Warkentine, and the brethren of Emporia Lodge No. 12 in Emporia, Kansas, and Mt. Zion Lodge No. 266 in Topeka, Kansas, provided me with substantial encouragement and support for which I remain profoundly grateful. I also wish to express my thanks to the very talented Patrick Craddock of Hiram Lodge No. 7, Franklin, Tennessee, for assistance with period regalia. In addition, I would be remiss were I to neglect to acknowledge the generous aid and assistance I received from two other notable Masons: Doug King of the Valley of Toledo, Ohio, who provided invaluable insight into Civil War customs and practices, as well as timely inspiration as tour guide to Johnson's Island, Ohio, and to the formidable Masonic scholar S. Brent Morris, for his sharp-eyed critiques, ready availability and unstinting advice and encouragement. Gentlemen: thank you.

I must also reserve special mention and heartfelt thanks to Michelle Rothenberger Combs of Syracuse University Libraries, my friend of nearly thirty years, who provided me with editorial advice throughout every stage of this project. Without her insight, keen eye for clarity, and her deep understanding of the beauty of English, this narrative would be a ragged, tattered thing.

Finally, let me thank my wife Mary, for her forbearance as well as her organizational and mathematical legerdemain, and my children Maura and Thomas, who, despite having little interest in minié balls or Masonic minutes sustained me with complete affection and unlimited patience.

Despite the contributions from all of these excellent friends, family and fellows, any errors that appear in the work that follows are mine alone.

—Michael A. Halleran

The Better Angels of Our Nature

Introduction

At dawn on New Year's Day 1863, Confederate Gen. John B. Magruder attacked federal forces occupying Galveston, Texas. It was a combined-arms assault using infantry and artillery coordinated with Confederate Navy "cotton-clad" gunboats—riverboats, fitted with guns and using bulwarks of cotton bales to protect their upper works and crews. After a sharp fight, the rebel forces overwhelmed Union troops stationed at the city wharf as well as five U.S. Navy ships in Galveston Bay.

Among the Union ships engaged that day was the USS *Harriet Lane*,[1] commanded by Capt. Jonathan Mayhew Wainwright II. During the action, *Harriet Lane* was boarded by the Confederate ship *Bayou City* and Wainwright was killed.[2] The following day, the Masonic Lodge in Galveston, Harmony Lodge No. 6, convened "a Lodge of Emergency," and in response to intelligence from some of the Union prisoners indicating that Wainwright was a member of the fraternity, the lodge buried him—a Union sailor and occupier—with full military and Masonic honors. Commenting in the minutes of the lodge, the master of Harmony No. 6 observed, "It does not conflict with [our] duties as patriotic citizens to respond to the calls of mercy by a prostrate political foe, or to administer the last rite of the Order to the remains of a Mason of moral worth, although yesterday they met as an armed enemy in mortal combat."[3]

Although not the first "Masonic incident" of the American Civil War, the funeral of Captain Wainwright is widely known in Masonic circles and is a fitting introduction to the subtle but pervasive influence of the Masonic fraternity during the war. Chivalry in wartime is of course nothing new. The ancient Greeks proscribed neglect of the dead, whether friends or enemies. Theseus is said to have magnanimously buried the slain Argives at Thebes; even the bitter Achilles was reportedly moved by pity to turn over Hector's body to his family for proper burial.[4] In later ages, the concept of chivalry developed and expanded to include a sense of fair play on the battlefield, an attitude reflected in the romance writing of Medieval Europe. French hero Roland was renowned for his chivalric bearing, the Arthurian legend is replete with examples, and even lesser-known tales like the English story of Sir Ferumbras (who had his helmet laced and tightened by his opponent Oliver before the two knights set about one another) embellished and preserved the tradition of decency in warfare.[5] Masonic forbearance, however, did not originate from chivalric tradition but stemmed from a fraternal obligation to look after one's own.

Examples of Masonic mercy are certainly not confined to the American Civil War. The American Revolution, the Napoleonic Wars, even the Franco-Prussian War of 1870–71 all contain similar accounts of Masons meeting in battle. But because American Masons—split apart by the secession of the Southern states—were members of the same culture and shared essentially the same antebellum heritage, chance encounters between antagonists who happened to be Masons were more likely in the American Civil War than in a conflict with a foreign adversary. Indeed, fraternal societies in general, and Masonry in particular, were pervasive in nineteenth-century American society, far more so than today, and the Masonic fraternity in prewar America carried with it the cachet of mystical secret society, the benevolence of the Kiwanis or the United Way, and the conviviality of a supper club all rolled into one. At the close of the nineteenth century one estimate suggests that one in five American men belonged to some fraternal organization, including Freemasonry, Odd Fellows, or an assortment of lesser-known organizations, which had the effect of making the war not only brother against brother, but Brother against Brother.[6]

Unfortunately, exact figures of Masonic membership during the war years 1861–65 do not exist. Although the governing bodies of the fraternity required (and still require) annual returns from each lodge detailing membership information, not all lodge returns, or indeed all lodges, survived the war. Many lodges in the Confederate states were destroyed and their records lost; lodges elsewhere disbanded as their entire membership went off to fight. Some information, however, has survived and lodge returns prior to 1861 are more or less complete. From these, we are able to gain a representative picture, which though approximate, provides us with information on membership that would be relatively accurate at the beginning of the war. In Georgia, for example, there were 261 Masonic lodges in existence in 1861, and 13,100 members, all of whom were free white males. The 1860 Census lists the total population of free white males in Georgia between the ages of eighteen and forty-five as 111,005. In 1860, a man was required to be twenty-one in order to join the Masonic lodge, and clearly there were members of the fraternity older than forty-five years, but extrapolating from the census figure yields an approximation of roughly 8.5 percent of free white men that were eligible for Masonic membership in that state.[7] As we shall discover in chapter 2, national Masonic membership as a percentage of the armies of North and South was closer to 4 percent. At the Battle of Gettysburg (July 1–3, 1863) nearly 93,000 Union troops faced roughly 70,000 Confederates. If 4 percent of those men were Masons, then in raw numbers more than 6,500 Masons were present in a small area of the Pennsylvania countryside during those three days—a significant number, and certainly far larger than the most optimistic attendance estimates for a Masonic conference.

It was inevitable that these Masons would interact with each other in one manner or another. And they did. In the chapters that follow, we shall see that on the most basic level, Masons sought out one another's company within their army units. They tented together, ate together, and socialized with one another while in camp or on the march. During periods of inactivity, many soldier-Masons formed lodges within their army units and met formally, initiating new members along the way. On some occasions, these men fraternized across the lines with Masons in the enemy army, and even crossed over to attend lodges in enemy territory. We will also examine evidence that proves that Masons also actively provided aid and assistance to other fraternity members, in many cases regardless of nationality. Such aid took various forms: funerary honors, both ad hoc and formal; fraternal courtesies toward members of the Craft and their property; and the rendering of aid to injured or endangered brother Masons in distress.

This crossing of the lines is a phenomenon that bears closer scrutiny, and we shall see that that in many instances, Masons were entirely willing to ignore the belligerent status of their enemies, regarding them merely as men. And this is curious. It is not unheard of, of course; mercy has been a component of warfare since its development, and although there is much that recommends the practice of it, all too often it is a quality in short supply. However, in the chapters that follow, we are presented with a systemic agent of mercy—Freemasonry—which, while it was an institution, issued no orders to its members to practice mercy. In fact, we will discover that the governing bodies of Freemasonry, while initially aghast at the prospect of a fratricidal war, later retreated along sectional lines in the character of passive observers. As we shall see, individual Masons acted rather differently.

Among all the expressions of Masonry in 1861–65 those who suspended hostilities to aid an injured Brother are perhaps the most sensational. This book does not attempt to analyze the motivations behind individual acts of Masonic kindness. No psychological theories are contained within, and no sociological motives are explored. The lens of the social sciences is absent here, in part because this is a history and not a series of cases studies, but also because the actions of these men were understood at the time as having but one motivation: the adherence to the tenets of a fraternity that preaches friendship, morality, and brotherly love.

Many of the men whose statements are contained within express gratitude to the Masonic order for enhancing the quality of their lives, and some of those who extended kindness to their enemies may have done so in repayment of that debt. Others seem to reach out in friendship to enemy Masons for the simple reason that they believed them to be fraternity brothers, as the lodge had taught them. A cynic might ascribe other motivations to the men, selfishness for instance, or a desire for praise, or honors. But these suspicions are non sequitur in the context of military service, where providing aid to the enemy is actively discouraged if not prohibited outright. Thus, although impure or selfish motives can never be discounted among men, Masons who extended charity to the enemy stood to gain little.

Hitherto, little serious scholarship has been undertaken on this subject. Within the fraternity, however, tales of Masonic compassion between Yankee and Reb have circulated for years, growing well worn in the telling. Many accounts, passed from lodge to lodge in newsletters and magazine articles, contain little more than hearsay, and previous book-length treatments of this subject have been decidedly nonscholarly. The most recent attempt, *House Undivided: The Story of Freemasonry and the Civil War* (The Ovid Bell Press, Fulton, Missouri, 1961) was written by Allen E. Roberts. Written by a Mason for Masons, the book recounts various Masonic stories about the war, but it contains so few annotations and references that it is of little use to the scholar. There is a paucity of critical analysis in Roberts's work, as well, and the reader is left with merely a recitation of interesting incidents, some of which are doubtless factual, but many others that require further investigation. *House Undivided* was reprinted in a second edition in 1990 by Macoy Publishing and Masonic Supply Co., in Richmond, Virginia, but the methodology remained the same.

Prior to that, the only monograph on this subject (beyond Masonic articles and circulars) was Jacob Jewell's *Heroic Deeds of Noble Master Masons During the Civil War From 1861 to 1865 in The U.S.A.,* privately published by that author in 1916. Jewell's effort was more modest; he simply solicited Masonic stories from veterans by advertising in newspapers and periodicals, collected the letters he received, and published them. Although quite valuable as primary source material, Jewell's role is one of curator, not academic, and nothing in the way of analysis or critical evaluation is offered in his book. Neither Jewell nor Roberts, it seems, put forth their books as scholarly treatments of the subject, and it is equally apparent that these books were not intended to be subject to peer review.

This treatment is an effort to provide a more evidentiary approach to documenting the intersections—and there are many—of warfare and Masonry during the American Civil War. Wherever possible, primary sources and firsthand accounts have been used, vanquishing the hearsay endemic to Masonic studies of the subject. In cases where names were not given, military records have been consulted in an attempt to prove or disprove the existence of the men in question and to provide the background and detail that previous treatments have omitted. Further, Masonic membership records have also been used to ascertain fraternal affiliation in an effort to prove a Masonic tie and to provide a scholarly context to what otherwise would be merely a fraternal tale. These records were also used to track down men who were not yet Masons: it was not uncommon for the participants to write of their intentions to join the Masonic order after witnessing an event with Masonic overtones. Grand Lodge returns have been reviewed to determine, to the extent possible, if these men actually did affiliate after the war.

Finally, this study has examined Masonic myths with a critical eye. Incidents that can be shown to be spurious, or to be factually inaccurate, have been identified and examined in detail throughout the text. The myths surrounding the death of Confederate Gen. Lewis A. Armistead at the Battle of Gettysburg—perhaps the most famous Masonic incident of the war—is examined separately in the prologue.

The analysis of Masonry in the Civil War requires that the reader know something about the fraternity itself, but this is problematic. As a secret society, the doors of Freemasonry are closed to all but members, and public inspection of the institution is neither encouraged nor allowed. This examination provides the backdrop to chapter 1, which offers a primer of general information, to acquaint the lay reader with the organization, structure, and terminology of Freemasonry that is apropos to this study. With the fraternity in proper context, we may then examine its role in the war

from the macro- to the microscale. Chapter 2 explores the big picture—
the role of the Grand Lodges and their reaction in 1860 to the looming
crisis on a national level. But as Freemasonry in America is not organized
along national lines, our focus must shift to the local level and to the actions of individual Masons. It is on this level that the practical effects of
the Masonic "code of conduct" is explored fully in chapters 3–6, which
detail how Masons responded to pleas for assistance made from civilians,
the wounded, and enemy combatants on the battlefield and in the prison
camps. Chapter 7 investigates the role and function of military lodges, and
the prevalence of the fraternity in camp and details African American Masonry in the context of military lodges.

For Freemasons in particular, of course, Masonry in the Civil War is a
subject of considerable interest. For the non-Mason, this collection illustrates an aspect of the war that has received little scholarly attention beyond the odd footnote or passing mention, which is regrettable. After
all, if a member of the Kiwanis club, to take a modern example, were
to suddenly stop fighting in Iraq, display his membership card, and utter
a "secret word," and be thereby conveyed safely from danger by his former enemy, it would assuredly make headlines, were it not deemed utterly preposterous. And yet, in 1861, on battlefield North and South, it
was not preposterous—such incidents happened not once but hundreds
of times. Masons make no claim that their fraternity altered the course of
the war or helped end the great debate over slavery and state's rights. But
they can claim, and rightfully so as this study demonstrates, that the fraternity in many small ways helped to ameliorate the suffering and misery
in America's Civil War.

Prologue
"The Widow's Son"—
Lewis Armistead at Gettysburg

The circumstances surrounding the death of Brig. Gen. Lewis A. Armistead at Gettysburg are the most famous Masonic "incident" of the American Civil War. According to the legend, Confederate General Armistead, a friend and Masonic brother of Union Gen. Winfield Scott Hancock, faced his estranged friend in the battle of Gettysburg in July 1863. Armistead was mortally wounded in an attack on Hancock's lines and *as he fell,* the story goes, he made a Masonic plea for assistance. A federal officer near him, Capt. Henry H. Bingham, also a Mason, and sometimes identified as an army doctor, immediately intervened, saved Armistead from further harm, and led him to a Union field hospital. Before he died, Armistead gave his personal effects, including his Masonic bible, to Hancock in care of Captain Bingham. Various permutations of the legend also suggest that Hancock supposedly met with Armistead before he succumbed to his wounds in a federal field hospital.[1]

Despite evidence to the contrary, this story has taken on a life of its own among Masons, and there is a monument at the Gettysburg Battlefield Park memorializing Armistead's encounter with Bingham. But what really happened? Did Armistead, in his last extremity, issue a Masonic distress call? Did Masons fly to his aid when he was shot down? Did he bequeath his Masonic bible to Union General Hancock with his dying breath? Previous treatments of this subject have not fully considered the evidence available

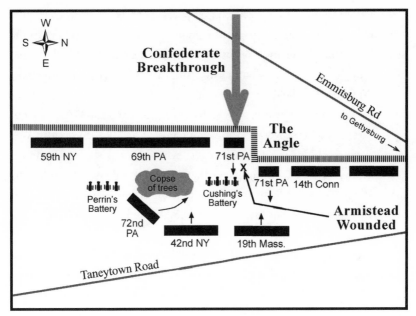

W

S ✦ N

E

**Confederate
Breakthrough**

Emmitsburg Rd

to Gettysburg →

**The
Angle**

59th NY   69th PA   71st PA

X

Perrin's
Battery

Copse
of trees

Cushing's
Battery

71st PA   14th Conn

**Armistead
Wounded**

72nd
PA

42nd NY   19th Mass.

Taneytown Road

Armistead's forlorn hope, the Confederate assault on the Angle.

to us. This preface will eliminate the speculation and establish, as closely as possible, the circumstances of Armistead's fall, and his eventual death, and the effect, if any, of Freemasonry on the outcome. It will also serve as prologue to an examination of the influence of Masonry in the Civil War itself, where the accounts of scores of other participants mirror the experience of Lewis Armistead.

A Career Military Officer

While the circumstances surrounding his death may be ambiguous, Armistead's biography is well established. He was born Lewis Addison Armistead at New Bern, North Carolina, in 1817, the son of career army officer Gen. Walker K. Armistead. Military tradition ran high in the Armistead family; young Lewis was also the nephew of Col. George Armistead, who led the defense of Fort McHenry against the British in 1814. At age seventeen, Lewis entered West Point but resigned two years later in the wake of escalating demerits and a disciplinary scandal.[2] He nevertheless pursued an army career and was commissioned in 1839 as a lieutenant in the 6th U.S. Infantry. During the intervening five years, Armistead applied himself to the profession of soldiering, and in 1844 he met and formed a friendship with Winfield Scott Hancock, a fellow subaltern in the 6th Infantry (of which more below). On active service, Armistead behaved well; he was brevetted for bravery in the Seminole War, and in the Mexican War he distinguished himself at Chapultepec, where he was slightly wounded as a member of the storming party that captured the citadel. Following the war with Mexico, he assumed the life of a frontier army officer, being posted to garrisons in Missouri, Minnesota, and Iowa and in the Kansas Territory at Fort Riley.

By late 1860, as secession and civil war loomed on the horizon, Armistead was a brevet major and post commander of New San Diego Barracks, California. When Virginia seceded on 17 April 1861 he resigned his commission. Following a lachrymose farewell to his friend and future antagonist Hancock in nearby Los Angeles, Armistead made his way east, accepting an appointment in the Confederate Army as a major, which was followed rapidly by a promotion to colonel of the 57th Virginia Regiment. By April 1862 he was a brigadier general in the Army of Northern Virginia.[3]

An Active Freemason

There is no doubt that Armistead was a Freemason. On 28 February 1839 he was initiated in the first degree of the Craft in Winchester Hiram Lodge No. 21, Winchester, Virginia.[4] Twelve years later, in part due to intervening military duties, including the war with Mexico, Armistead petitioned Alexandria-Washington Lodge No. 22 of Arlington, Virginia, to complete his Masonic work. The minutes of the Lodge for 19 September 1851 read in part:

> The Master stated the object of the meeting was [to] confer the FC
> Deg. & Master's Deg. On Bro. Lewis A. Armistead, he being duly
> initiated in E. A. Deg. in Hiram Lodge No. 21, Winchester, Vir-

ginia. He presented a certificate from said Lodge No. 21 with its seal & signed by the W. Master, Bro. F. W. Carson.

Ordered that the certificate be filed. The W. Master appointed a committee to examine Bro. Armistead. They having performed that duty, returned to the lodge room, stated they had performed that duty and [were] satisfied he was E. A. Mason. On motion ordered that the Lodge proceed to ballot for Bro. Armistead to take FC degree when he was duly elected. Bro. Lewis A. Armistead being in waiting was introduced and received the FC Degree and took his seat with us as FC Mason. The FC Lodge was then closed in AF [Ancient Form] and the Master's Lodge resumed business.

On motion the Lodge proceeded to ballote for Bro. Armistead to take the Master's Deg. when he was duly elected. He being in waiting, was introduced and raised to the sublime degree of a Master Mason. Nothing further appearing the Lodge was closed at ¼ of eleven O'clock.[5]

In 1856, while serving as commandant of Fort Riley, near present-day Junction City, Kansas, Major Armistead and several other Masons on the post petitioned the Grand Master of Kansas, Richard R. Rees, for a dispensation to form a lodge from scratch. The request was granted on 29 October 1857, and the provisional lodge formed there was given a charter and a new name, Union Lodge No. 7, A.F. & A.M.[6] The minutes of Union Lodge for 20 June 1857 show Armistead serving as Senior Warden, and lodge tradition has it that his wife, Cornelia, had on at least one occasion served as Tyler.[7]

In sum, we know a good deal about Armistead. At least two photographs of him exist; one photograph portrays him as a dapper man in civilian walking-out attire, with a top hat, cane, and serious mien, but the portrait most often seen of him presents a stern visage without the slightest hint of good humor. His age is exaggerated by the tonsorial fashions of the 1860s and by the bags under his eyes. It gives the impression of an older man, yet at his death at Gettysburg he was only forty-six. We may accurately picture him, however, as balding, with a prominent forehead, his cheeks ample without being fat. His nose is broad, perhaps once broken, and lends seriousness to the eyes that stare out fixedly and without compromise. His beard, grizzled and though short by the standards of Hood or Stuart, is nonetheless full, rendering his mouth invisible. The cravat and high collar he wears in the photograph suggest a certain tightness, both of dress and manner.[8]

One might ascribe this appearance of ill humor to the formalistic posing typical of photography of the period, but there are hints that his temperament was habitually stern. The men under his command commented about him in letters and diaries, describing him as a strict disciplinarian, crusty, brusque, and rather gloomy, and there is evidence that his troops complained about him.[9] Apparently Armistead commanded the respect of his men, but not their love. During the war, his leadership had attracted some criticism at the battle of Malvern Hill in 1862, for ordering an ill-advised piecemeal attack against a strong federal position. The assault failed and there were many casualties. Nevertheless, by the third day of Gettysburg, he was assigned a leading role in the rebel attack: a headlong rush at the center of the federal line that would, if successful, smash open the Union defenses, destroy Meade's army and maybe even win the war.

Pickett's Charge

The assault on the third day at Gettysburg was planned to converge on a small section of the federal line along Cemetery Ridge south of the town of Gettysburg, an area dominated by a stone fence along the ridge and punctuated at a critical point by a copse of trees. In one of the war's many ironies, this section of the Union line was overseen by Armistead's close friend, Hancock, commanding the federal II Corps. The ground between the Confederate positions and the Union line comprised at least a mile of relatively featureless terrain, "quite open, gently undulating and exposed to artillery the whole distance," according to Colonel Fremantle, an English observer of the Confederate army.[10] "The area covered by the Confederate infantry during the charge formed a trapezoid. It extended along

Seminary Ridge from the MacMillan house to the swale on the south side of the Spangler farm, a distance of 2,000 yards; from the swale to the stone wall, some 1500 yards; and from the stone wall to the MacMillan house, a distance of 1,333 yards. The stretch of the federal line they hit, along the stone wall from the Brian barn south to just past the copse of trees, is about 450 yards. The total ground covered is approximately one-half of a square mile."[11]

Over this ground, some eleven- to twelve-thousand infantry—estimates vary significantly—would cross, supported by massed artillery, in a bid to crush the Union center.[12] Yet, the massive preliminary rebel bombardment of the federal position, while impressive by the standards of 1863, had not suppressed the Union defenders, and their serried ranks stood more or less intact as the rebel line of battle advanced inexorably forward.

The Confederate advance was labeled ever after as Pickett's Charge, a nomenclature that rankles descendants of the other participants. Pickett was not the only divisional commander on the field during the attack; divisions commanded by Confederate generals Pettigrew and Tremble also participated, but no matter. The sobriquet has become fixed in the American imagination, as immovable as the marble monuments marking the battlefield today, and so the dash, verve, and eventual failure belong to Pickett.

Pickett's command formed the tip of the rebel spear. They were Virginians, led by three brigade commanders: James L. Kemper, Richard B. Garnett, and with Armistead in support. More importantly, they were fresh troops, having seen no action in the preceding two days. Armistead personally commanded five regiments, arrayed from right to left: the 14th, 9th, 53rd, 57th, and 38th Virginia. These regiments in support of Garnett's and Kemper's troops began the assault by moving northeast from the Confederate positions. Pettigrew and Tremble's commands, men from North Carolina, Tennessee, Mississippi, and Alabama, started to the left of the Virginia regiments and advanced southwest to the same objective: the stone wall near the wooded copse. Under ferocious defensive fire, Armistead exploited a gap in the line caused by a precipitous retreat of some of the Union defenders and forced his men through the federal defenses at the "Angle," an 80-foot jut of the stone fence immediately west of a copse of scrub oak trees.[13]

This patch of trees, known forever after as The Copse, was the focal point for the final act of Armistead's attack but once he and his men enter the "Angle," the fog of war descends, and the events surrounding his death become less clear. A less visible figure would have faded at this juncture, but Armistead was a commander, known to his men and noticed by the enemy. He was observed by many eyewitnesses, and through their cumulative testimony it is possible to reconstruct—to a reliable degree of certainty—the circumstances of his death.

A Few of Us Followed Him

At the start of the assault, Pickett's brigades were arrayed with Kemper on the right, Garnett to his left, and Armistead immediately in the rear.[14] W. Stuart Symington, a captain of Pickett's staff, recalled the placement, stating, "When we started Garnett and Kemper's brigades were a first line, and Armistead's brigade was in the rear, forming a second line. After moving forward some distance the troops on our left wavered, and finally broke badly. Pickett then ordered Armistead to move up and take position on the left of our first line. This movement was made promptly, and while we were still moving to the front. Almost as soon as Armistead came on line with the other two brigades, the direction of the charge was changed somewhat to the left."[15]

Robert A. Bright, another captain on Pickett's staff, concurred with Symington:

[A]fter our left supports retired, Armistead moved into line with Garnett. He was placed as you see in the diagram for the purpose of taking said position . . .

> *Garnett.*   *Kemper.*
> *Armistead.*

Bright reported to J. H. Stine, the Union historian, that he transmitted the order to charge to Kemper, assigning as his objective a red barn near the federal line.[16]

It is unknown exactly how many of Pickett's men completed the advance and pressed forward against the stone fence; estimates range from 1,000 to 4,300 of all ranks. Of those in Armistead's immediate contingent, however, the number is far smaller; Confederate survivors indicate that perhaps 150 to 300 men participated. Of those, 100 men, more or less penetrated the Angle. Forty-one died there, not counting the general. Of the sixteen rebels present with Armistead whose names are known, two were killed outright, one was wounded but managed to return to the rebels lines, seven were wounded and captured, six were captured unharmed, and one man survived without a scratch.[17] The statements of the Union witnesses bear out the rough math of the Confederates. Gen. Alexander Webb, whose Philadelphia Brigade directly confronted the Virginians, estimated Armistead passed over the fence with "probably over 100 men of his command and several battle flags."[18]

The contested ground inside the Angle was quite small. At the end of the fight Pickett's men had advanced only about twenty yards into the federal position where they stayed and fought for approximately ten minutes, perhaps fifteen, before the federal fire fatally wounded Armistead and destroyed his men or drove them back.[19] It is not known, however, who crossed the stone fence first, although at least one eyewitness stated that Armistead was in the van of the assault. Capt. Thomas C. Holland, of Company G of the 28th Virginia (Garnett's brigade), pinpointed himself and two rebel subalterns, John A. I. Lee, of Company C, and John J. Eakin, of Company B, of the 28th as among the very first to cross the stone fence. "[A]ll rushed to a battery which proved to be Cushing's of Philadelphia. Quite a number of us crossed the wall at the same time. I could not say who was first. Perhaps Lee was, but if so, he had many very close seconds."[20]

The 56th Virginia—part of Garnett's command—also reached the stone wall, and Lt. Henry C. Mitchie of Company H was with it. He reported that Armistead brushed his right elbow as the general clambered over the wall right beside him. He later wrote that Armistead cleared the wall with his hat held aloft on the point of his sword, a detail that is corroborated by many other witnesses. Lt. George W. Finley, also of the 56th in Company K, wrote a detailed account of what followed:

> [Armistead] on foot, strode over the stone fence, his hat on his sword and calling upon his men to charge. A few of us followed him until, just as he put his hand upon one of the abandoned guns, he was shot down. . . . the Federals advanced in heavy force. The bullets seemed to come from front and both flanks, and I saw we could not hold the fence any longer. I again looked back over the [stone fence] to see the chances of withdrawing. The men who had begun to fall back seemed to be dropping as they ran, like leaves, and in a very few moments the number on the ground was four or five times as great, apparently, as when I had looked before. It seemed foolhardy to attempt to get back. The Federal line pressed on until our men fired almost into their faces. Seeing that it was a useless waste of life to struggle longer I ordered the few men around me to "cease firing" and surrendered. As we walked to the rear I went up to Gen. Armistead as he was lying close to the wheels of the gun. On which he had put his hand, and stooping looked into his face, and I thought from his appearance and position that he was then dead.[21]

James T. Carter, a corporal of the color guard of the 53rd Virginia, was also in the van of the assault and he also saw Armistead cross the fence. Carter was near the wall when his regiment's color sergeant was shot down. He seized the flag, only to have it torn from him by another member of the color guard who was also killed, whereupon his comrade, Robert Tyler Jones, of Company K, retrieved the color from where it had fallen and advanced to the stone fence accompanied by Carter. From his vantage point in front of the wall, Carter saw Armistead only yards away: "When the brigade reached the wall there were very few men left, and Armistead, turning to Lieut. Col. R[awley] W. Martin, said: 'Colonel, we can't stay here.' Col. Martin replied, 'Then we'll go forward!' and over the wall the remaining few went, but there were only seven or eight left—Gen. Armistead, Col. Martin, Lieut. H. L. Carter, Lieut. J. W. Whitehead, Thomas Treadway, James A. Coleman, and some others. . . . Gen. Armistead was killed while trying to turn one of the guns on the enemy."[22]

Three other Confederates corroborate this detail, and each remarked on Armistead's call to turn the Yankee guns. Capt. Benjamin L. Farinholt of Company E of the 53rd Virginia reached Cushing's guns with Armistead as did Lt. James A. Harwood of Company K. Both officers heard Armistead order the federal cannons turned to face the Yankees.[23] Erasmus Williams, a private in Company H, 14th Virginia, was also present. He heard the general yell "Turn the guns!" in reference to Cushing's unmanned federal artillery, and Williams complied. Moments later, he saw both Armistead and Colonel Martin of the 53rd Virginia shot down.[24]

Corporal Carter was captured and lived to tell his tale, and despite having seventeen bullet holes in his clothing, he escaped without serious injury—a charmed life, to be sure. Captain Holland, noted earlier, was not so fortunate. He crossed the wall with Armistead and was shot in the face and neck. He lay nearly unconscious next to Armistead and was captured.[25]

Struck in the Breast and Arm

Moments after entering the Angle, Armistead was seriously wounded. Milton Harding, a private under Lieutenant Lewis of Company G, 9th Virginia Infantry, was present. "I was within six feet of him to his left, and observed that he staggered painfully, and could barely keep his feet until he reached the enemy's guns (Cushing's, I think), some sixty feet from the wall, although he continued to lead the charge like the hero he was. As he slapped his left hand on the gun he sank to his knees, and then fell full length to his right. I asked him if I could do anything for him. He requested me to get a small flask of brandy from the satchel he had carried by a strap from his shoulder, and from this he drank a swallow or so. I asked where he was wounded. He replied that he was struck in the breast and arm. In answer to my offer to assist him, he advised me to look out for myself. About that time the enemy recaptured the guns, and I, with others, retreated to the stone wall, where I was taken prisoner."[26]

The most persuasive (and often repeated) account of the fall of Armistead comes from Sgt. Drewry B. Easley, Company H, 14th Virginia. Easley advanced with his regiment but was slowed slightly in reaching the Angle by a crowd of Union soldiers who were trying to surrender blocking his advance. He ignored them and clambered over the stone fence directly in front of Cushing's abandoned Battery A. "I mounted the fence and got one glance up and down the line, while General Armistead mounted it just to my left, with only a brass cannon between us. I forgot my company and stepped off the fence with him. We went up to the second line of artillery and just before reaching those guns a squad of twenty-five to fifty Yankees around a stand of colors to our left fired a volley back at Armistead and he fell forward, his sword and hat almost striking a gun." Easley had no indication that Armistead was wounded—rather he thought him dead.[27]

> I dropped behind the gun and commenced firing back at them till they located me and poured in another volley. They shot my ramrod off where it entered the stock. I then ran back to the stone fence to get another gun. General Armistead did not move, groan or speak while I fired several shots practically over his body; so I thought he had been killed instantly and did not speak to him.[28]

Easley, who had enlisted as a student, was only seventeen years old at the Angle, and his account is particularly useful because he later became a Freemason, a member of South Boston (Virginia) Lodge No. 91. No records exist to indicate when Easley joined the fraternity, and he was too young to have been a Mason during the battle, but almost certainly he joined after the war.[29] Writing in 1913, he again recalled Armistead's wounding:

The order was "Guide center," and just as I was catching up the 57th Va. gave way to the right, and closed up the little space between the regiments; first pressed against my company and then lapped behind it cutting me off. I then dived through a little gap in the company to our right, and ran to the front looking back, but my company seems to have disappeared, I do not know how far I ran but not far till I ran into a squad of Yankees. I did not do anything brave or desperate, my only idea was to locate my company and get with them, and I do not recollect hearing a ball whistle from the time I ran forward to the volley was fired which killed Armistead. I ran squarely into the Yankees before seeing them and brought down my bayonet before seeing they had up *the sign of distress*" [emphasis added]. There was nothing for me to do but crowd through them, and then I struck the stone wall. I glanced to the right and left but the wall was vacant with the exception of two squads, and my recollection is that they huddled around the colors, and they seemed to have given us a little more breathing room to our right. I could not locate our left. I struck the wall with two brass guns to my right, and two to my left pointing over the wall.

There were others to my right and left. I took in all this at a glance and then saw Armistead. We went up to the second line of guns almost as close together as if we had been marching in ranks. He fell to our left of the gun and I stepped in to the right. I might say here that our line was crossing the wall when I looked back; possibly half of them over. They went back to a man. The squad that killed Armistead was just about where the monument of the 71st Penn. is located. . . . Armistead did not groan or move while I fired several shots near him, and I thought him dead.[30]

Easley's mention of "the sign of distress" is proof that Armistead made no gesture, Masonic or otherwise, when he fell. In William Morgan's *Illustrations of Masonry*, published in 1827, the author suggested that the Masonic distress signal, also called the Grand Hailing Sign of Distress, was made by holding the arms aloft in the "I surrender" position. Morgan also claimed that a Master Mason was required to immediately render assistance upon seeing the signal.[31] From membership in the fraternity, Easley would have been well acquainted with the Grand Hail, and although Easley was not then a member, we can be certain that he would have recalled the gesture once he was made a Mason. The gesture would also have been significant to non-Masons; from their perspective, Armistead would have appeared to be trying to surrender. Up until the time he was struck down, there are no verifiable Confederate reports that he made any Masonic gestures whatsoever, and no reports exist that indicate Armistead appeared to surrender before being shot down.

I Fired at Armistead with My Pistol

Accounts of federal troops who faced the rebel assault bear out the assertion that Armistead made no extraordinary gestures during the fight. On breaching the stone fence, the rebels met with fierce resistance from several federal units under the command of Union General Alexander Webb. Among them, two regiments in particular devastated the advancing Confederates; the 72nd Pennsylvania, who were clad in obsolete, albeit debonair, Zouave jackets and white gaiters, and companies A and I of the 69th Pennsylvania who were oblique to Armistead's troops. In addition, there were some members of the 71st Pennsylvania still fighting—it was their earlier retreat that had caused the gap that Armistead had exploited. On the fringe of Armistead's penetration were also elements of the 42nd New York and the 19th Massachusetts who added firepower to the federal defense. And finally, Hall and Harrow's brigades and the remnants of Cushing's gun crews were also in the vicinity and actively resisting the Confederate advance.[32] In short, the area was a beehive of activity. Through the smoke and confusion, which must have been intense, several federal observers caught sight of Armistead. None of these witnesses reported that he made any physical gestures that could be characterized as a secret Masonic signal or as a surrender.

Sgt. Frederick Fuger of the 4th U.S. Artillery (Cushing's battery) found himself directly opposite Armistead and since the battle some historians have placed him at the center of the Armistead myth. Fuger had earlier fired the last of his artillery ammunition with another surviving gunner and sought shelter in the rear. As the Confederates broke through, he found himself in pistol range of the rebel general.[33] In *The Gettysburg Campaign, June–July 1863,* historian Albert A. Nofi suggested that Fuger and Armistead were acquainted.

> As Confederate Brigadier General Lewis A. Armistead lay mortally wounded in the middle of the Angle atop Cemetery Ridge he uttered a cry for help, adding the phrase "as the son of a widow." As the Rebel tide was ebbing by then, some men on the line received permission to go to his aid. A romantic tradition has it that one of them was First Sergeant Frederick Fuger of Cushing's battery. Fuger had known Armistead in the prewar Army, when both had served in the *6th Infantry* and in Utah. According to one of Fuger's fellow gunners, Christopher Smith, Armistead said to Fuger, "I thought it was you, sergeant. If I had known that you were in command of that battery I would never have led the charge against you."[34]

Nofi suggests that the account was "romantic" in that it expressed Armistead's regret for ordering the charge, but Nofi does not appear to refute the connection between Armistead and Fuger. Fuger's own sworn testimony, however, directly contradicts Nofi's assertion of a prior relationship. "I did not know Armistead; I saw him come over but did not know who he was then but found out afterwards that it was Armistead; I saw him fall near the point in advance of where Cushing fell. . . . I fired at Armistead with my pistol; if he was hit by it I do not know. I was about ten feet from where Armistead fell when I shot at him, in rear of gun No. 3. I was about six or seven feet from where Cushing fell, and Armistead fell between Cushing and the wall."[35]

Although it is certainly possible that Fuger and Armistead had words after the attack—Nofi does not provide any attribution to the statement, nor is this variance with eyewitness accounts the only inaccuracy present in Nofi's recounting of the incident (see below). Furthermore, there is no evidence presented by Fuger that Armistead made any Masonic distress call during the attack itself. Another federal witness corroborates this. Anthony W. McDermott, Company I, 69th Pennsylvania, was also in the thick of things and he had a clear view of Armistead at the fateful moment: "We poured fire upon him (the enemy) until Armistead received his mortal wound; he swerved from the way in which he winced as though he was struck in the stomach, after wincing or bending like a person with a cramp, he pressed his left hand on his stomach, his sword and hat (a slouch) fell to the ground. He then made two or three staggering steps, reached out his hands trying to grasp at the muzzle of what was the 1st [*sic*] piece of Cushing's battery, and fell. I was at the time the nearest person to him."[36]

The combination of federal and Confederate accounts make clear that Armistead made no appeal for Masonic aid during the actual attack; at most, Armistead placed his hand on one of Cushing's guns, issued a command, and was shot down: nothing more.

The Son of a Widow

Once the rebel attack was dispelled, there is credible evidence that Armistead made a Masonic appeal after he was carried from the field, although not, as is claimed, to Frederick Fuger. According to Charles Banes, at that time a captain and a staff officer of Union Brig. Gen. Alexander Webb's Second Brigade, Armistead, prostrate and wounded by Cushing's No. 3 gun, made a Masonic allusion to an anonymous soldier, possibly from the 72nd Pennsylvania. In his *History of the Philadelphia Brigade*, Banes claimed that "General Armistead, who was in the Confederate front, fell mortally wounded, close to the colors of the Seventy-Second. One of the men of that regiment who was near him, asked permission of the writer to carry him out of the battle, saying, '*He has called for help, as the son of a widow*' [emphasis in original]. An order was given to take him to an ambulance, and when his revolver was removed from his belt, it was seen that he had obeyed his own command, 'to give the cold steel,' as no shot had been fired from it."[37]

According to William Morgan's *Illustrations of Masonry,* the phrase "son of a widow" has a particular meaning among Masons, and when spoken it signals distress and constitutes a call for immediate assistance.[38] Following the publication of his *History of the Philadelphia Brigade,* Banes gave testimony in a lawsuit concerning the placement of battlefield monuments in the Gettysburg battlefield. Under examination by counsel, he testified about the location of Armistead when he was shot down and again mentioned the "widow." "I was so near that one of the Seventy-second regiment men said he heard a man calling for his mother, who was a widow, and I saw them carrying him off the field. Three men of the Seventy-second regiment carried him up and he had his revolver, and I took it and looked at it and every shot was still in it. I gave the revolver to somebody to hold and he is holding it still for I have never seen it since."[39]

In what might constitute a historical red herring, or possibly the origin of the Armistead legend, Capt. John C. Brown, Company K, 20th Indiana, also claims credit for finding Armistead wounded on the field, although his claim is, by his own admission, less certain. The 20th under Col. John Wheeler formed part of Ward's brigade attached to the II Corps and were placed in support of the main line of resistance behind the Pennsylvania troops. Writing to John B. Bachelder in 1887, Brown claimed his recollection of the events of Pickett's charge had been refreshed by attending a battlefield tour conducted by Bachelder for a party of dignitaries including the president and vice president of the United States. In his letter, Brown recalls having heard Bachelder make the following remarks during that tour: "I think it is not unbecoming, or improper for me to say here, and thus publicly, that Genl. Armistead was lifted up and borne from the field by virtue of the grand hailing sign of a Mason."[40]

According to Brown, shortly after the repulse at the Angle he encountered a wounded Confederate officer whose identity he never ascertained, and who clearly identified himself as a Mason and requested help as such:

I walked out among the dead and wounded of bothe forces as they lay intermingled upon, and near, our line. . . . I heard a groan on

my left and turned to see what it meant, and saw a Rebel Officer lying upon his right side, his cheek resting upon his right palm, and his
elbow resting upon a slight elevation that surrounded some kind of
fruit tree, I think it was, and seeing evidences of great suffering expressed upon his face. I asked him if he was seriously hurt, and he
responded to the effect that he was, and that, as he believed he was
"pierced through" the boddy twice, and was bleeding profusely. I in-
tuitively expressed my strong sympathy for him, and he then said to
me, "Are you a mason?" and I responded "I am." Then having become
possessed of the knowledge that he was a Mason, and he had appealed
to me as such, I instantly resolved to fly to his relief.

I turned back after telling him that I would return to him very
soon, and went to my own Co . . . and selected two of its members,
and instructed them to procure a stretcher, we went to the wounded
Officer, tenderly lifted him from the ground and laid him upon the
stretcher and the two soldiers bore him to our hospital and in my
name & with my compliments, placed him in its official charge. I did
not ask him to tell me his name or his rank . . . I wish to learn if it
was Genl. Armistead that I relieved.[41]

Although many accounts agree that Armistead made some conversation
with a federal officer as he was being evacuated, it was almost certainly not
with Brown but with a Union adjutant named Henry H. Bingham, a captain in the 140th Pennsylvania.

On 3 July Bingham was attached to the II Corps as an aide to General
Hancock.[42] Bingham was a Pennsylvania man, and also a Freemason.[43] He
came upon Armistead being borne from the field by some enlisted men
whom he stopped and questioned. Bingham is often erroneously described
as a physician in the popular Masonic accounts and indeed in Nofi's *Gettysburg Campaign,* but he was in fact the furthest thing from a doctor; he was
an army lawyer.[44] Describing his meeting with Armistead in a letter to
Winfield Scott Hancock in January 1869, he related:

I think I found you [Hancock] in about 15 minutes after I got Armistead's message and effects. . . . I saw Armistead first at the high point of the enemy's repulse. . . . I met Armistead just under the crest of the hill, being carried to the rear by several privates. I ordered them back, but they replied that they had an important prisoner and they designated him as General Longstreet. . . . I dismounted my horse and inquired of the prisoner his name he replied General Armistead of the Confederate Army. Observing that his suffering was very great I said to him, General, I am Captain Bingham of General Hancock's staff, and if you have anything valuable in your possession which you desire taken care of, I will take care of it for you. He then asked me if it was General Winfield S. Hancock and upon my replying in the affirmative, he informed me that you were an old and valued friend of his and he desired for me to say to you, "Tell General Hancock for me that I have done him and done you all an injury which I shall regret or repent (I forget the exact word) the longest day I live." I then obtained his spurs, watch chain, seal and pocketbook. I told the men to take him to the rear to one of the hospitals.[45]

Bingham is a reliable source. He would later be awarded a Congressional Medal of Honor for his actions during the Battle of the Wilderness in May 1864 and he was promoted to the rank of brevet brigadier general by war's end. Following his military service, he was elected to Congress in 1878 and served as a representative for Pennsylvania for thirty-three years until his death in 1912. He makes no mention of receiving a Masonic bible from the rebel general, and writing to Hancock—also a brother Mason[46]—he makes no mention of any Masonic communications from General Armistead.

Some accounts report that the physician who treated Armistead's wounds also came to his aid through a Masonic Communication. These stories, like those of Armistead's battlefield Masonic appeal, are unfortunately unsubstantiated; in fact, firm evidence exists that disproves them.

Daniel Garrison Brinton, who would later become a famous ethnologist and anthropologist,[47] was a surgeon at Gettysburg at the 11th Corps field hospital set up at the George Spangler farm. Brinton was another Pennsylvanian, and although it is possible that he was a Freemason, there is no record of his membership in the fraternity in that state. Nevertheless, he treated Armistead personally after the battle and wrote in 1869 concerning Armistead's wounds, which he recalled were non-life-threatening. He conceded that he kept no notes as to individual patients, but recalled that Armistead was brought to his field hospital around 4:00 p.m. on 3 July:

> [M]yself & Dr. Harvey . . . examined & dressed his wounds. They were two in number, neither of them of a serious character, apparently. The one was in the fleshy part of the arm, the other a little below the knee in the leg of the opposite side. Without being positive, I think the leg wound was in the left side. Both were by rifle balls, and no bone or leading artery or nerve was injured by either.
>
> In conversation with the General he told me he had suffered much from over-exertion, want of sleep, and mental anxiety within the last few days. His prospects of recovery seemed good, and I was astonished to learn of his death. It resulted not from his wounds directly, but from secondary fever & prostration.[48]

Armistead died in a federal field hospital on 5 July 1863.

The Burden of Proof

From a careful examination of the facts, it is clear that the longstanding legend of Armistead's Masonic appeal is not what it seems. He made no appeal, either verbally or by gesture, when he was wounded that could rationally be deemed to have any Masonic significance. Furthermore, the oft-repeated claim that he cried out that he was "the son of a widow" on being shot is clearly false. Equally spurious is the assertion that *Doctor* Bingham sprang to his aid. Although Capt. Henry Bingham did encounter Armistead being borne to the rear by federal soldiers, Bingham was no doctor, and the encounter occurred by the purest chance. In his letter to Hancock, Bingham described taking Armistead's spurs, watch chain, seal, and pocketbook—but no Bible. No Masonic doctor appears in the record, either. When the rebel tide receded, however, there is some evidence that something Masonic occurred.

Capt. John C. Brown's account, while tantalizing, leaves many questions unanswered. The identity of the wounded officer is never established. Furthermore, Brown reports that Armistead was carried off by two men of the 20th Indiana. This conflicts with the testimony of Banes, who said he directed *three men* of the 72nd Pennsylvania to evacuate the wounded rebel general, whom he positively identified as Armistead. Brown's account also conflicts with Bingham's report, in which he states that he encountered Armistead being carried by *several men*. The location that Brown describes is also suspect. Brown makes no mention of Cushing's battery in his description of the area. The guns of Cushing's battery, remarked upon by virtually all the witnesses to Armistead's fall, form a landmark to the location of his body, yet Brown does not remark on them, mentioning instead a fruit tree. Assuming that Armistead had not moved from the position described by Easley and Fuger—an assumption that may be logically borne out by the testimony of Banes who found him near the 72nd Pennsylvania's line—and assuming that the guns had not been repositioned, and there is no evidence at all that they were, Brown's omission of Cushing's guns casts grave doubt on the usefulness of his testimony for our purposes and makes it far more likely that Brown's wounded rebel, while certainly a Mason, was not Armistead.

Charles Banes is the linchpin of the legend. The enticing reference made by Bachelder probably resulted because of something Banes mentioned. Banes's statements form the strongest argument that Armistead ever called for Masonic relief, yet even here the burden of proof is not completely met. In his book, Banes recalls that an anonymous man "from that regiment"— the 72nd Pennsylvania—reported hearing a man ask for help as "the son of a widow." Under direct examination in court, Banes told of hearing a soldier report "a man calling for his mother, who was a widow," a slight variation on his earlier statement. It would be intriguing if Banes, a Pennsylvania man, was a Mason, but there is no record of his affiliation with the Order at the Grand Lodge of Pennsylvania, so we must surmise that he was simply repeating what he had heard without possessing any deeper Masonic understanding of the phrase. The fact that the phrase was altered in its retelling bears this out. A Mason would have made no mistake about it. Unlike Brown's statements, however, there is no difficulty in establishing that Banes identified Armistead. Rather, the problem is that Banes is reporting hearsay. He did not witness the statements—he heard them secondhand. In a court of law, Banes's testimony would be inadmissible to prove that Armistead said anything about a widow at all.

There is more to the story, however. Writing in 1958, historian Glenn Tucker made the assertion that a certain Union soldier actually heard Armistead speak the words "the widow's son." According to Tucker, "Armistead fell in the midst of a group of five Federal soldiers, only one of whom, Private Wildemore of the 71st Pennsylvania, claimed to have caught words spoken in a whisper by Armistead, asking help and saying, as Wildemore repeated the words to his comrades, that 'he is the son of a widow.' Wildemore was wounded almost at once and the others, understanding the fraternal implications of the call, carried Armistead back, where he died."[49] Tucker's statements, though, are also problematic. Most notably: there is no attribution in his text as to the source of this statement. Conceivably it could have come from Wildemore, if he survived, or any of the other four soldiers referenced, but we have no information of them at all. Another problem is that Wildemore does not appear on the rolls of the 71st Pennsylvania Infantry; however, there is a Pvt. Jacob Wildemore who does appear on the muster rolls of Company I, 72nd Pennsylvania Infantry—the regiment referred to by Banes. Consequently, if we assume by his membership in the Philadelphia Brigade that he was a local man—and it appears that he was—his affiliation with the Masonic Order would be significant. Unfortunately, there is no record of Jacob Wildemore in Pennsylvania Masonic records. Tucker's statement, that "the others" understood the fraternal implications of the call, appears to bear out this supposition—Wildemore was no Mason, but someone nearby must have been. Those considerations aside, Tucker's narrative provides supporting evidence to Banes's claims, and most importantly provides us with a name of a purported witness who was present and who actually heard the words firsthand, and it is upon these words that the legend rests. It is flimsy stuff, however.

So what really happened? We know that nothing of Masonic significance occurred during the fighting in the Angle. While wounded and prostrate, Armistead spoke to at least one of his men, Milton Harding; he asked for brandy and told Harding to look after himself, but he did not ask for help. Drewry Easley thought Armistead dead as he fired his rifle over his body. Lieutenant Farinholt of the 53rd saw him shot down, and noticed nothing extraordinary. From the Union vantage point, the view is the same as what the Virginians saw. Sergeant Fuger looked right at Armistead, possibly even shot him, and saw nothing, and Private McDermott, from the ranks of the 69th Pennsylvania witnessed, and described minutely, Armistead's appearance when he was shot down. Nothing Masonic occurred up to that point. Bingham, likewise, made no report of any Masonic communication despite the fact that he was a Mason. He might have been understandably reticent if he were describing the incident to the general public, but not to a brother Mason: General Hancock. But Bingham gives not even a hint of any Masonic communication in his correspondence to his commander.

The unmistakable conclusion is that the legend of Armistead's dramatic Masonic death scene simply didn't happen. Without question he made no gestures when he was shot down and no evidence exists to contradict that statement. He was not rushed from combat by anyone. There was no Masonic huddle with *Doctor* Bingham, no handoff of a Masonic bible, and no meeting with Hancock. Something of Masonic significance probably occurred as Armistead lay wounded after the assault—and he very likely made the Masonic allusion to "the widow's son." But absent evidence to the contrary, any claims beyond that are unsupportable or spurious.

For many readers, the Masonic legend of Armistead's death is the first, and often the only, story of Masonry's role in the Civil War they encounter. Although not as dramatic, the real events surrounding his death merit remark, but his case is by no means isolated or extraordinary. As the following chapters will show, Masonry's influence on the individual level was profound, encompassing not only soldiers resorting to Masonry to secure aid and comfort on the battlefield, but also Masonic funerals attended by soldiers from both sides, prisoners invoking the fraternal tie to stave off starvation in prison or to effect escape from capture, and Masonic signs given to preserve cherished personal effects from thieves and freebooters. These incidents—to which the Armistead account is merely prologue—illustrate the remarkable effect of America's oldest fraternity on America's greatest national calamity.

I

Masters and Fellows

A good true oath he must there swear
To his master and his fellows that be there;
He must be steadfast and true also
To all this ordinance, wheresoever he go,
And to his liege lord the king,
To be true to him over all thing.
And all these points here before
To them thou must need be sworn,
And all shall swear the same oath
Of the masons, be they lief be they loath
—The Regius Poem (Halliwell MS) ca. 1390

What Is Freemasonry?

The history of Freemasonry is beyond the scope of this work, yet in order
to determine its influences during the American Civil War, some brief explanation of the institution is required. Variously known as Freemasonry,
Masonry, or the Craft, its beginnings are lost to history. Although its
members claim to be the oldest surviving fraternal organization in the
world, with a heritage stretching back to early medieval or even Biblical times, there is little solid evidence to support that assertion. Freemasonry can, however, be easily traced to sixteenth-century Edinburgh,
although the first Masonic governing body was not founded until 1717 in
London. By 1723, the *Constitutions of the Freemasons* were assembled and
published and although that document explicitly refers to an alleged meeting of stonemasons in England assembled by Prince Edwin, the son of the
tenth-century Saxon king Athelstan, there is no supporting evidence to

this claim.[1] Despite this, theories that the fraternity is much older than the Age of Enlightenment exist, and most historians accept that the Craft is descended from the medieval stonemason's guilds. According to historian David Stevenson, the starting point in tracing the origins of Freemasonry can be found in the medieval trades in England. "Like other Medieval trades the masons had their craft organisations or guilds, and their mythical histories stressing the antiquity and importance of their crafts, closely linking them with religious and moral concepts." But, he states, the English masons were particularly elaborate in their mythical trade history, and these contributions—of legend and organization—formed the perfect ingredients for the development of the fraternity, which took place, he argues, not in England, but in Scotland.[2] Scholars of Freemasonry appear to agree with this assessment:

> Relatively little is known about the origins of Freemasonry. It is clear that the fraternity has, to some extent, its antecedents in the ancient stonemason's guilds of medieval Europe, but an exact pedigree has thus far eluded Masonic scholars. What is known is that Scottish Freemasonry transitioned from a trade guild into a social club. It may be assumed that English Freemasonry followed suit at a similar time and in like manner, but this remains unproven. It is clear however, that the social club reflected Enlightenment sensibilities while retaining the organizational structure of a union. The most notable of these labor features are three levels, or "degree," of lodge membership corresponding to a typical craftsman's career; 1°, Entered Apprentice, 2°, Fellow Craft (or Journeyman), and 3°, Master Mason.[3]

Historian Margaret Jacob asserts that no proof exists to place Freemasonry in a medieval context but supports the conclusions of Stevenson that Freemasonry was refined in Scotland. "That evolution, to this day only partially understood, makes for a fascinating story . . . with the example of one Scottish lodge. The lodge in Dundee, Scotland, experienced the transformation from a guild, or lodge, of workingmen—'operatives' as they are called in Masonic literature—to a private society of 'free and accepted' masons within a few decades, from roughly 1700 to 1730."[4]

Although its origins remain disputed, it is clear that during the Enlightenment, new lodges sprang up throughout Europe and America and membership grew. The first American lodge was chartered in Boston, Massachusetts, in 1733.[5] As Masonry became a new social force, Masons were at pains to demonstrate its respectability. According to Jacob, "in the face of rival and purely aristocratic orders of medieval origin, Continental Freemasons sought a careful reconstruction of a history they believed extended back to Hiram, the builder of Solomon's Temple. They went on to tie the history of their fraternity to the Crusades, then to the Knights Templar, and finally they picked up the story again in seventeenth-century England. We have manuscript histories by French Freemasons stating, almost in passing, that Freemasonry was associated with Oliver Cromwell."[6] These reconstructionist tendencies, endemic in the fraternity to a certain extent even today (see chapter 7), have frustrated serious scholars of Freemasonry and have defied attempts to explain its significance.

A great many definitions have been applied to Masonry over the last three hundred years, but these descriptions are of little utility. Many are heavily tinged with dubious assertions, and popular accounts in print or on screen focus on ritualistic bric-a-brac that contributes little to our understanding of the nature of the fraternity. Masonic authors, to be sure, have written voluminously about the character of the institution, but many of them fall victim to their preoccupation with exploring mystical esoterica, or attempting to antedate the origins of the Craft to ancient rites of the classical or preclassical world. These "histories" are so couched in the arcana of the fraternity as to be almost useless. The Masonic scholar Samuel Hemming (1757–1828), for example, declared that Freemasonry was a "system of morality, veiled in allegory and illustrated by symbols," and while this definition has been widely accepted by Masons the world over, it reveals little.[7] Another prominent Masonic scholar, Albert G. Mackey (1807–81), declared that Freemasonry was first and foremost "a science which engages us in the search after divine truth, and which, if rightly understood, enables us to assist that search by a knowledge of what was done in the same great labor [by] the symbolism of the ancient sages," but that the institution was also religious in character. "The very science which it inculcates is in itself the science of religion. Not a religion of forms and creeds, but a universal religion, whose theology embraces the important dogmas of a Supreme Creator, and of a future existence . . . and, hence, the religion of Freemasonry is its science, and its science is its religion."[8]

Mackey maintained that Masonry was a dual-purpose social institution. On one level, the organization functioned as a charitable institution providing for the relief of members and nonmembers alike. On another level, Masonry met mankind's instinctive need to associate. This association, according to Mackey, allowed Masons to shed individual social distinctions and prejudices—"the imbecility of the individual"—and meet one another as equals "upon one common level of brotherhood and equality." In the lodge, he wrote,

> friendship is cemented by a mystic bond, and strifes, and envies, and jealousies are discarded, while the only contention that exists is that noble emulation of who can best work and best agree. And this 'mystic bond' is not local nor confined in its influences to any narrow limits . . . in every nation a Mason may find a friend, and in every climate a brother.
>
> And thus, within these fraternal associations, spreading over the whole face of the globe, and existing in all the great national confederacies of the world . . . are to be found men of all political parties, and of every religious faith, bound together for one common purpose. . . . And when 'wars and rumors of wars' are desolating the nations of the earth, in their happy retreats of peace and concord, the brethren of the mystic ties assemble to meditate on the sublime truths of religious science, and to promote those virtues, whose fruits are friendship, morality and brotherly love.[9]

Yet Mackey's definition, as well as the theories propounded in the bulk of Masonic writing, convey little real information about the particulars of the organization, and until recently the non-Masonic academic world offered little more. Despite the fact that formally organized Freemasonry has existed since at least 1717, the fraternal structure and its implications in society have attracted little attention or interest from scholars, and social scientists have only recently regarded Freemasonry as a worthy subject for investigation.[10] In 1875, Charles W. Heckethorn authored one of the first notable studies concerning Masonry and similar groups yet, to the modern reader, his *Secret Societies of All Ages and Countries* is practically unintelligible—as a sample of his explanation on the origins of the institution demonstrates. "Freemasonry was early mixed up with the *compagnonnage,* and the construction of the Temple, which is constantly met with in the former, also plays a great part in the latter—a myth, undefined, chronologically irreconcilable, a poetic fiction, like all the events called historical that surround the starting-points of various sects; for sects, existing, as it were, beyond the pale of official history, create a history of their own, exclusive of, and opposed to, the world of facts."[11]

Although Heckethorn may be correct that the origins of Masonry are not to be found in the biblical or classical world (of which, more below), his presentation and analysis is so stilted as to be completely obscure to all but the most dedicated reader. Not until the twentieth century do any modern analyses place Freemasonry in context within American society. In a 1940 inquiry titled "Secret Societies: A Cultural Study of Fraternalism in the United States," sociologist Noel P. Gist defined Freemasonry in America as a "benevolent and philanthropic society," a cooperative brotherhood that provided companionship, charitable work on behalf of the needy and the unfortunate, social activities, and to a limited extent a guarantee of social and economic well-being among its members who had fallen on hard times. In short, what we have come to understand as a fraternal organization.[12]

Gist's work was followed forty-four years later by that of the talented historian Lynn Dumenil. Her *Freemasonry and American Culture, 1880–1930* provided students of fraternalism with a modern study addressing the fraternity in a scholarly manner without the allegorical mysticism of previous treatments. Dumenil summed up mainstream American Freemasonry succinctly as an all male, primarily native, mainly Protestant society concerned with meeting the social and personal needs of its members. She held that the "order was a quasi-religious secret society dedicated to the ideals of fraternity, charity, and moral behavior. It offered sociability, relief in times of distress, as well as possible financial and political advantages, but the most important aspect of Masonry was its commitment to moral uplift and self-improvement." As part of its message of moral rectitude, Dumenil found that Masonry used traditional values of "sobriety, thrift, temperance, piety, industry, self-restraint and moral obligation," a theme that had tremendous appeal in nineteenth-century America because it mirrored values that its members identified with.[13]

With the insight offered by Dumenil, Gist, and others, then, it is possible to characterize Freemasonry in nineteenth-century America as an exclusively male fraternal organization of a spiritual or quasi-religious nature, which conducted its business behind closed doors. That this organization—which at first glance appears little more than a boys' club—should have any influence whatever during America's Civil War is a function of the popularity of fraternalism among nineteenth-century American men and the resulting large number of Masons directly involved in the conflict.

The Fraternal Culture

Fraternal organizations were increasingly popular by the middle of the nineteenth century, and their importance stems from the sheer number of men who belonged to them. The most prominent secret society in this period besides Freemasonry was the Independent Order of Odd Fellows. Claiming a similar pedigree to Masonry, the first recorded Lodge of Odd Fellows began in England in 1745, and the first American lodge, Washington Lodge No. 1, was founded in Baltimore in 1819. Odd Fellowship quickly attracted new members because it was a benefit society. Odd Fellows who were taken sick could claim financial benefits from the lodge in the form of cash stipends paid weekly according to a scheduled table of benefits. Benefits paid to members were not considered charity, but rather a "right" of membership.[14]

Beyond the Odd Fellows there were a dozen or so lesser-known fraternities such as the United Ancient Order of Druids, founded in London in 1781; the Ancient Order of Foresters, established in 1813; the Society of Red Men, also founded in the same year; or the Ancient Order of Hibernians, organized in 1836. Occasionally, fraternal societies evolved from social clubs and became political actors. The nativist Order of the Star Spangled Banner, often referred to as the Know-Nothings, originated in 1849 as an oath-bound secret society but later became a political party enjoying brief success and some regional and national prominence, whose members were instructed to claim that they "knew nothing" about any secret society. The Knights of the Golden Circle was another political society. It advanced an agenda that included expansion of Southern American interests in a "golden circle" that included Mexico, the Caribbean, and parts of Central America, and later became enmeshed with the Northern Copperhead societies.[15] Despite the varying attraction of these societies, Freemasonry stood apart and its appeal was less tangible. Although Masonry was regarded as a charitable institution, it was not, unlike Odd Fellowship or other similar organizations, a benefit society. Masonry recognized the right of brethren to ask for, and receive, relief—financial or otherwise—but Masonry dispensed no stipends as rights of membership, nor did it have a schedule of benefits for sickness, disability, or death. While lodges could, and did, contribute to the relief of destitute brethren, their widows, or orphans, the payment of benefits was, and remains, outside the scope of the fraternity.

Anti-Masonry and Masonry Rejuvenated

The fortunes of Freemasonry declined sharply—following one hundred years of steady growth—in 1826 when William Morgan, a disgruntled former Mason in Batavia, New York, announced his intent to publish and expose the Masonic ritual. Local Masons were outraged, and when Morgan disappeared suspicion fell upon the fraternity. It was claimed that a Masonic conspiracy had organized his kidnapping and eventual murder, and despite the fact that Morgan's body was never found, six men, all Masons, were brought to trial. Four were convicted but sentenced to only minor terms in jail. Subsequent disclosures that the sheriff, prosecutor, and many of the jurors were members of the fraternity ignited an anti-Masonic backlash that quickly spread across the country. The concept of the secret society was branded as subversive, and those associated with Masonry were publicly excoriated as corrupt and suspected of cronyism, or worse. Preachers railed from their pulpits that Masonry was sin, editors fulminated and published detailed exposés of Masonic rituals, and Masons in public life were openly questioned about how they could reconcile their secret obligations with their public duties. As a consequence, many men left the fraternity to avoid criticism.[16]

By 1828, a full-fledged political party—the Anti-Masonic Party—formed, with the extraordinary goal of eliminating Masonic influences from public life. When the anti-Mason firestorm finally burned itself out in 1836, in part because of the dishonest motives of its political leaders, American Masonry was moribund. Membership plummeted as lodges and Grand Lodges across the country shut their doors.[17] In New York alone between 1828 and 1835 the number of Masonic lodges fell from 490 to just eighty, and active membership declined from 20,000 to 3,000.[18]

By the late 1840s, however, a renewed popular interest in Freemasonry emerged as anti-Masonry and hostility to secret societies that had riveted the national attention span were replaced, at least in part, by other perceived threats, among them Irish-Catholic immigrants and the simmering national debate over slavery. Between 1850 and 1860 Freemasonry rebounded vigorously, tripling its membership from 66,000 to 200,000 members in over 5,000 lodges nationwide. Masonry's reputation was restored, if only because so many men chose to become Masons, providing the American public with the indisputable respectability of numbers. Although it was still a secret society, for the first time in twenty years men openly wore the symbol of the fraternity—the square and compasses—from their watch chains and on their lapels.[19]

Although benefit societies certainly appealed to the mercenary motives of members, fraternal stipends do not explain the attraction of fraternalism in general, and Freemasonry in particular. Social scientists and historians have speculated that the ceremony and rituals of the fraternal orders, whether Freemasonry, Odd Fellowship, or the other less populous groups, in fact served a valid sociological function, filling a void and reinforcing a spirit of community. In Dumenil's terms, fraternalism gave men a "sacred asylum" in a world fraught with change and upheaval. The tradition-laden initiation ceremonies, ritualism, and open hierarchical structure of Masonic order created in a sense an artificial society, which both intensified bonds of comradeship among the initiated and reinforced a shared set of values that insulated its members from the vicissitudes of life. However chaotic the outer world, the lodge remained firm, inviolate, and intact.[20]

Is He Worthy and Well Qualified?

Popular imagination held that fraternal ritual required men to assemble in their lodge rooms, don ridiculous garb and funny hats, and subject one another to practical jokes—often termed "riding the goat"—all this horseplay and tomfoolery made even more ridiculous by being cloaked in the guise of somber biblical, Oriental, Druidical, or Native American mysticism. While doubtless some of this occurred, the emphasis in many of the fraternal orders was on moral uprightness and rectitude of conduct, as opposed to practical jokes and pranks, and most rituals share remarkably similar themes. The initiation ceremony of the Freemason contained similar elements to the ceremony of the Odd Fellows, with both emphasizing the theme of death and rebirth and the transition from a profane world of ignorance into a select circle of knowledge.[21]

An 1831 exposé of Masonry, Odd Fellowship, and other secret societies published by Avery Allyn, an old-line Anti-Mason, described the initiation ceremony of the Odd Fellows in full, and typifies the initiations that Civil War soldiers would have undergone upon acceptance into the fraternal culture. At the beginning of the ceremony, the candidate

is taken into the preparation room, by the one who proposed him, and prepared by blindfolding. He is then conducted to the door of the lodge, by the outside guardian, who knocks on it three times, on hearing which, the inside guardian answers the raps by three more, opens the door, and inquires, "Who comes there?" The outside guardian replies, "A Stranger, who wants admission to this ancient and honorable order of firm and independent odd fellows." The inside guardian returns to the lodge and says—

"Most Worthy [Vice Grand—an officer's title], a stranger wishes to enter." The Vice Grand inquires—"Is he duly and truly prepared?"
[Inside Guardian]:   He is.
[Vice Grand]:   Is he worthy and well qualified?
I.G   He is.
V.G.   Then admit him.

He is then admitted, conducted three times around the lodge, and halted. The conductor then steps up to him and gives him a violent blow with his hands, on his shoulders, and at the same time exclaims, in a vehement tone, "Stand! presumptuous mortal! and forget not, in the dreadful scenes you have to pass, to show you have the fortitude of a man! Stranger! before you further go, a warning you must take! Behind your back is fire! Under your feet is a yawning gulf! And before your breast is a pointed instrument of death."[22]

Following a dialog between the conductor and the entire lodge as to whether the blindfolded candidate (termed "hoodwinked" in fraternal parlance) is to be tortured or shown mercy (the verdict is invariably that he should be tortured), the candidate is asked what he most desires, and is prompted to answer "Light!" His blindfold is then removed and he is confronted by a member of the lodge in the guise of Death who reminds the candidate of his own mortality. After being admonished to keep the secrets of the fraternity on pain of death, the candidate is then required to swear an oath of secrecy before being taught the *signs, grips,* and *words* of the society.[23]

Period exposés of Masonry tell us that the nineteenth-century Masonic experience was substantially similar. Ralph Lester's *Look to the East!* (1876) declared that the candidate would be placed before the Masonic altar, his hands positioned on the Bible, and upon giving his name would recite,

> Of my own free will and accord, in the presence of Almighty God, and this worshipful Lodge, erected to him and dedicated to the Holy Saints John, do hereby and hereon (Master presses his gavel on the candidates knuckles) most solemnly and sincerely promises [sic] and swear that I will always hail forever conceal, never reveal any of the secret arts, parts, or points of the hidden mysteries of Masonry which have been heretofore, or shall be, at this time, or at any future period, communicated to me as such, to any person or persons, whomsoever, except it be a true and lawful brother Mason, or within the body of a just and lawfully constituted Lodge of Masons.[24]

This Masonic obligation continues for some length and is repeated and augmented with each degree, but it is not designed, according to Joshua Gunn, to protect a profound secret truth, but rather to "impart the gravity and significance of *the act of swearing.* In this respect the Masonic oath is the classic social contract; however, it is peculiar in its literal and figurative blindness. Before passwords or handshakes are revealed to a Masonic candidate—before any secret content is revealed—he is asked, blindfolded, to make the obligation *first.*"[25]

Common to most fraternal orders of the nineteenth century, signs, grips, and words were simply recognition signals. *Signs* were gestures, usually made with the hands, that allowed a member to signal his affiliation without verbal cues. *Grips* were handclasps—the much talked-about secret handshakes of the fraternal orders—indicative of membership in the fraternity and also used for recognition. *Words* were certain phrases that betokened membership and enabled a man to prove his affiliation so that he might attend a lodge despite being a stranger, or solicit aid from members who did not know him. Grips and words are also sometimes referred to as *tokens*. In Odd Fellowship,

> one of the *signs* is made by raising the right hand, the forefinger open; all the rest, and thumb, clenched: touch the end of the finger to the eye-brow; then drop the hand by the side. This is done with a quick motion, as a salute, on entering a Lodge. On examining a Brother, sometimes the finger touches the side of the nose; and in some lodges, they use two fingers instead of one. . . . [Another] sign is made by placing the right hand on the left breast, and at the same time pronouncing the words—"*upon my honor.*" Another sign is made by taking hold of the lower part of the left ear, with the thumb and forefinger of the right hand.
>
> . . . The *grip* is made by locking the two first fingers of the right hand [as though you were taking hold to pull, or try the strength of them,] so as to make the end of your two fingers and thumb meet around the two fingers of the one you are receiving the grip.[26]

Besides being inherently attractive to the adolescent boy in most men, all of these gestures and phrases had a basic utility vis-à-vis the secret society; they maintained the secret and exclusive nature of the group. Although perhaps never intended, they were also, as we shall discover, unusually useful in wartime.

Membership and Its Privileges

Some benefits of fraternal associations were obvious. Upon initiation, a new member was provided with instant companionship, a gamut of social functions from which to pick and choose, and a network of fraternity brothers who obligated themselves to provide assistance to him, moral or material, should he find himself downtrodden, destitute, or injured.

Another benefit, perhaps less obvious, was the hierarchy of the fraternity. This was a closed system in which otherwise average men could distinguish themselves. In the United States in 1860, the body of Free-masonry had a simple hierarchy (as is similarly the case today). At the local level were the independent lodges. A small county or town might have a single lodge, while more populous towns or cities might have several, each wholly independent of one another. All lodges in a given state were nominally beholden to a single superior body known as the Grand Lodge of that state, but it was the local lodge that was the base operating unit of the organization. In the lodge, ordinary business was conducted: bills for lodge supplies such as paper, ink, and fuel were paid upon a vote of the members; social functions were scheduled; and most importantly, new members were voted on and admitted, or in some cases denied admission altogether.

The number of members in any given lodge varied widely by jurisdiction. Some metropolitan lodges had hundreds of members, while country lodges could have a score, or less. A random sample of lodge membership returns from 1857–59 confirms this. The Grand Lodge of Louisiana reported 4,238 members in 102 chartered lodges for an average number of members per lodge of 42 in 1859. Georgia's Grand Lodge reported their totals in 1857 as 216 chartered lodges with 12,027 members for an average of 56 members per lodge. In Massachusetts in 1858, 90 chartered lodges held regular meetings with a total of 5,899 members paying dues to chartered lodges, for an average of 66 members per lodge. The largest lodge, Columbian Lodge in Boston, reported 222 members; the smallest lodge, Eureka, in New Bedford, and chartered for only six months at the time of the survey, counted just 13 men.[27]

The lodge was under the leadership of the Worshipful Master who functioned as president. He was assisted by two wardens, Senior- and Junior-, who acted as vice presidents, and by a lodge Secretary and a Treasurer. These officers were elected to fixed terms that varied by the jurisdiction from six months to two years, with one-year terms being the most common. It was (and remains) common for Secretaries and Treasurers to be reelected year after year; the duties involved being tedious in the extreme, and the list of applicants willing to undertake them being rather short. Besides the local elected officers, the Master of the lodge appointed other lesser officers, including Senior and Junior Deacons, Stewards, Chaplains, and the Tyler whose function was to guard the door of the lodge from the outside. Beyond the local level, other offices and titles were attainable to the ambitious Mason among the larger Masonic districts, and at the state or territory level in the Grand Lodges.[28]

In 1860 as today, each state or Masonic jurisdiction (for example, the District of Columbia) had its own Grand Lodge, the supreme Masonic body under which all subordinate lodges are constituted. As in the case of the local lodges within its jurisdiction, each Grand Lodge was, and remains, wholly independent of every other. (America, unlike most other countries in which Masonry is prevalent, has no federal or "general" Grand Lodge, although discussions about the establishment of one have surfaced within the American branch of the fraternity nearly continuously since 1790.[29]) The Grand Lodge system mirrored the organizational structure of the local lodges, with the "state president" being titled "Grand Master" and his officers "Grand Senior Warden," etc. It was therefore possible for a clerk or a merchant, a cooper or a tanner, to rise from the ranks of ordinary Masons and become Grand Master, and many ordinary and average men were attracted by the opportunities for distinction that the fraternity offered.

Masonic Regalia

Masons met in various locations—in rented space, over a store or a tavern, or sometimes in their own building, which was often termed a Masonic Hall or Temple.[30] Masonic custom dictated the presence of certain furnishings in the lodge room, including chairs for the principal officers and an altar, upon which must be placed a holy book that in nineteenth-century America would have invariably been interpreted to mean the Bible. Laid with the Bible on the altar would have been two stylized stonemason's tools—the square and compasses that make up the emblem of the fraternity. Candles or lamps stood nearby to light the scene. Additional paraphernalia in the form of aprons—the apron being a badge of membership of the fraternity, and emblematic of the stonemason's garb—were also required, along with badges of office, known as *jewels*.

Period sources frequently mention Masonic pins and during the war Masons placed a good deal of importance in them as identifying marks signaling their membership in the fraternity to others.[31] That they were worn in battle suggests that soldiers recognized them, at least subliminally, as a talisman that might aid them in the event of being wounded or disabled, or insurance of a last resort that might induce a fellow Mason to bury them and mark their grave.

One example featuring a Masonic emblem of this kind is the account of Alabama officer William H. May, who was offered a Masonic pin in exchange for rescuing a wounded federal. "I was put in command of the 3rd Alabama Regiment September 19, 1864. Before the command was turned over to me I had found a badly wounded color-bearer of the 26th Massachusetts Regiment. His leg was broken and wounded in three places. I had a breastworks of rails placed before him for protection from his own men who kept up a constant fire, both of musketry and cannon. His name was John A. Brown, a nice man, and he told me he was a Mason. Wanted to make me a present of something, but had nothing but his Mason's pin. I told him my father was a Mason and not to let it trouble him, for what was done was for no purpose or reward."[32]

Additionally, many Masons went armed with a diploma—the nineteenth-century equivalent of a dues card. Referred to as a *Ne varietur,* Latin for "it must not be altered," these documents were the forerunners of membership cards, and were printed on vellum or parchment as a certificate. The phrase alludes to the Masonic custom of requiring a member, when he receives the certificate, to affix his name, in his own handwriting, in the margin, as a precautionary measure that enables other lodges and brethren, by a comparison of the handwriting, to recognize a true brother and detect any imposter who may have obtained one unlawfully. Carried by soldiers, doubtless in part to prove their membership and admit them when visiting a lodge in a nearby town, they also indicated affiliation in the chaos of battle. An editorial in the *Masonic Review* in 1865 describes one such diploma found in the field:

> Some time since a brother presented us with a Master Mason's Diploma, on parchment, neatly filled up, and attested by John Dove, Secretary of the Grand Lodge of Virginia. It is dated the 31st of December, 1855, and was granted by Equality Lodge No. 136, to Thomas E. Buchanan, whose signature is on the margin. Its history is curious: some time ago, after one of the battles in Virginia . . . a rebel soldier was found on the battle-field. Being fatally wounded, and feeling that he must soon die, he had taken this (his) diploma from his pocket, opened and spread it out beside him on the ground so that it might attract the attention of some Mason among the conquering forces and—died. [33]

The unspoken implication here, which would have been understood by all Freemasons, is that the former owner of the parchment was taken up and buried by Union Masons.

One Common Level

By the nineteenth century, Freemasons characterized their fraternity as an organization that "brings men of all religions, of all politics, of all manners, and of all habits to one common level." [34] This was achieved by the standardized process of initiating all men alike and through identical rites; in theory a farrier was socially indistinguishable from a judge within the confines of the lodge, each free to call one another "Brother." Through longstanding tradition, Freemasons did not recruit new members; a man was required—on his own volition—to apply for membership. If, after his application, two or more members would recommend him, he was considered for membership by the local lodge in a formal session. On approval by a unanimous vote, he was said to have been "elected to receive the Mysteries of Freemasonry," and was initiated as a first degree, or Entered Apprentice, Mason. This practice, centuries old in 1860, has continued more or less to the present day.[35]

The first three degrees of Freemasonry, referred to as *Blue Lodge* Masonry, were (and remain) the bedrock Masonic experience; before becoming full members with all the rights and privileges thereof, all Masons had first to complete the degrees of Entered Apprentice, Fellow Craft, and Master Mason. Upon being deemed proficient in the customs and traditions of the fraternity relative to the first degree of Entered Apprentice, as proven by his knowledge of a catechism, the newly admitted man received the second degree and was "passed to the degree of a Fellow Craft." Following a similar test of his proficiency at that level, he received the last degree offered in Blue Lodge—the "sublime degree of a Master Mason" which, once conferred, entitled him to full membership in the Order. Beyond the spiritual and moral significance of the ritual process, the act of initiation was also a homogenizing event bringing together and treating equally men from all walks of life, who in ordinary circumstances might barely cross paths.

Once a man was a Master Mason, he could join additional Masonic organizations separate and distinct from Blue Lodge, among them the York Rite and the Scottish Rite. York Rite Freemasonry, often termed the American Rite, offered additional degrees in three separate but related lodges known as the Royal Arch (degrees 4–7), Royal and Select Master (degrees 8–9), and the Knights Templar (degrees 10–12). American Freemasons could also affiliate with the Scottish Rite of Freemasonry, which offered a total of twenty-nine degrees beyond those obtained in the Blue Lodge (as well as an honorary 33rd degree), and during the last third of the nineteenth century millions of members underwent repeated initiations, with some men joining the Blue Lodge and some who went on to join one, or both additional Rites.[36]

An Army of Masons

The immense amount of fraternal activity all but guaranteed the success and popularity of the Masonic fraternity during the mid-nineteenth century, and the membership rolls demonstrate the degree to which American men embraced fraternalism in general and Masonry in particular. By 1860 the fraternity, without any single source of national guidance (for it had none), had subtly changed from an elite club to a more open society, which while still exclusive in a technical sense, no longer catered to the rich or privileged.

The fraternity in 1860 was on the surface the same fraternity as the 1717 model, but during the post-anti-Mason resurgence subtle changes had crept in. The most significant was in the nature of its membership: once the exclusive province of the patrician class, American Masonry shed its elitist attitudes after the Morgan affair and became a popular social organization of middle-class men.[37] Between 1853 and 1864 the twenty-nine degrees of the Scottish Rite were rewritten, and the York Rite was also substantially remodeled to reflect contemporary values. Combined with a revision of the Blue Lodge ritual ceremonies that occurred from 1840 to 1860, Masonry gained considerable appeal with the American middle class. These changes, "which included the near total prohibition of alcohol in lodges, and the importance of ritual as mirroring desirable social mores worked. Membership skyrocketed and the fraternity became a mirror for middle class sensibilities."[38]

After the long, dark winter of the anti-Masonic period, the fraternity reemerged with new members, each of whom had to be initiated into the Order through a series of lengthy and complex ceremonies. The result, as we shall see, was an army of Masons.

2

Plures Ex Uno

More than any other conflict, the American Civil War was a war between brother Masons. When secessionist forces fired on Fort Sumter in Charleston Harbor, South Carolina, on 12 April 1861—Confederate Gen. P. G. T. Beauregard, a Freemason and a Knight Templar,[1] drew his sword not only against the federal government, but also against a brother Mason—Maj. Robert Anderson, a member of Mercer Lodge No. 50, Trenton, New Jersey.[2] Members of the fraternity served in every capacity and at every level in the armed forces of both North and South, and in every theater of the war members of the fraternity confronted one another in combat. Some played important roles and their names are easily recalled—Armistead, Buckner, Butterfield, Cameron, Cleburne, Hancock, Heth, Houston, Johnston, McClellan, Pickett, Price, Thomas, Toombs, and Wheeler[3]—but the majority were ordinary men unknown to history. Masonic symmetry was present at war's end, as well: when the Army of Northern Virginia surrendered on 9 April 1865, the "last salute" was exchanged between Union Gen. Joshua Chamberlain[4] of United Lodge No. 8, Brunswick, Maine, and Confederate Gen. John B. Gordon of Georgia of Atlanta Lodge No. 59, a minor example of how Masonry confronted its mirror image during the war.[5]

When South Carolina seceded on 20 December 1860, American Freemasonry was in the midst of resurgence. Despite a temporary public opposition to Masonry and other secret societies during the anti-Masonic furor that peaked in the 1830s, the fraternity had established roots in every corner of America. Since colonial times, when lodges were often established on the arrival of military units in each new territory or colony, Masonry had organized itself along state lines, with each state forming its own sovereign jurisdiction and having its own Grand Lodge. Often viewed as an elite fraternity of patricians, the Craft had become more accessible to a wider range of men in the period immediately prior to the war, and membership rolls reflected a consistent annual increase in the number of Masons by the middle of the war. On the eve of war, the fraternity was booming.[6]

By the 1850s and 1860s Freemasons were active in all areas of society, in civil as well as military life, and their numbers were at all-time highs. In 1859 a convention of Masonic Grand Lodges was held in Chicago to explore the formation of a national Grand Lodge. As part of that process—which failed, incidentally—a Masonic census was taken. By comparing those figures with the U.S. Census figures for the male population of the nation, one can estimate the percentage of Freemasons in American society immediately before the war. Two caveats should be borne in mind. First, the Masonic census is likely based on 1858 membership numbers, two years prior to the national census and three before the war. Second, the U.S. Census provides a breakdown of male population aged eighteen to forty-five, which at first glance seems an appropriate age bracket; yet in 1860, unlike today, a man was required to have attained the age of twenty-one years before he could join the fraternity. Furthermore, many men over forty-five years of age belonged to and were active in lodges. That being said, these numbers, without being definite, provide some perspective on how pervasive Freemasonry was during the war (see table 1).[7]

These figures correspond with another prominent American fraternal society, the Independent Order of Odd Fellows. The American branch of the Odd Fellows was first established in Baltimore in 1819—in a single lodge comprised of five members. By 1850, that fraternity numbered 174,637 members gathered into 2,354 lodges and distributed nationally,

Table 1. Masonic membership in 1858 compared with the 1860 Census

State	No. of Lodges	No. of Members	1860 Census Male Population 18–45	% of Masons by Population
Alabama	230	7,260	99,967	7.26%
Arkansas	151	4,383	65,231	6.72%
California	122	4,727	169,975	2.78%
Connecticut	87	5,224	94,411	5.53%
Delaware	19	505	18,273	2.76%
D. Columbia	11	673	12,797	5.26%
Florida	49	1,628	15,739	10.34%
Georgia	230	12,006	111,005	10.82%
Illinois	341	12,053	375,026	3.21%
Indiana	257	9,382	265,295	3.54%
Iowa	148	4,577	139,316	3.29%
Kansas	14	374	27,976	1.34%
Kentucky	366	10,319	180,589	5.71%
Louisiana	162	3,979	83,456	4.77%
Maine	97	3,762	122,238	3.08%
Maryland	36	1,941	102,715	1.89%
Massachusetts	95	5,929	258,419	2.29%
Michigan	128	5,816	164,007	3.55%
Minnesota	28	926	41,226	2.25%
Mississippi	195	9,587	70,295	13.64%
Missouri	195	6,916	232,718	2.97%
New Hampshire	41	2,039	63,610	3.21%
New Jersey	52	2,492	132,219	1.88%
New York	491	28,370	796,881	3.56%
N. Carolina	114	4,994	115,369	4.33%
Ohio	311	12,105	459,534	2.63%
Oregon	26	623	15,718	3.96%

Continued on the next page

Table 1. *Continued*

State	No. of Lodges	No. of Members	1860 Census Male Population 18–45	% of Masons by Population
Pennsylvania	156	11,428	555,172	2.06%
Rhode Island	16	1,391	35,502	3.92%
S. Carolina	82	3,500	55,046	6.36%
Tennessee	288	10,500	159,353	6.59%
Texas	237	7,160	92,145	7.77%
Vermont	48	2,411	60,580	3.98%
Virginia	182	5,529	196,587	2.81%
Wisconsin	108	3,363	159,335	2.11%

Total Lodges:	5,113			
Total Members:		207,872		
Total Male Population 18–45 in 1860:			5,547,725	
Average total % of Masons by national population (approx):				3.75%

suggesting that Odd Fellow membership equaled approximately 3.14 percent under the same analysis as above.[8]

A glance at table 1 shows that Masonry was particularly common in parts of the future Confederacy, with Mississippi, Florida, and Georgia having by far the largest percentages of Freemasons within the eligible male population. These numbers are supported by empirical evidence. An anti-Masonic observer in the 117th New York Volunteers who marched through Georgia near the end of the war remarked,

> Much surprise was expressed at the great number of Masonic Lodges met with. They appeared more plenty in that region [the South] than they are in the North. In and about some of these lodges applications for membership were picked up in which the applicant had unreserv-

edly expressed a purpose to comply with all the requirements of the society. The order, it seemed, had accepted without discrimination, a majority of the "poor white trash," a class, which, before the war were never annoyed with solicitations to join. On witnessing this aggressive feature, this unparalleled democratic tendency, which it had so suddenly acquired in that latitude, and the diligent attention it had received, at a time when the public mind must have been very much pre-occupied, it was difficult to avoid the conclusion, that the order had been an effective promoter of the interests of treason. This conclusion seems supported by the law of probabilities. Is not the order beautifully adapted to the work of moulding and directing its members with reference to a given object? Is not the form ominously similar to that of a conspiracy? That the confederates realized their need of a cementing agency will not be questioned and that men sufficiently corrupt were numbered among its members, is also patent.[9]

Although it is possible that Masonic affiliation in the South was inordinately comprised of men predisposed toward secession, the sentiments of Masonry's governing bodies do not bear out the theory that Masons formed the nucleus for political change at any time. By ancient tradition, the fraternity was opposed to rebellion against the government, although the actions of an individual member in rebellion would not in and of themselves bring about the sanction of the Order. "If a Brother should be a Rebel against the State, he is not to be countenanc'd in his Rebellion, however he may be pitied as an unhappy Man; and, if convicted of no other Crime, though the loyal Brotherhood must and ought to disown his Rebellion, and give no Umbrage or Ground of political Jealousy to the government for the time being; they cannot expel him from the *Lodge,* and his Relation to it remains indefeasible."[10]

Let Us Agree to Separate Amicably

As the secession crisis deepened in 1860, Freemasonry's response was as fractured as that of the rest of the country. On the eve of war, many in the fraternity actively sought conciliation and compromise to avert a national disaster, while others urged that Masonry take no side concerning secession. Early on, the Grand Masters of Kentucky, Ohio, and Indiana attempted reconciliation through a general Masonic conference to diffuse the secession crisis.[11] The Grand Chapter of Royal Arch Masons in Virginia—an appendant body to regular, or "Blue Lodge," Masonry—expressed a different but not bellicose view: "When we have exhausted every effort at compromise and reconciliation, and the very last ray of hope is about departing . . . Let us agree to separate amicably, as brothers, each traveling a different road, and each having a different aim to accomplish amongst the great family of nations."[12]

In December of 1860, John Dove, the Grand Secretary of Masons in Virginia, wrote an open letter to the Craft warning of the impending disaster:

> The patriot Mason stands appalled, and his heart sinks almost to suffocation when he beholds this majestic edifice scathed and scattered into fragments by the vivid lightning of intemperate zeal; and, straining his tearful eyes he beholds amid the lurid and angry flames of civil revolution, every star and stripe transformed into a red and angry ground, fit emblem of the precious blood of martyrs shed in its defense; and gazing still again intently, he beholds the dark Demon of Discord, with exultant and hell-inspired satisfaction writing on this once sainted banner, *Plures ex uno*. Shall this be? Forbid it. . . . Oh! let it not be torn asunder by the convulsive and sickening throes of popular revolution.[13]

A week after South Carolina seceded, the Grand Master of Pennsylvania, Henry M. Phillips, echoed Dove's remarks and pleaded for national reconciliation to avert a catastrophe, making an "affectionate and a Masonic appeal to practice out of the Lodge those principles of forbearance, generosity, charity and brotherly love as they are taught within it, to unite as a brotherhood to preserve the glorious work in which so many of our honored brethren participated, and to aid in restoring peace, harmony good will and friendly relations that should exist among the whole American people."[14]

Initially, the Grand Masters of the several states held out hope that peace would be restored and that an amicable solution could be achieved, but as the reality of war's inevitability became apparent, doubts about the preservation of the Union began to be openly discussed. In a letter dated 31 December 1860 to Winslow Lewis, Grand Master of Massachusetts, from John R. McDaniel, Grand Master of Virginia, McDaniel wrote, "the Union is beyond doubt dissolved, and the only hope that remains is, that a peaceful separation may be effected, and the conservative elements of both sections may so exert themselves, as to secure the most friendly relations."[15]

The lack of central control over Freemasonry added to the confusion over secession, and no consensus of Masonic thought emerged even up to the first summer of the war. In May 1861, the Grand Lodge of Tennessee expressed its dismay over civil war and declared its hopes for a speedy return to peace.[16] Likewise, in the pro-Union *Masonic Review,* an anonymous editorialist declared in mid-1861: "Some Grand Lodges have given expression to their opinions, while others have declined to agitate the question entirely, though no less loyal than the former. We, however, should seek to mollify the passions, and smooth the asperities of this fratricidal contest; and do all we can to bind up the wounds that may be made. Peace and fraternal fellowship should be the object of Masons everywhere—not peace at the expense of principle and right, but in contradistinction to hostility and hatred."[17]

Masonry, in short, had no answer to the question of civil war, and indeed was as powerless as any other institution to halt the calamity.

Shock, or perhaps stunned silence, characterized official Masonry during the early months of the war, and Masonic vilification of the enemy during those early days was a rare thing. But, as the initial optimism of a quick victory faded and the casualties mounted on both sides, the attitudes of the grand jurisdictions, commentators, and editorialists began to harden. The Grand Lodge of Ohio, noted earlier for its supplications in support of peace, became intransigent, communicating to its members that "a Mason is to be a peaceable subject to the civil powers, and is never to be concerned in plots and conspiracies against Government . . . and that it is the duty of every worthy Mason . . . to stand by the general government even at the expense of fortune and life."[18] Likewise, the Grand Lodge of Virginia stated flatly, "if our soil be polluted by an invader's tread, be he Mason or Profane, drive him back."[19] Once the shooting started, the Grand Lodges, like the rest of the country, became embittered by the divorce and sought solace in victory. Southern grand lodges, like the Grand Lodge of Virginia, for example, which had been among the early voices calling for peace and harmony, had, by the third summer of the war, reexamined the traditional teachings of Freemasonry that were hostile to rebellion and arrived at a political justification for secession and civil war.[20]

> The Constitutions of Masonry teach us,
> "Whoever will be a true Mason is further to know, by the rules of his art, his allegiance as a subject and citizen will not be relaxed, but enforced. *He is to be a lover of quiet, peaceable and obedient to the civil powers which yield him protection and are set over him where he resides or works,* so far as there is no infringement of the limited bounds of reason and religion."
>
> This duty as Masons we honestly perform by adhering to the sovereign power of our own State. It is under our State government we hold all our rights as husbands, fathers, and owners of property. It is by its benign laws that the purity, honor and fair character of families are preserved. It is by its laws all our affairs with our neighbors are regulated and the rewards of our industry secured. It is under it we reside and work.
>
> The United States government has infringed the bounds of religion and reason by attempting to set over us an usurped and tyrannical despotism. Masonry does not require us to yield allegiance to usurpers and tyrants.
>
> We think it behooves us to put this vindication of ourselves as men

and citizens on our records and permit it to go down to our successors. For while Masonry has nothing to do with war or politics, the vindication of our characters as honest men and good citizens is dear to us, and we feel we are doing justice to Masonry in preserving our fair fame from men who have borrowed the garb of Masonry to make the assault.[21]

While the Grand Lodges repositioned themselves and issued political screeds to support their individual positions on the war, it was left to the individual members of the fraternity to put the tenets of Masonry— brotherly love, relief, and truth—into practice.

The Rebellion Came On like a Cyclone

Yet at the local level, lodges had difficulties reconciling the political climate with the aims of Masonry. The onset of hostilities tore many lodges apart, diverting the energies of the members and leaving empty chairs in the lodge halls. According to Calvin Smith, one of the founders of Smithville Lodge in Smithville, Missouri, when secession became a reality the lodge at Smithville simply disbanded "when the war of the rebellion came on like a cyclone. Some of the brethren were for the Union, some for secession. So brethren disagreed out of the lodge and on the street. In the lodge we said brethren should agree in and out of the lodge. But a storm was too plainly brewing and the shock was at hand; so we passed a resolution to surrender our charter back to the Grand Lodge of the State of Missouri, instructing our secretary to send the charter and jewels to the Grand Lodge. This was in October, 1861, or thereabouts."[22]

And so the Craft went to war. But although the Grand Lodges had thrown up their hands, and the local lodges folded, the individual Mason in the ranks took another approach and, as we shall see, the fraternity continued to thrive and nurture the ideal of brotherhood despite the conflict. As the Masons left their lodges and joined up, many organized traveling "Military Lodges" that held regular meetings, initiated new members, and provided for the wants of less fortunate soldiers and civilians, whether members or not. In those regiments where traveling lodges were not permitted, Masons messed together, tented together, and, the evidence shows, maintained close associations within the military organization. Although Masons needed the permission of their Grand Lodge to form a regimental lodge (see chapter 7), once granted Masonic soldiers had little if any contact with Grand Lodge supervision, and the evidence suggests that Masons coalesced without any centralized authority whatsoever.

Not Permit It to Be Done by Others

Although the war unquestionably killed thousands of members and disrupted normal operations at the home lodges, not only of Masons but of other fraternal societies as well, it also brought to the forefront a unique facet of the fraternal organization: mutual aid. As described in chapter 1, fraternal orders—the Masons and the Odd Fellows in particular—had long-established traditions of aiding fellow members away from home or in distress. In Odd Fellowship, the system was quite formal and provided for stipends, assistance in obtaining work, and other prerogatives typical of a benefit society.[23] Masons, although similarly inculcated to aid a distressed worthy brother, had no such benefit schedule; each Mason was only obligated to aid another if in so doing he would not injure himself (see chapter 3).

But whether or not the fraternal aid was to be dispensed formally as with the Odd Fellows, or in a less structured fashion by Freemasons, one still had to be sure if the recipient was a brother, and this required a test. In some instances a member could prove membership by asking other members to vouch for him, if they knew him. In other instances he could produce paperwork (see below) that demonstrated his affiliation, but in strained circumstances, bereft of supporting documents, and often among strangers, fraternal signs and tokens were called upon to verify affiliation. Originally intended for use by stranded travelers or a fraternity brother beset by highwaymen, these significations—consisting of secret phrases or specific gestures taught within the lodges—could be used to prove membership and summon assistance in a military context. Although such communications were almost certainly never intended for use in warfare, soldiers and sailors on both sides "requisitioned" Freemasonry when the occasion required it.[24]

These Masonic ties were invoked in camp, in the field, in prison, and in battle. One example of how Masonry influenced events in the field occurred at the Battle of Gettysburg (1–3 July 1863). A private, Anson C. Miller, of Company J, 151st Pennsylvania, was shot four times near the Lutheran Seminary. Left behind by his retreating comrades, he was set upon by a group of rebel troops who stole his clothing, blankets, and food until he made a Masonic appeal: "He used those words which a Master Mason hears and heeds, even amid the fury and din of battle. Immediately there stepped out from among the Rebel soldiers one who remember his duty to a needed brother. He was a Tennessean—Menturn by name. He declared that he had never robbed a wounded foe, and that he would not permit it to be done by others."[25]

Incredibly, Anson's property was restored, he was evacuated and despite dim prospects, he survived the battle.[26]

A second example is found during the Second Battle of Manassas (29 August 1862) where one of Jackson's "foot cavalry" described a furious charge that routed a federal regiment. "They turned and ran," he wrote, "leaving many dead and wounded on our side of the railroad. Approaching these men, lying on the ground about one hundred yards from us, I noticed one of them on his back, gesticulating with his hands, raising them up, moving them violently backward and forward. I thought he was trying to attract our attention, so that we might not injure him in our advance. When I reached him, I recognized by his shoulder straps that he was a Yankee captain, and one of our captains, who was running on my left, said he was making the masonic sign of distress."[27] Although the report contained no clue if the distress call was ultimately answered, the fact that it was noted and recorded by an ordinary soldier provides some insight into the pervasiveness and influence of Freemasonry.

It is manifestly evident that the fabric of America was torn apart by the Civil War. That Freemasonry formed a significant part of that fabric has not been readily recognized. Although it is easy to dismiss the role of the Masonic fraternity during the war as just another social club with grandiloquent titles and preposterous costumes, that assumption is false. The chapters that follow show the particular ways in which individual Freemasons translated their Masonic experience from a peacetime social function to an indispensable resource in war. Masonic aid took many forms. In some cases, it preserved property from the unsparing hand of war by guarding a fellow Mason's house, safeguarding his personal possessions from looters or thieves, or protecting a Masonic lodge in a captured town. In other instances, Masons cared for the wounded—often unasked, but many times in response to a fraternal call for help. Masonic prisoners of war were beneficiaries of fraternal kindness, receiving food, clothing, and medicines from their warders who were also members of the Craft. In startling examples of Masonic interventions during actual combat, Masons more than once saved the lives of their brethren along the front lines. Despite the indecision and oftentimes powerlessness of the Grand Lodges in ameliorating the suffering and hardship of war, individual Masons took it upon themselves to inject their concept of brotherhood into the war with, as we shall see, remarkable results.

3

"If That Is Masonry
I Will Take Some of It Myself"

Returning from a raid at Grenada, Mississippi, in August of 1863, the 9th Illinois Infantry passed through the village of Holly Springs, and the officers of the 9th were nervous. Recent operations in Mississippi had shown the citizenry to be openly hostile to Union troops, and several towns had been burned in retaliation. To prevent this, guards were posted at the houses as the infantry passed through, but an enterprising soldier, intent on dinner, not revenge, had circumvented them and was in the process of raiding a chicken coop. The woman of the house inquired loudly, "is there a Mason here? I am the widow of a Mason! I wish to know if there is a Mason here? I wish protection!" When no Freemason appeared, she set about the robber with a stick, and drove him from her chicken coop unaided.[1]

A similar scene occurred in Albemarle County, Virginia, in March of 1865. Faced with Union soldiers ransacking her home and smokehouse, Mrs. Meriweather Anderson produced a Masonic apron and called out, "is there no one here who can protect the widow of a Mason?" But in this instance, a rescuer was at hand; a passing cavalryman dismounted, grabbed the apron, examined it, then went inside and ordered every soldier out.[2]

These widow's pleas are examples of yet another peculiar aspect of the fraternity—the obligation of a Mason to render aid when called upon by a fraternity brother, his wife, widow, or children. Inculcated to practice charity through fraternal ritual, charity was, and is, esteemed by Masons as the greatest of virtues. A Masonic publication in 1859 explained,

> The Masonic creed is Faith, Hope, and Charity. Faith in God: Hope in Immortality, and Charity to all mankind. A Faith, which has a living, abiding and active reliance upon all the promises of God. Hope, which takes hold of those promises of that blessed life and immortality which was brought to light by Him who put death under his feet. And Charity, which consists not and contents not itself alone in alms-giving, or in the still more grateful and noble office of administering consolation to the weary and afflicted soul but a charity that leads us to judge of others with lenity and to speak of them without reproach.[3]

Another Masonic tract—among many published after the war—held that Masonic charity did not extend merely to almsgiving but rather should be "that nobler charity which teaches us to feel another's woe, to hide another's fault. Tolerance that permits the exercise of reason and the free expression of thought, and that true spirit of Fraternity which is wide enough to embrace in its arms the whole world."[4] A source of constant comment within the fraternity, Masonic commentators have devoted considerable thought to the importance of benefaction; even the formidable Albert G. Mackey, Freemasonry's Dr. Johnson, counted "relief" as of the four great rights of the fraternity, and he commented at length on how Masonic charity must be given.

> One of the great objects of our institution is, to afford relief to a worthy, distressed Brother. In his want and destitution, the claim of a Mason upon his Brethren is much greater than that of a profane. . . . This claim for relief he may present either to a lodge or to a Brother Mason. The rule, as well as the principles by which it is to be regulated, is laid down in that fundamental law of Masonry, the Old Charges, [which state:]

"You are cautiously to examine him, in such a method as prudence shall direct you, that you may not be imposed upon by an ignorant, false pretender, whom you are to reject with contempt and derision, and beware of giving him any hints of knowledge.

"But if you discover him to be a true and genuine Brother, you are to respect him accordingly; and if he is in want, you *must* [emphasis added] relieve him if you can, or else direct him how he may be relieved. You must employ him some days, or else recommend him to be employed. But you are not charged to do beyond your ability, only to prefer a poor Brother, that is a good man and true, before any other people in the same circumstances."[5]

Practicing charity in peacetime is vastly different from charity in war, and Masons found themselves asking how they could reconcile their principles with the political reality of open war. In October of 1861, the Grand Master of New York, Finlay M. King, supplied his jurisdiction with the answer. Arguing that Freemasonry was in a unique position to mitigate the horrors of war, being pervasive on both sides of the Mason-Dixon line, he urged greater Masonic participation in military units, and called for an increase in charitable efforts on the battlefield and in military hospitals, letting "the light of Masonic charity and mercy shed forth their cheering beams, bringing balm to the sufferer, comfort to the sorrowing, and sustenance to the poor and hungry."[6]

Although American Freemasonry was not under King's exclusive control, individual Masons did in fact put the tenets of the fraternity into practice, and many accounts exist of Union or Confederate Freemasons who did just that, by providing aid and assistance to brother Masons on the other side. These contemporary accounts indicate that Masonic charity came in several distinct forms—all of which received considerable attention in period sources—and though many Masons who engaged in these acts of mercy may not have heard King's call, their own Masonic instincts made them act accordingly.

These instincts manifested themselves in many ways but the most basic was forbearance by the victors toward the vanquished. Although history provides many instances of victorious troops sparing towns and villages from pillage and looting, plunder is the time-honored prerogative of the victor. The Masonic affiliation, however, tempered this tendency, and Masons in the conquering forces were at great pains to spare the property of their vanquished brethren. A famous example concerns Confederate Gen. Albert Pike's house (and impressive Masonic library). Pike, who later would become arguably the most famous American Mason, had incited Union wrath by securing Indian allies for the Confederacy, and Union troops sought to wreak their revenge by burning his house in Little Rock to the ground. Apprised of the fact that the house and its contents would be destroyed, a Union officer—Col. Thomas Hart Benton Jr., of the 29th Iowa infantry, who was also the serving Grand Master of Masons in Iowa at that time—intervened and took the house for his headquarters. Benton's actions saved Pike's house and preserved for Masonry a pearl of great price. Pike's collection of books and manuscripts later became the library of the Supreme Council (Southern jurisdiction) of the Ancient and Accepted Scottish Rite.[7]

Masonic property in the form of jewels and regalia also summoned Masonry's "better angels," and to prevent their theft or destruction Masons went to extraordinary lengths. In some cases, officers suspended hostilities until Masonic regalia could be transferred to its rightful owners, as in the case of Confederate Col. H. H. Miller. While in command of rebel forces defending Ponchatoula, Louisiana, on 1 April 1863, Miller reported to his superiors that he met under flag of truce one "Colonel Smith" of the 165th New York (2nd Battalion, Duryee's Zouaves), who, among other things, returned to him some Masonic jewels stolen from an area lodge. Miller gratefully accepted the stolen badges, gave his compliments to the federal colonel, whereupon the fighting around Ponchatoula resumed shortly thereafter.[8]

Noncombatant Masons also took great pains to make known their affiliation with the fraternity to insure their homes and personal property from the ravages of war. Watching federal troops marching down the road in front of his house, a plantation owner in St. Landry Parish, Louisiana, made a Masonic gesture from his balcony, which was observed by the Union commander who immediately ordered the house and property off limits to his command.[9] A similar situation was reported near West Point, Mississippi. A Masonic apron "of curious workmanship and material" and of antique origin was uncovered by marauding Union troops, some of them Masons, as they ransacked a private home while holding the occupants, a mother and child, at gun point. When the apron was discovered, one of the looters, who was perhaps brought to his senses by the fraternal trappings, conversed in whispered tones with the lady of the house before leaving and returning with a federal officer. At once, order was restored and an apology issued to the owner of the home.[10] Offers by the Union commander to pay for the damage were cut short, however, by the arrival of Confederate forces under Gen. Nathan Bedford Forrest who drove the invaders away.[11]

Sometimes, Masons had no property to protect, being entirely destitute. A peculiar codicil of the Order requires each individual Mason, should he chance upon a poor and penniless "worthy brother" to contribute to his relief as liberally as possible without injury to themselves. Future U.S. president William McKinley was so impressed by the generosity of one particular Freemason that he joined the fraternity before he left the army. At the Third Battle of Winchester (Virginia),[12] twenty-one-year-old McKinley was a staff officer in the Union Army of the Shenandoah. Following the fight, he accompanied a federal surgeon on a visit to Confederate prisoners. In a conversation after the war, McKinley described his first impression of Freemasonry. While visiting Confederate POWs with a federal doctor, McKinley observed the physician handing out money to the rebel prisoners until he had none left. On the way back to camp, McKinley inquired of the doctor if he knew the men or if he had seen them before. On hearing the doctor answer that he did not know the men, McKinley persisted, pressing the physician for his motives. "They are Masons," the doctor replied, "and we Masons have ways of finding that out." McKinley, surprised at this generosity to strangers, asked whether the doctor ever expected repayment. "Well," said the doctor, "if they are ever able to pay it back, they will. But it makes no difference to me; they are brother Masons in trouble, and I am only doing my duty." "If that is Masonry," McKinley observed, "I will take some of it myself."[13]

Eight months later, after the surrender of Lee's army at Appomattox, while McKinley remained stationed at Winchester, Virginia, he petitioned Hiram Lodge No. 21—which was comprised of Southerners—and was initiated. He took his first degree on 1 May 1865, his second the next day, and his third degree on 3 May 1865.[14]

He Made Some Sign to a Passing Rebel

The foregoing examples illustrate Masonic charity during periods of relative quiet, but fraternal concerns for the property of Masons did not stop at the edge of the battlefield. At Chancellorsville on 3 May 1863, Lt. Col. Guy H. Watkins of the 141st Pennsylvania Infantry was seriously wounded and left behind as Confederate infantry advanced. Rebel troops captured him and were in the process of stripping him of his clothes and valuables when "on making himself known to the Lieutenant of the company as a Free Mason, [the lieutenant] also belonging to that same fraternity, he was sent to the headquarters of General Longstreet," where he immediately received medical treatment.[15]

Similarly, at the Battle of Corinth, 3 October 1862, Lt. Samuel A. Tinkham of Company B, 14th Wisconsin, received a gunshot wound to the leg, followed shortly by another to the body.[16] "He made some sign to a passing rebel—which was said to be a Masonic sign of recognition. The rebel immediately came to Tinkham's side, and rendered him all the assistance in his power."[17] Before he died, Tinkham gave the Confederate soldier his watch and money to forward to his family. The rebel then pinned a small piece of paper on the Union officer's coat, to aid in identifying him postmortem. Tinkham's body was found after the battle and buried by his comrades. Nine months later, at the capitulation of Vicksburg, the rebel Mason who aided Tinkham was captured. He reportedly sought out the 14th Wisconsin and discharged Tinkham's property to them.[18]

Countless reports illustrate soldier's concerns—often their last wishes—that their keepsakes be returned home in the event of their deaths, yet a great many witnesses report that all too often these small treasures became the spoils of war as the victorious robbed the dead or dying. Charles Dana, Lincoln's assistant secretary of war, saw the last wish of a dying man fulfilled when he witnessed an incident after the Battle of Champion's Hill.[19] Following the Confederate withdrawal, Dana toured the field with federal staff officers, among them Lt. Col. John A. Rawlins. Riding through a field of Confederate dead where the thickest of the fighting had occurred, the group discovered a mortally wounded rebel soldier, who raised himself up and asked, "For God's sake, gentlemen, is there a Mason among you?" Rawlins answered affirmatively, dismounted, and knelt by the dying man. The soldier pressed a memento into Rawlins's hands, requesting it be sent to a loved one back home. According to Dana, Rawlins accepted it and a short time thereafter succeeded in sending on the keepsake as instructed.[20]

Our Mystic Circle

Masonry's reputation—well known during the 1860s—as charitable benefactors did not spare the fraternity from pillage and looting, and many lodges were destroyed during actual battle, or by marauding troops either during or after the investiture of their towns. The town of Yellville, Arkansas, is a typical example. A small hamlet of no strategic importance, the town was set upon by pro-Union guerillas of one Captain Webb, in November of 1862, who, in the process of the raid, burned down thirty-two houses, two hotels, the Methodist church, and the Masonic hall, all of them destroyed deliberately.[21]

By contrast, when Baton Rouge surrendered to Union troops in May 1862, Masons in the conquering forces stepped forward to protect fraternal property. The master of St. James Lodge reported that "brethren of the [Masonic] order in the ranks of the army restrained those outside our mystic circle," and his lodge was spared destruction by freebooters.[22] The lodge at Fredericksburg, Virginia, was also spared destruction when the colonel of the 10th New York, John E. Bendix,[23] a Freemason, caught soldiers cavorting through town dressed in Masonic regalia. He ordered the troops to "carefully replace" the stolen articles, which were later forwarded to the Grand Lodge of Virginia for safekeeping.[24]

During the Peninsula Campaign, another Masonic lodge was equally fortunate. In November 1861, federal troops encamped near Fortress Monroe, Virginia, passed through the looted and deserted village of Hampton. Among the ruins of the town stood St. Tammany Lodge No. 5, which had survived the worst of the pillage. As luck would have it, one of the federal officers in the advance was Lt. Jackson H. Chase, a member, and past Master, of Temple Lodge No. 14, Albany, New York, and an officer in the 3rd New York Volunteers. With little time left to postpone the advance, Chase quickly contacted the commanding general, Benjamin F. Butler,[25] another prominent Mason, to request a detachment to secure the lodge against further looting. Describing his visit to Tammany Lodge, and seeking some place to store the lodge property, Chase wrote to the nearest friendly Grand Officer he could—John S. Berry, the Grand Master of Maryland. His unusual account, reproduced here in full, demonstrates the particular care with which Chase and his fellow officers took to secure the looted lodge.

M. W. [Most Worshipful] Sir and Brother:—The 3d Regiment, New York Volunteers, to which I am attached, encamped in June last at Camp Hamilton, Va., some two miles from Fortress Monroe, and about one mile from the village of Hampton. This village has been deserted by its inhabitants, a short time previous to our arrival, and in such haste as to leave libraries, furniture, &c., exposed to the pillage and plunder of the hordes of negroes who congregated there immediately on the departure of the citizens. Much valuable property had been taken and destroyed by them. Learning that there was a Masonic Hall in the place, and fearing its safety, I reported the fact to Major General Butler, and obtained from him an order to take "a sufficient force, proceed to Hampton, and take possession of such property belonging to the Masonic Order as was thought proper, and report to him." In accordance with this order, Col. S. M. Alford, commanding the 3rd Regiment, provided a detachment commanded by John E. Mulford, W.M. of Mystic Lodge, No. 131., N.Y.; and Lieutenant William E. Blake, S. W. Excelsior Lodge, No. 195, N.Y., accompanied the detachment. We proceeded to Hampton, and with the officers referred to, visited the Hall of St. Tammany Lodge, No. 5. Nearly all the Lodge furniture was found, including the Records and Warrants, one Warrant bears the date 1787. The Jewels had been removed, probably by some member of the Lodge.

The property thus found I have retained in my possession, hoping that a favorable opportunity might present itself to forward it directly to Richmond. But not having had such an opportunity, I take great pleasure in transferring the effects to you for safe keeping, subject to the order of the Grand Lodge of Virginia. Since taking this property, the hall, together with the entire village, was destroyed by fire; and my associates with myself congratulate ourselves that we were the humble instruments in rescuing the Records and Warrants from that conflagration. When this property shall be returned to our brethren in Virginia, please to convey to them our fraternal regards, and say that although we come in defence of our just rights, as we honestly believe, still we come not to wage war upon an Order expressly founded to inculcate the exercise of Brotherly Love, Relief, and Truth.[26]

Shortly thereafter, the Grand Lodge of Maryland received word from James B. Campbell, the Deputy District Grand Master (District 1) of the Grand Lodge of Virginia, that the Virginia Masonic authorities acknowledged their property to be in the keeping of the Grand Lodge of Maryland and that he was authorized to request that "the furniture, Warrant and Records, be forwarded by Adams' Express Co., to me, at the earliest convenience, as the proper custodian of such articles, by the Grand Lodge of Virginia." Campbell also wrote that "[o]n behalf of the Masonic Fraternity of this State, and especially the members of St. Tammanys Lodge, No, 5, let me thank you . . . and Lieut. Chase, for the care and preservation of these articles. A circumstance which beautifully exemplifies the principles of our noble Order, amidst the fierce and sanguinary warfare now raging."[27] That Virginia and Maryland were then in a state of war, and Campbell's correspondence through enemy lines concerned not affairs of state, but Masonic jewels and paperwork, underscores the importance of the Masonic bond on both sides of the conflict.

But the case of St. Tammany Lodge was not an isolated incident. Union officers in Georgia in November of 1864 acted similarly to safeguard the Masonic regalia of a lodge looted in the wake of Sherman's March to the Sea. In an undated account, published in 1885, anonymous female correspondent "L. F. J." described federal officers—Masons—visiting her home during the occupation and depositing with her the Masonic jewels they had rescued from the unidentified lodge. "These officers told me their men had rifled the Masonic hall before they could prevent it, and they had gathered up all the jewels they could find, and having been told my husband was a Mason, they brought them to me. I ripped open a feather-bed, hid these jewels and returned them afterwards in safety to our village lodge." To ensure the home, and the Masonic property, would not be disturbed, the officers detailed a soldier to guard the house.[28]

The Masonic "jewels" referenced here and elsewhere are badges of office, which in America generally conform to specific styles regardless of the jurisdiction. A typical lodge of the period might have six officers at a minimum: the Master, Senior and Junior Wardens, Secretary, Treasurer, and the Tyler, although well-established lodges might perhaps include deacons, a chaplain, and other officers as well. The Master's jewel, for instance, was (and remains) invariably in the shape of a stonemason's square; the jewel of the Senior Warden was a stylized level, the Treasurer's jewel an emblem consisting of two crossed keys, the Tyler's a pendant displaying a sword. These emblems could have been worn in any number of ways—suspended by a cord or chain and hung about the neck, or pinned on the breast of the wearer. Depending on the relative wealth of an individual lodge, they may have been made of precious metal and comparatively ornate, or crudely fashioned out of tin or sheet metal.

The regalia of a lodge, which is also sometimes referred to as the "furniture," includes not only the chairs, podiums, and fixtures within the hall itself but also equipment used in ritual work—a sword, the Bible, and the square and compasses. De rigueur in all Masonic lodges, these items possess great significance to members of the fraternity.

The lodge charter was also of great concern to Masons. A formal certificate, often on sheepskin or vellum, it bore official language and signatures and was easily recognizable to members. Masonic soldiers who chanced upon them in the ruins of demolished temples took extraordinary steps to insure their survival, for they were sine qua non to any Masonic lodge. Issued by the governing body of the Masonic jurisdiction, it was similar, though not identical, to a business license. Without a charter, a Masonic lodge could not conduct business, initiate new members, or even meet officially—they were therefore (and they remain) indispensable to the Craft. Charles Moore, the editor of Boston's *Freemason's Monthly*—a staunchly pro-Union Masonic magazine—from 1842 to 1873, was Grand Secretary of the Massachusetts Grand Lodge during the Civil War. In the September 1863 issue of the *Monthly,* he published a letter from a surgeon attached to 17th Massachusetts—William Hinds—who recounted the plunder by Union forces of Conoho Lodge No. 131 in Hamilton, North Carolina, on 4 November 1862. Hinds, who was also an officer in his regimental lodge, wrote as follows:

> While on the recent expedition under Gen. Foster, we passed through the village of Hamilton, N.C. Our regiment being in the rear, it was sometime after the arrival of the head of the column before *we* reached the place. When we did arrive, I found that the building occupied by the Masonic Fraternity had been broken open by some New York soldiers, and much of the regalia, and all of the Jewels carried off. With the assistance of some Brethren I succeeded in getting

a guard placed over what was left, while the troops were in the town. In looking over the articles that were left, I found the Charter of the Lodge, which being in quite a fine frame, I feared might perhaps be taken possession of by some one who might make an improper use of it: and there being no one in the town with whom it could be left, by the advise of some of our Fraternity, I took possession of it, and herewith enclose it to you. You will please make such disposition of it as you may deem proper under the circumstances.

I could find no trace of the Jewels, but should I succeed in getting possession of them hereafter, I will send them to you to be deposited with our Grand Lodge until such time as they can be returned.[29]

Without hesitation, Hinds recognized the importance of the discovery and took immediate steps to safeguard the charter, delivering it from the war zone to Moore's office in Boston. Moore received Conoho Lodge's charter and noted that it was dated 1850, "given at Raleigh, the 5th day of December and signed by Alonzo T. Jerkins, as Grand Master."[30] At some later point Moore also received the jewels of Conoho Lodge as well, consisting of a silver set of badges for the Master, Wardens, Treasurer, Secretary, and Tyler, along with the seal of the lodge and two Masonic tools from Maj. Andrew A. Elwell of the 23rd Massachusetts.[31] Moore wrote that he would hold the charter and jewels of the lodge in a "sacred, brotherly trust," in the hope that the owners could receive them and be reunited to their brethren in the North and, he added, to "the Flag of his Fathers."[32]

Nor was this the only reported incident involving the looting of Southern lodges by federal troops. Just over a year after the incident in Conoho Lodge, the lodge in Washington, North Carolina, about thirty-five miles south of Conoho Lodge in Hamilton, suffered likewise when it was ransacked by Union troops on 27–30 April 1864. This lawlessness, however, attracted official notice and prompted the issuance of General Order No. 5 by the Union commander, Gen. Innis N. Palmer. Palmer was outraged at the firing of the town and at the deliberate targeting by lawless troops of the "the charitable institutions . . . bursting open the doors of the Masonic[33] and Odd Fellow's lodges, pillaged them both, and hawked about the streets the regalia and jewels." Referring to the culprits as "thieves and scoundrels, dead to all sense of honor and humility, for whom no punishment can be too severe," Palmer identified two of the regiments involved and ordered ten days dress parade for the entire complement of the 17th Massachusetts Volunteers and the 15th Connecticut Volunteers—during which the entire order would be recited each day—until the guilty parties were found.[34]

The board of inquiry formed to investigate the incident identified culprits not only in the 17th Massachusetts—Surgeon Hinds's (of Conoho Lodge fame) own regiment—and 15th Connecticut, but also in the 58th Pennsylvania Volunteers, 21st Connecticut Volunteers, two companies of the 5th Rhode Island Volunteer Artillery, Ransom's New York Battery, two companies of the 12th New York Cavalry, the cavalry company of the 1st North Carolina (Union) Volunteers, as well as sailors, freed slaves, transport corps personnel, and citizens of the town.[35]

In North Carolina at least, Masonry had friends in high places. General Palmer was reputedly a Freemason, and he would use his influence again on at least one other occasion to safeguard a Masonic lodge, in Elkin, North Carolina, in April of 1865.[36] His commander, Maj. Gen. Benjamin F. Butler, was unquestionably a member of the Order. In April 1864, Butler had formally intervened concerning property taken from the lodge at New Bern, North Carolina, ordering Maj. Gen. John Peck to secure any Masonic property found and to arrange for its return to local Masons.[37]

Butler was so well known as a Freemason that his official correspondence included several letters with requests for favors or assistance couched in Masonic terms. One letter sent to him in 1864 requested leniency for a certain Captain Swift, accused of serious crimes, and presumably slated to be punished. The letter from Swift's would-be benefactor is lost, but Butler's reply survives.

You appeal to me in behalf of *Capt. Swift* by a tie which never should be lightly invoked, and certainly not for an unworthy object.

If you have taken the obligations which you claim, you know that they do not call upon either of us to interfere to protect the criminal or defend the wrong. We should go many miles, aye even *bare foot* and *over frozen ground,* to aid a worthy brother; but not one inch outside the path of duty to aid an unworthy one.

If I could believe for a moment that this was *Capt. Swift's* first offense, without any appeal to my Masonic obligations I would overlook it, but I am well assured that it is not; and charges for other like offenses are against him, previous to this time. Therefore I must do my duty by sending him to a Court Martial.[38]

The *Experimentum Crucis*

Plunder and pillage, the handmaidens of war, were never officially condoned by either army, although certainly in many instances commanders turned a blind eye toward these activities. In certain circumstances, however, seizure of private property—particularly foodstuffs, military supplies, and forage for animals—was official army policy. Special Field Order 120, issued on 9 November 1864, by Union Gen. William T. Sherman prior to his "March to the Sea," provided that no general train of supplies would follow the army and that the army should "forage liberally on the country during the march." Sherman instructed that each brigade would organize its own foraging party to secure provisions and forage from among the civilian population sparing them only a store of ten days' provisions at any one time. Although the orders prohibited entering or breaking into homes, civilian gardens were fair game. Livestock and other supplies were also openly sought, and Sherman's order targeted rich Southern citizens "who are usually hostile" as opposed to "the poor or industrious," who it was judged were either neutral or kindly disposed toward the invading army. The only restriction as to the amount of provisions garnered from any one source was that the foraging parties should "*endeavor to leave with each family a reasonable portion for their maintenance.*"[39]

An unnamed doctor in Cheraw, South Carolina, saw this order firsthand when a federal foraging party appeared at his door in February of 1865.

On the day after the appearance of the army in the town, I was standing at the door of my mansion, when an army officer approached, accompanied by a guard and followed by a large baggage wagon. He introduced himself as Lieut. B - - -, of Wisconsin, when the following conversation took place.

"Have you any specie in your house?"

"I have not."

"Have you any gold or silver?"

"Yes, I have a gold watch, and my wife has another; and I have the usual plate of a respectable family—some silver forks and spoons and things of that kind."

"Well, I will attend to those matters in time. What provisions have you in the house?"

"About enough to last my family a year."[40]

Shown the provisions by the doctor and his wife, the Union officer commandeered the lot and ordered his men to begin loading the supplies, excepting ten days' provisions for the doctor and his family. With the transportation system in ruins, and with no means of obtaining a fresh supply, the prospects were grim. Faced with the reality of starvation, the doctor resorted to Freemasonry.

I thought that if he were a mason there was still some small hope of saving myself and family . . . and for the first time in my life, long as I have been a member of the Order, I determined to have recourse to it for that aid which it had always promised to me in time of peril and danger. I commenced, therefore, in the mute but expressive language of our institution, to inquire if Lieut. B - - - was a brother of the mystic tie. To my first signals he promptly responded and in a few minutes I was convinced that he was a Master Mason. I proceeded in the same mysterious manner with my investigations, and was satisfied that he was also a Royal Arch companion. . . . Having learned this much, I resolved to try the *experimentum crucis,* and to make that last appeal, to which I hoped he would not be inattentive. . . . The position of things at this time was thus: I was standing in the centre of the room where the provisions were stored; on my right hand was my wife; opposite me was the lieutenant, the soldiers had just left with the first load of provisions . . . I availed myself of the opportunity afforded by their absence, and by the fact that my wife was intently looking on the floor in a pensive attitude, to move back a step and to make that signal to which no true mason can, without perjury, refuse to respond.

The lieutenant, as he recognized the hail, seemed for a moment surprised, and perhaps confused. He turned rapidly on his heel and retreated to a window, where he sat down and leaned his head upon his hand, apparently in deep thought. After a few minutes the soldiers who had deposited their first load in the wagon returned, and were preparing to throw another load upon their shoulders. At that moment the lieutenant arose from his seat, and in a gruff voice exclaimed:

"Men, put those things down. You can go."

In response to their look of surprise he continued: "I guess there isn't more here than is sufficient for the family."

The mystic sign had prevailed.[41]

In direct contravention of orders, the doctor was left with more than ten months of provisions, solely due to the influence of Masonry. For good measure, "Lieut. B - - -" posted a sentry at the door of his house during the remaining stay of the army to guard against any further foraging attempts.[42]

Stripped of its fraternal trappings, the Masonic obligation to render assistance to a fraternity brother in distress is really nothing more than a restatement of the ethic of reciprocity found in Judeo-Christian tradition.[43] Although Masonry requires an affirmative request before a member is obligated to respond with assistance, the fundamental teachings of the fraternity echo nineteenth-century American religious practice and urges

Masons to practice charity liberally without being asked. The exhortation of New York's Grand Master King reinforces the perception that while Masonry is often thought of as little more than a back-scratching boy's club, many Masons felt the need to actively practice charity as part of their particular expression of Freemasonry. Some Masons, as we have seen, were exemplars of chivalry and charity, and their good deeds stood in stark contrast to the ugliness of war that surrounded them.

Others were not so praiseworthy. The fact that looters recognized Masonic regalia and aprons or that Masons on scores of occasions happily stripped a prisoner of clothes and valuables is de facto evidence that Masons could and did loot, pillage, and despoil their enemies. It proves, if there were any question to the contrary, that Masons were, and remained, ordinary men, subject to all the frailties of the human condition and as disposed toward the savagery of war as non-Masons. Indeed, many of the incidents here show that individual Masons appeared to have engaged regularly in the brutal mechanics of warfare without restraint. Yet, once the Masonic tie was invoked the evidence suggests that invariably an epiphany occurred, which halted and even reversed the actions of the malefactors. The effect of these epiphanies, then, are the noteworthy aspect of Masonry in warfare, and by the volume of the incidents reported, the effect of Masonry on the conduct of the American Civil War was without precedent.

4
Saving the Life of the Enemy

During the war, Masonic aid took many forms. In some instances, fraternal courtesies extended only to Masonic funeral ceremonies; in others, Freemasons spared the homes and possessions of brethren in enemy territory. A great many accounts, however, tell of members of the Craft who went out of their way to spare, or even rescue, brother Masons in the enemy ranks. Under normal circumstances, attracting the attention of the enemy in battle is inadvisable, but many Masons, in peril or wounded, certainly did so in order to appeal for help.

The accounts related here refer regularly to Masonic "signs of distress" and other signals given by members of the fraternity. Descriptions of the various signals and gestures of the fraternity do not appear in print in primary source material owing to the vows of secrecy that Freemasons take upon initiation, although one account from before the war describes how a Masonic sign might have been given. In 1855, the future Georgia governor, Joseph Emerson Brown, was a circuit judge in Gilmer County, Georgia. In a commemorative address given after the war, a commentator described an encounter by the judge with an overenthusiastic supporter who was at pains to demonstrate his familiarity, and presumably his influence, with this important man.

> Bob Ralston, a famous character of Gilmer County . . . presuming upon [the judge's good humor] . . . bet a friend a pint of apple brandy

that he (Bob) could with impunity go into court and give "Joe Brown" the Masonic sign. While not a Mason, Bob conceived that he had detected and acquired one of the most important signals of that ancient order. This was a snap of the finger and at the same time a wink of the eye. Bob repaired to court, leaned against the bar, caught the attention of his honor, snapped his finger, and winked his eye. "Take that gentleman to jail until he cools off," was the unappreciative response from the bench.[1]

Over Thar' a Little Way

Gestures of this kind as well as Masonic emblems or jewelry served as recognition signals on the battlefield to attract the attention of Masons in the enemy ranks. A well-known example involves Lt. (later Colonel) William H. Raynor of Company G, 1st Ohio Volunteer Infantry.[2] Raynor's story received considerable publicity in the 1860s, the details appearing in the *Masonic Review, Harper's Magazine,* and elsewhere. During First Manassas—also called the First Battle of Bull Run, 21 July 1861—Raynor and two sergeants, separated from their unit on a watering detail, were attacked by rebel horsemen. Raynor was wounded by a gunshot to the foot and a blow to the head, the latter rendering him unconscious.[3] When he awoke,

the rebel cavalry returned, and one of them discovering him, dismounted and approached to make him a prisoner. As he came near, Raynor discovered on the person of the rebel soldier a watch key, pin, or other jewel bearing a masonic device. Instantly it flashed upon him to try the influence of Masonry upon his captor. . . . He did so and the intimation was promptly recognized. Just then more of the rebels approached and, seeing him, called to their comrade to stand out of the way that they might "shoot the Yankee." Raynor began to think his time had come, but his rebel captor kept near him and, appealing to his comrades, declared the wounded officer was his prisoner, and that as a prisoner he should be spared.[4]

Following his deliverance, Raynor's captor brought him to a rebel field hospital.

His wounds were washed, and he was made as comfortable as the circumstances would permit. The generous guard, J. H. Lemon, of Radford's Cavalry[5] . . . inquired if he had any money, evidently intending to give him some if he were destitute. In reply to Raynor's earnest expression of gratitude he said: "I only hope to get the same treatment from your men if I ever fall into their hands. If you will relieve the distresses of a suffering brother mason when in your power I shall be well paid." . . . As he said this he pointed to a masonic pin on . . . Raynor's shirt bosom, and hastily mounting his horse rode away.[6]

A Masonic pin triggered another instance of fraternal forbearance during the Battle of Shiloh. The 15th Michigan, commanded by Col. John M. Oliver, met Confederate troops on the 6th and 7th of April, 1862, having arrived in the vicinity only the day before the battle. Hotly engaged, the regiment suffered two officers and thirty-one men killed in action, one officer and sixty-three privates wounded, and seven other ranks missing.[7] Among the casualties was Capt. George A. Strong, who was mortally wounded and left on the field.

Captain Strong was a Mason—a Knight Templar [an appendant body of Freemasonry]—and was the Recorder of Monroe Commandery, No. 6, Monroe Michigan, when he joined the army. When he received the fatal wound, and fell on the battle-field, he wore on his person a fine gold watch, and wore a Masonic breast pin set with brilliants. A Captain of a company of Texas Rangers approached him, after he fell, and discovered the Masonic emblem. . . . Knowing the wounded officer would be robbed, perhaps murdered, if left where he fell, the Texan had him carried to a tent, bound up his wounds as well as he could, furnished him with water, and took means to protect him from insult and robbery. The battle was still raging, and was renewed the next day, Monday, when the national troops succeeded in repulsing the rebel army. . . . On Tuesday, Capt. Strong was found in the tent where the Texan officer had left him, still alive and fully sensible and with his valuables safe upon his person. He was able to detail the whole transaction to his friends, and attributed the protecting kindness of the Texan officer to the magic influence of the Masonic jewel worn upon his person.[8]

A similar example is recorded at the Battle of Fredericksburg in December 1862. Following the disastrous assault on Marye's Heights at Fredericksburg, Sgt. Charles Hollands of Company K, 34th Pennsylvania Regiment, 5th Reserve, was badly wounded. By nightfall, the rebel troops had come out of their prepared positions and were plundering the dead and injured. Hollands gave "the sign of Masonic recognition, which was responded to by the rebel bending over him." Immediately following this exchange, Hollands was evacuated from the field and taken to Richmond as a prisoner of war. He was shortly paroled, but he never recovered from his wounds and died a few months after his release.[9] Oddly, in that same battle Charles M. Hamilton, of the same regiment, also claimed he owed his life to a Masonic appeal. A color bearer, Private Hamilton was shot in the leg and claimed he was left on the field for five days. His calls for aid attracted a rebel Mason and, like Hollands, he was taken to Libby Prison in Richmond and later exchanged. Hamilton survived the war and became a member of congress for the state of Florida.[10]

William A. Morgan, a lieutenant with the 23rd Kentucky Volunteers (U.S.), and a member of Zeredatha Lodge No. 80, Cottonwood Falls, Kansas, corresponded after the war with Masonic historian Jacob Jewell about an incident he witnessed at the Battle of Stones River on New Year's Eve, 1862. In a letter dated 26 September 1914, Morgan who was not a member of the fraternity during the battle, related that he was awake following the day's fighting and, "About 10 o'clock I heard a peculiar cry for help, apparently coming from the farthest side of the field." According to Morgan, a

fellow lieutenant, who was a Mason, on hearing the same cry located another Mason and together proceeded across no-man's land in the direction
of the cry for help. They traveled "until more than half way across the field;
then crawling on their hands and knees, with the utmost caution, until they
thought themselves as far as they dared go, one of them repeated the cry
in a low voice." This call was answered not by the wounded man, but by a
rebel picket near them, who also proved to be a Mason. The Confederate
informed them that "two of your men are lying right over thar, a little way."
Thus directed, the two Masons, with the aid of a blanket borrowed from
the rebel sentry reached the wounded men and evacuated them to safety,
and incredibly, returned the blanket to the rebel picket. The significance
of those events were lost on Morgan at the time, but "ten years after, when
I became a mason, I heard the same cry [as part of the Masonic ritual], and
the field of Stone River [sic], and the awful night of December 31, 1862,
passed before my mental vision as vivid as an event of twenty-four hours
previous."[11]

The Battle of Chancellorsville provides another example. In 1887, Asa
W. Bartlett, formerly a captain of the 12th New Hampshire, described
a Masonic incident involving a comrade, Capt. John M. Durgin, of his
regiment:

He was shot through the body [and] left for dead on the field and reported in the list of the killed. Helpless and almost speechless he lay
on the field where he fell, begging in vain of every rebel that came
near enough to make himself understood for a drink of water, until
nearly night, (he was shot in the morning about 8 o'clock,) when seeing a rebel officer not far off he happened to think, as the last resort,
to make the Masonic sign of recognition. The officer, who was about
to pass by without halting, at once stopped, turned about and went
up to him. Finding that he was actually dying for want of water to
quench the burning fever that was rapidly consuming him, the officer
told him that, if possible, he would bring him some water, but that

his own men were dying everywhere for want of the same thing. As good as his word . . . he soon returned with a canteen nearly full of water . . . this drink of water from the canteen of this rebel officer, who chanced to be also a Masonic brother, was what Captain Durgin says saved his life.[12]

Durgin was a member of Strafford Lodge No. 29 in Dover, New Hampshire. He was initiated on 14 May 1857, took his second degree on that same date, and was raised to a Master Mason one week later.[13]

Elsewhere on the field at Chancellorsville, Capt. Joseph H. Durkee, of Company A, 146th New York State Volunteers, was seriously wounded and captured by Confederate troops. By means of a Masonic gesture, he attracted the attention of a rebel surgeon, who found that he was in danger of bleeding to death. The doctor amputated the arm successfully, saving his life, and Durkee was then paroled and carried by rebel stretcher-bearers to the Union picket lines and released. The surgeon was Dr. George Rodgers Clarke Todd, chief surgeon for Kershaw's brigade and Abraham Lincoln's brother-in-law.[14]

Some Mystic Signs in a Circle

Masonic credentials proved useful even in the most bitter fighting. During the Battle of Fort Pillow (12 April 1864) in Tennessee, where Confederate forces were accused of massacring black Union troops following their surrender, a Kansas Mason, Charles Harris, of Emporia Lodge No. 12, Emporia, Kansas, and formerly of Company F, 21st Iowa Infantry, reported third-hand that at least one white officer was spared and allowed to escape after making his Masonic connection known to a rebel Mason.[15]

At the Battle of the Wilderness in May 1864, a rebel private, Clement J. "J. C." Allen, sustained horrific wounds—both his eyes were "shot out"— yet he remained alive. Sgt. Simon F. Culpepper of Company D, 8th Georgia Infantry, told of Allen's rescue by Union soldiers in a letter dated 9 September 1914:

Federals got possession of the woods where he was . . . and two soldiers were looking over the ground to see what they could find and
came across [him].

They talked with him a little while and he insisted that they take
him out where he could receive assistance, but they told him they believed he would die and that it was useless. . . . After they had passed
by a little ways, he made himself known as a mason, and they at once
returned; took him to their hospital. . . . He lived several years, but
was always blind.[16]

Mystic signs drawn in blood enliven another account that occurred earlier in the war at Antietam. Members of the 5th New Hampshire were on
picket duty in the Miller cornfield on the day after the battle, still bedev-
iled by rebel marksmen who had not yet retreated.

Early in the morning one of the wounded rebels, who lay just outside the pickets, called one of the New Hampshire men and handed
him a little slip of paper, on which he had evidently, with great difficulty, succeeded in making some mystic signs in a circle with a bit of
stick wet in blood [emphasis in original]. The soldier begged [him] to
hand the paper to some Freemason as soon as possible, and he took
it to Colonel E[dward] E. Cross of his regiment. The Colonel was a
Master Mason, but could not read the mystic token, it belonging to
a higher degree. He, therefore, sent for Captain J[ames] B. Perry, of
[Company C] the Fifth Regiment, who was a member of a higher degree of Freemasonry, and showed him the letter. Captain Perry at
once said there was a brother Mason in great peril, and must be rescued. Colonel Cross instantly sent for several brother masons in the
regiment, told the story, and in a few moments four "brothers of
the mystic tie" were crawling stealthily through the corn to find the
brother in distress. He was found, placed on a blanket, and at great
risk drawn out of the range of the rebel rifles, and then carried to
the Fifth New Hampshire hospital. He proved to be First Lieutenant

[John Oden of Company K, 10th Alabama Infantry], badly wounded in the thigh and breast. A few hours and he would have perished.[17]

Also on the field at Antietam, Capt. (later Brevet Major General) Newton M. Curtis, of the 16th New York Infantry, received a report from a subordinate, Lt. William L. Best, concerning a wounded rebel calling for aid:

[Best said,] "Captain, just beyond where I found the one I last brought to the surgeons is a man who plaintively repeats something that I do not understand, except that he said he was the son of a widow. I will show you where he is." I followed . . . and carried to the surgeons a seriously wounded soldier. . . . The next day, referring to the incident, Best said, "Captain, you took great chances last night bringing off that wounded Confederate. Was he a Mason?" I replied, "I did not ask him but your statement that he was a widow's son caused me to suspect he was."[18]

At the battle of West Point, Virginia, on 7 May 1862, Cpl. James Cook of Company F, 16th New York Infantry, was shot in the leg and left on the field by his retreating comrades. Robbed by a Confederate of his watch, purse, and Masonic ring, he called out for aid. His call was answered by a rebel Mason nearby who brought him water and restored his property to him. "We are enemies in honorable warfare," the Confederate told him, "but on the plane where your disabilities have placed you, the laws of humanity and charity prevail."[19]

All too often, however, a Masonic appeal could not be answered. George W. Bynum of the 2nd Mississippi Infantry told of one such instance. "At the battle of South Mountain, Va., when we were obstructing the advance of Gen. Hancock, on the night of Sept. 14, 1862, in the heat of battle, I heard a brother on the Federal side in distress, calling for help. But the chances of losing my life were too great, greater than those of saving his, and I could not give the help."[20]

While these accounts of fraternal kindness toward wounded fellow Masons are of interest to Masonic scholars, one might naturally surmise that, with or without fraternal bonds, medical aid to wounded enemy soldiers might normally be granted once the shooting stopped. Clearly, there are manifold examples of medical aid of this nature that bear no stamp of Freemasonry. However, the degree of personal risk willingly undertaken by the rescuers in many of the preceding stories suggests something more than simple compassion. In addition, period sources indicate that Masons actively intervened to protect brother Masons in dire peril, as we shall see in the following section.

He Brought Masonry into Requisition

By 1862 Confederate military and political leaders began exploring the use of irregular troops. While the politicians realized that guerrilla warfare could not be used in or near the major Southern population centers—Richmond, Nashville, Atlanta—without endangering popular support for the Confederate government, the government's attitude toward unconventional warfare had shifted. At the outset of the war, Confederate military thinking did not contemplate the use of irregular troops, preferring to encounter the Union invaders with conventional forces employed under traditional nineteenth-century military doctrine. But by the spring of 1862, following the Confederate defeat at the Battle of Pea Ridge, Arkansas, guerrilla warfare—which promised that small, loosely organized forces could stymie a larger opponent—became official Confederate policy, particularly in the Trans-Mississippi Department. Shortly thereafter, in January 1863, Col. John S. Mosby was given official sanction to operate a cavalry force of partisan rangers in Northern Virginia. Before long, rebel guerillas were operating in all theaters.[21]

Federal commanders reacted harshly. Gen. William T. Sherman's response was typical. Writing in September 1862, he commented darkly on what rebel partisans could expect if captured. "Whether the guerillas or partisan rangers, without uniform, without organization except on paper, wandering around the country plundering friend and foe, firing on un-

armed boats filled with women and children and on small parties of soldiers, always from ambush, or where they have every advantage, are entitled to the protection and amenities of civilized warfare is a question
which I think you would settle very quickly in the abstract." Confederate
commanders countered Sherman's threats to execute captured rebel guer-
rillas with retaliation, man for man.[22]

For the common solider, the odds of surviving a guerrilla encounter had
just gone down. To counter this situation, many soldiers resorted to Masonry. Captured by rebels, Lt. Mathew J. Borland of the 10th Ohio Volunteer Cavalry did just that:

> I make the following statement, as much to combat the impression
> that Masons in the rebel army would not recognize "the yankee ma-
> sons" (as they call them,) as to show the benefits of Masonry under
> certain circumstances. While out on a scouting party on the 3d day
> of August, 1864, I was surprised and attacked by four times our
> number, and myself and two men taken prisoners. I expected to re-
> ceive very severe treatment, as our captors were a roving band, and
> not under very good discipline. The private soldiers had taken from
> me all my valuables before the commanding officer made his appear-
> ance. When he came up (it was a Col. Andrew Young) he recognized
> me at once as a Mason, secured and returned to me all my personal
> effects that could be found, and allowed me to ride in his company
> and share his rations. When we reached Gainesville, Georgia, he in-
> troduced me to prominent masons—among others the D. G. Master
> of South Carolina. . . . I am glad to say that I received very kind treat-
> ment from every Mason I met.[23]

Informed that he must be executed in retaliation for federal treatment of
Confederate prisoners that was "contrary to the uses of war," Borland again
invoked his fraternal connection. "The officer who was intrusted with the
execution of this duty discovered that I was a Mason, and instead of shooting me as ordered, gave me an opportunity to escape, and furnished me

with a hundred dollars in confederate money—which was of great service to me, for I was penniless."[24]

John S. Mosby and his partisan rangers appear frequently in Masonic stories about the war. In November 1864, a series of reprisals occurred between Mosby's men and Union forces under Brig. Gen. George A. Custer. Custer had executed seven of Mosby's men at Front Royal, Virginia, a few days before, and Mosby ordered the execution of seven Union prisoners in reply. Twenty-seven prisoners were assembled and a "lottery of death" was conducted to determine which would die. One of those chosen revealed himself to his captors as a Freemason and was spared.[25] A contemporary illustration of the lottery was drawn by James E. Taylor, an artist for *Frank Leslie's Illustrated Newspaper.* Taylor's sketch shows a line of distraught federal prisoners drawing chits from a hat, a rebel officer drawing out names, and a federal prisoner embracing a rebel guard in a display of Masonic fellowship.[26]

Another Mosby incident, widely reported in period sources, relates to an unnamed Union surgeon who escaped hanging by Mosby's rangers. In the *Masonic Review* in 1864, an anonymous correspondent described the event.

The distance between Martinsburg and Winchester, some 22 miles, is infested by Moseby and his band, and [it] is not safe to travel over it without an escort. Dr. - - -, surgeon of - - - Regiment, started from the latter place with an escort of ten men to go to Martinsburg. When about half way, a man in our uniform rode up to him from a house near by, and informed him that a soldier there was very sick, and requested the Doctor to ride over and prescribe for him: he did so, taking four men with him. When he entered the room in which the supposed sick man was in bed, the latter rose up with revolver in hand and ordered the Doctor to surrender, which he was obliged to do. His men, outside the house, were also captured. At this juncture the redoubtable Moseby made his appearance; and on the Doctor asking what was to be done with him, Moseby replied that he hung all Federal officers, and was immediately hurried towards the woods as he supposed for that purpose. Concluding all was lost, he brought Masonry into requisition, which was immediately recognized by Moseby. Proceedings were at once arrested; and although his watch and other valuables that had been taken from him were *not restored,* his life was spared, and he was taken back within five miles of Winchester and allowed to return.[27]

Curiously, Mosby is not believed to have been a Mason. However, at least one of his aides, Capt. Richard P. Montjoy, certainly was,[28] and he is credited with saving two federal soldiers and fellow Freemasons from hanging on Mosby's orders. This earned him a rebuke from Mosby: "Remember Captain, in the future, that this command is not a Masonic lodge!"[29]

A Beautiful Illustration of the Work of Masonry

The signs and symbols used in Masonic lodges, however, were often used as survival tools by soldiers facing an enemy onslaught. During the Battle of Fort Gregg, part of the Petersburg campaign, on 2 April 1865, Joseph B. Thompson, a sergeant in Company F of the 16th Mississippi, recounted how Confederate troops from Harris's brigade of Mississippians, outnumbered nine to one, repelled two federal charges by infantry of the 24th Corps before finally succumbing to the third federal assault. Writing in *Confederate Veteran* magazine in 1921, Thompson wrote that of three hundred rebel attackers only "twenty-seven [survived], nineteen of them badly wounded. Among the eight unwounded was M. G. Turner, a Freemason. He gave the Masonic sign of distress to a Federal colonel who grasped him by the hand and drew him from the crowd and protected him from massacre."[30]

Masonic forbearance on the battlefield was also reported by Henry W. Graber, of Company B, 8th Texas Cavalry (Terry's Texas Rangers), an account widely referenced on the Internet. Graber relates an extraordinary incident he witnessed near Macon, Georgia, probably in the fall of 1864, where one Mason intervened in combat to save the life of another. While

awaiting a farrier to shoe his horse, he and a comrade named Jim Freeman heard federal cavalry attacking the Confederate line. "We immediately mounted our horses and dashed over there," he wrote, "and just as we
got in sight of the roadway through the breastworks we witnessed a lone
trooper of Kilpatrick's cavalry coming up the road through the works, having his horse shot just as he reached inside." Trapped by his wounded horse,
the Union trooper was in danger of being killed by the southern militia,
"when Jim put spurs to his horse and with his pistol raised, dashed up to
where this man lay under his horse, and drove off the excited militia. I, of
course, followed him. He called up a lieutenant, asked his name, company,
and regiment; told him to take charge of that prisoner and see that he was
well treated, that he would hold him personally responsible for his safety,
and immediately wheeled his horse, I following him, and returned to town
without giving the lieutenant a chance to ask questions." On their return,
Graber asked Freeman his reasons for risking his own life among the un-
trained militia to save an enemy soldier.

> He answered, "He is a brother Mason." I asked him if he had ever met
> him before. He said, "No, but I saw him give the grand hailing sign of
> distress, which obligates a Mason to save the life of a brother, at the
> risk of his own." . . . Here was a beautiful illustration of the work of
> Masonry, and I told Jim Freeman the first opportunity I had of join-
> ing the Masons, if I lived through the war, I intended to be one, which
> resolution I carried out, joining the Masons at Rusk, Texas.[31]

Graber did in fact petition Euclid Lodge No. 45 in Rusk, Texas, and was
initiated on 4 July 1868.[32]

Another cavalry action—this time at Waynesboro, Virginia, on 28 September 1864, also featured an intervention by a brother Mason in the heat
of battle. Capt. George N. Bliss of Company B, 1st Rhode Island Cavalry,
was engaged with rebel troopers of the 4th Virginia Cavalry; Bliss's horse
was shot and he was thrown to the ground.

Before I could rise two of the enemy reined in their horses by me, and leaning over their saddle struck at me, one with a carbine, and the other with a sabre. I could parry but one, and with my sabre stopping the crushing blow from the carbine at the same instant that the sabre gave me a cut across the forehead. I at once rose to my feet and said to the soldier who had wounded me, "For God's sake do not kill a prisoner." "Surrender then," he said; to which I replied, "I do surrender." He demanded my sword and pistol, which I gave him, and had scarcely done so when I was struck on the back with such a force as to thrust me two steps forward.

Upon turning to discover the cause of this assault I found that a soldier had ridden upon the trot and stabbed me with his sabre, which would have passed entirely through my body but for the fact that in his ignorance of the proper use of the weapon he had failed to make the half-turn necessary to give the sabre smooth entrance between the ribs. I also saw at this moment another soldier taking aim at me with a revolver.

There was only one chance left for me; I called for protection as a Freemason, and Capt. Henry C. Lee, the acting adjutant-general of the enemy's force, at once came to my assistance, ordered a soldier to take me to the rear and see that my wounds were dressed. . . . Later in the evening I was put into an ambulance with Capt. William A. Moss [of the 4th Virginia Cavalry], at that time a lieutenant, and rode several miles to a small house in the mountains. I found Captain Moss to be a brother Mason, who did everything possible for my comfort. He had received a bullet wound from some other soldier in addition to a sabre-cut from me, but happily recovered his wounds.[33]

The universal currency of Masonry was not only confined to battles on land and at least one account tells of the influence of Freemasonry at sea. On 27 June 1863, the Confederate schooner *Archer* attempted a cutting-out expedition against the federal revenue cutter *Caleb Cushing,* then at anchor in Portland, Maine.[34] After the moon had set, at about one o'clock in the morning, the watch on board *Cushing* were surprised by Lt. Charles W. Read, C.S.N., and twenty-five to forty armed rebels, who poured over the side, overwhelmed the crew, and captured the ship. The night was calm, however, and the lack of wind hampered their escape. Despite spreading every scrap of canvas, Lieutenant Read was obliged to put some of his men in boats to tow the *Cushing* out of the anchorage—a circumstance that allowed his federal pursuers to hastily commandeer three civilian steamships, *Forest City, Casco,* and *Chesapeake,* as well as a detachment of federal troops and cannon and to chase them.[35]

Lt. James H. Merryman, of the U.S. Revenue Marine, pursued *Read* and his men on board *Forest City.*

> After much delay off Fort Preble taking on board two 12-pounder field guns, 35 soldiers, and 40 muskets for my crew and our volunteers, we started in pursuit of the cutter, which was then in plain sight [at] the mouth of the harbor and standing to the westward. Steaming rapidly after her, we ran within 2 miles of her by 11:20 a.m., when she commenced firing her pivot gun, throwing well-directed line shots to within 70 yards of us. As we approached her she fired five shots in rapid succession, the last one falling within 30 feet of us. At this moment we observed the propeller *Chesapeake* coming to our assistance . . . and we therefore bore away, and meeting the *Chesapeake,* which was admirably prepared for action on such short notice . . . held a short consultation, and together started for the *Cushing.* As we again approached her she fired three shots, the last a stand of grape, and all ineffectual.[36]

Lieutenant Read, seeing the three steamers bearing down on him, abandoned ship and, with his crew and the federal prisoners from the *Cushing,* fled in the ship's boats. Merryman reported that "smoke and flames were seen bursting from her wardroom and cabin companionways. By the aid of my glasses I perceived that her decks were deserted and that the *Cushing* was doomed to destruction. Expecting every moment to see her blown to atoms, for I had learned that her magazine contained 500 pounds of powder, I advised Captain Lipscomb to bear away for the boats containing the pirates and run them down. As we neared them however, they frantically displayed white handkerchiefs and masonic signs, and the steamer was therefore sheered clear of them and stopped."[37] Read and his men were spared and taken aboard alive.

We Will Some Day Meet Again

There is little doubt that battle in the Civil War was an experience of great intensity. Sights, sounds, and smells recorded by diarists and participants, often many years after the event, recall the events in exacting detail. Correspondingly, many soldiers wrote detailed accounts of the enemy, recalling a close encounter minutely, but rarely does the researcher encounter a tale of former antagonists meeting again in peacetime. Although certainly possible—it is the stuff of dime novels and fraternal after-dinner yarns—these stories continue to circulate. We close this chapter with two examples of former enemies reunited despite the intervention of many years of peace, accompanied by an analysis of the veracity of each account.

The first account is a common theme—wounded soldiers rescued by a fellow Mason on the victorious side. At the Second Battle of Bull Run (28–30 August 1862), Capt. Thomas D. Mosscrop, of Company F, 10th New York Volunteer Infantry, and his comrades, Capt. Robert A. Dimmick of Company B, and Color Cpl. Edward A. Dubey, were each wounded and left for dead on the field. They were chanced upon by Capt. Hugh Barr of Company A, 5th Virginia Infantry, who, it was subsequently claimed, was a member of the fraternity. The regimental history of the 10th New York asserted that

> on the evening of the third day, after they had suffered almost unendurably, and had submitted to the robberies of Rebel prowlers and marauders (with the exception of Dubey, who by sheer boldness

and hard words enlisted the admiration of the thieves), and when it seemed that death must soon ensure, the attention of a passing Rebel officer was attracted by a masonic pin worn by Lieut. Mosscrop. He interested himself in the three comrades: their wounds were dressed and they were conveyed in an ambulance to a neighboring house, where they were, in a day or two, paroled, and managed to reach Washington.

Sixteen years afterwards Capt. Dimmick met Capt. Hugh Barr, their masonic friend, in Winchester, Va., and recognized him.[38]

According to Barr family history, after the meeting with Dimmick, the three Union men presented him with a painting "about the size of a door" depicting Barr administering aid to them on the battlefield. In addition, they also sent him (and after his death, his widow) a twenty dollar gold piece each year. The painting is still in the possession of Captain Barr's descendants.[39]

Barr was a musician and part of, or possibly the commander of, the regimental band, and as such would have been tasked with assisting in tending the wounded after battle. Curiously, however, Masonic records do not confirm that he was a member of the fraternity during the war, and in fact show that Barr was only initiated as a Mason in 1870.[40] Although it is not difficult to guess his humanitarian motives in providing aid and succor to three prostrate enemy soldiers, the role—if any—that Masonry played in his actions is impossible to judge. Despite the factual difficulties concerning his Masonic affiliation, the story of Captain Barr has circulated since 1882 and is cited by respected academicians as indicative of Civil War Masonic fraternization. Whether it is entirely true or not is impossible to verify.

Finally, there is a dramatic story that appeared in the March 1893 issue of *Confederate Veteran,* which like the account of Captain Barr also prompts many questions for the scholar. Appearing under the headline "The Blue and the Gray," a soldier known only as "J. W. T., Co. A., 15th Texas," described going forward on the attack at Chickamauga.

My company was ordered out with the skirmishers, and we were soon engaged in a rambling fire. The Federal skirmishers soon gave way before us, leaving here and there a dead or wounded comrade. I discovered immediately in front of me a soldier dressed in blue, prostrate, and attempting to rise. He turned his eyes toward me, gave the Masonic sign of distress, and asked me for water. I hastily placed his head on his knapsack, gave him my canteen of water, and ran forward to join my company. The enemy was reinforced and we were driven back over the same ground. Again I saw the wounded Federal soldier and stooped over him a moment to hear what he might say.

As near as I can remember these were his words:

"Brother, something tells me that we will live through this battle, and that we will some day meet again."

I clasped his hand and hastily joined my command.[41]

"J. W. T." wrote of the aftermath of this brief encounter twenty years after the war.

While perusing a newspaper my eyes fell upon the following item: "If the Confederate soldier belonging to company A of the Fifteenth Texas, who gave a wounded Federal soldier a canteen of water during the battle of Chickamauga, will write me at - - - - Hotel, New Orleans, he will learn something of interest to him.
—JOHN RANDOLPH."

I wrote immediately and received a telegram to go to New Orleans at once. . . . I arrived at the Hotel about 2 o'clock, registered, and inquired for Randolph. The clerk informed me that such a man was there, but confined to his room and in the last stages of consumption. I asked to be shown to his room. I was met at the door by a middle aged gentleman, who invited me into the room. On the bed a gray haired man was reclining, who at my approach held out his hand and scrutinized my features intently . . . he requested his com-

panion to bring from a wardrobe in the room a canteen. It was old
and worn, but on the cover was plainly marked, "J. W. T., Co. A.,
15 Tex." I recognized it as the same that I had left with the wounded
United States soldier during the battle of Chickamauga.

Is this your canteen? the sick man inquired. I told him that it
once was mine, but that I had given it to him. I now return your
property, he said, and, clasping my hand, he feebly ejaculated, "My
brother!"[42]

The story concludes with a dying bequest of $10,000 from Randolph to
the author. "J. W. T." reported that he assisted with funeral preparations
and arranged with surviving family for shipment of the body to Illinois for
burial.[43]

Unfortunately, this romantic tale is not easily verifiable. The 15th Texas
Cavalry (dismounted in April 1862) formed part of Brig. Gen. James Desh-
ler's brigade, Hill's Corps, at the Battle of Chickamauga on 19–20 September 1863. A search of the muster rolls of Company A, 15th Texas
Cavalry, does not reveal any potential candidates for "J. W. T." "John
Randolph" may have been John M. Randolph of Company B, 79th Illinois,
who according to the muster rolls of the regiment joined up on 28 August 1862 and was "absent—sick" at the mustering out of the regiment in
June 1865. The 79th Illinois were engaged at Chickamauga and therefore
it is possible, although by no means certain, that John M. Randolph is the
man we seek.

The questions raised in the tales of Captain Barr and John Randolph may
never be answered with any degree of scholarly certainty, but they should
not be entirely dismissed. Beyond being ripping yarns, accounts like these
underscore the romanticism of Freemasonry that has fascinated the public
since the day the war began. Heretofore, little scholarly attention has been
paid to incidents of Masonic intervention in wartime—perhaps because
the anecdotes were so sensational that scholars viewed the entire subject
with circumspection. And yet, most of the narratives involving Masonry
on the battlefield are fully verifiable, and for that reason, all the more
astonishing.

The Mirror Image

The phrase "brother against brother" has long been associated with the Civil War. But as the foregoing examples attest, more than one kind of brotherhood was often involved. Freemasons on both sides reached across the lines of battle, sometimes at great personal risk, to aid their fellow Masons *in extremis* and fulfill their fraternal obligation to assist a worthy brother in distress. Considerable documentary evidence exists to prove that these fraternal acts were not isolated to the American Civil War, yet the sheer number of incidents among both Union and Confederate combatants is startling. Clearly the influence of Freemasonry in American society in the period immediately preceding the war helped ensure that there were many Masons in the ranks of both armies. That Masons, or any other identifiable group with a strong sense of identity and belonging, might naturally protect the property of other members is not unheard of. Neither is the fact that a soldier might stop and render aid to an injured antagonist. But accounts of one Mason saving the life of an enemy brother while literally under fire occur rarely in other wars. That they occurred with persistent frequency in the American Civil War is a function of the unique nature of civil war itself, combined with the prevalence of fraternalism in American society at that time, and a testament to the seriousness with which the nineteenth-century American Mason treated his fraternal obligations.

Gentlemen of the White Apron

Approximately 410,000 soldiers were taken prisoner in the Civil War, and roughly 56,000 died in prison.[1] The ordeal of Civil War captives is a subject that received considerable treatment immediately following the war, and renewed scholarly interest in the last twenty years. Scores of titles have been published about Civil War prisons, yet only tantalizing fragments illustrate the influence of Freemasonry inside prison walls. Notwithstanding its paucity, the evidence that does exist shows that the Masonic tenets of brotherly love and relief found a perfect field of expression in Civil War prisons, where food, shelter, and compassion were in short supply. Although ignored by scholars, there is considerable evidence that Freemasons in prison went to great lengths to care for their own, and that this fraternal concern transcended Union or Confederate affiliation. The vignettes presented here make plain that apart from being a mere social phenomenon, Freemasonry was a lifeline to prisoners of war—nearly all of whom were confined in unwholesome and unsanitary conditions, and the fraternity provided not only actual necessities that sustained life—food, blankets, clothing, and medicine—but also psychological support that sustained men under the bleakest of conditions.

I Immediately Commenced My Free-Masonry

Just as in actual combat, many Freemasons resorted to appealing for aid when captured, sometimes to assure their personal safety—and sometimes to avoid capture entirely. Lt. Col. Homer Sprague, 13th Connecticut Volunteers, was taken prisoner by Ramseur's brigade in the 3rd Battle of Winchester on 19 September 1864. Following a long march with his fellow captives, Sprague's strength failed him and he collapsed in a roadside ditch. A rebel officer took pity on him and he was allowed to ride in an ambulance.

> Into the ambulance I climbed with some difficulty, and immediately commenced my free-masonry on the driver. He responded to the signs. . . . He gave me some nice milk and some fine wheat bread. "As a Mason," said he, "I'll feed you; share the last crumb with you; but as a Confederate soldier, I'll fight you till the last drop of blood and the last ditch."[2]

While the chances of a modern soldier meeting any success by "commencing his Freemasonry" is undoubtedly slim, in nineteenth-century America, the fraternity, and its reputation for solidarity between brethren was well known. During the Petersburg campaign, John Floyd, a captain in the 18th South Carolina Infantry, described a successful sortie against a federal position that illustrates the reputation of Masonry among frontline troops. Floyd had ordered his troops to approach the Union position stealthily to within 30 yards, then to yell with all their might before falling "flat on their faces." The federals fired en masse at the commotion, but the shots passed harmlessly over the rebels. "I then ordered my men forward at the run, and before the enemy could reload their guns we were on them. They commenced begging for quarter and inquiring for Masons and Oddfellows. We captured all of them."[3]

Floyd doesn't comment on whether the men he captured were actually affiliated with either fraternity, and his affiliation with the Craft is not known. It is possible that these men were Masons and Odd Fellows, but it is equally possible that they were not affiliated with either group but were aware that the qualities of fraternal mercy were not strained.

A federal officer caught napping hazarded his luck on Masonic mercy near Tuscumbia Landing, Alabama. On 12 April 1864, Confederate troops from the 27th and 35th Alabama regiments captured the entire complement of Company G, 9th Ohio Cavalry, known as the "White Horse Company," in a midnight raid on a farmstead where the federals were camped. As dawn threatened to expose the rebel column, consisting not only of federal prisoners but also their horses, baggage, and a herd of cattle, the jubilant rebels hurried to cross the Tennessee River to return to rebel lines. Midstream the raiders realized that they had not captured the federal officers who had been sleeping apart from their men. The rebel commander, Col. Samuel S. Ives, decided to go back for them. With several hand-picked men, including Lt. Albert Goodloe, of the 35th Alabama, Ives returned, and "lantern in hand, rushed into the room where they were, finding them still asleep, notwithstanding what had just transpired" in the farmyard. According to Goodloe, the colonel "aroused them from their slumbers and dreams of conquests and Rebel scalps to the wakeful consciousness of the fact that they were in the gentle grasp of chivalrous Southrons. The captain made the Masonic sign of distress, thinking that his life was in immediate peril. Col. Ives answered him that he was in no danger of personal violence, but that his presence was needed instanter within the Rebel lines."[4]

A similar incident was told by Dewitt Gallaher, a former Confederate staff officer who resigned his commission and enlisted as a private soldier in Company E, 1st Virginia Cavalry. In his diary, he related a conversation with Dr. Hunter H. McGuire regarding the Southern physician's escape from Union forces in 1865. Dr. McGuire, formerly surgeon to Stonewall Jackson and at the time attached to Confederate Gen. Jubal Early's staff,[5] was captured by a Union officer following a pursuit on horseback.

> [Dr. McGuire] told me he was trying to escape and had reached a piece of woods . . . and finding his pursuers very close behind him tried to jump his horse over a low rail fence and get into the woods. But alas! His horse fell with him! An officer told the fellow to put his gun down, saying "He's MY prisoner." The Dr. told me he was a

Mason and that he made a Masonic sign and the Yankee officer being a Mason also had saved his life. He said the enemy treated him very nicely and paroled him.[6]

Civilians also made use of Masonic ties to avoid entanglements with the enemy army. A Southern man with a wagonload of sorely needed cloth and fabric ran afoul of a Union patrol in Patterson, North Carolina. Clem Osborne was a private citizen but he was also an ardent Confederate sympathizer, and the load of supplies was intended for rebel troops nearby. Spotted by Union cavalry under the command of Gen. George Stoneman Jr. the Union troopers seized his wagon and team, and tried to seize Osborne himself, but Osborne ran and, eluding his pursuers, climbed into the bell tower of the town's woolen mill to hide. Frustrated federal troops searched the building and grounds of the mill, but failed to locate him. Reporting their failure to their officers, they were ordered to fire the mill. "Realizing that there was nothing else to do . . . Osborne made known his hiding place and the Yankees brought him down. The command was that as [Osborne] reached the last step he was to be shot. Before reaching this last step, however, Mr. Osborne gave the Masonic distress sign and a member of the enemy forces who was also a Mason gave the order that no harm come to him."[7]

Sometimes confusion resulted from all these secret signs and gestures. Lt. Alonzo Cooper, of Company F, 12th New York Cavalry, was captured at the Battle of Plymouth (North Carolina) on 19 April 1864. He was imprisoned at Andersonville for a brief period before being transferred to Camp Oglethorpe in Macon, Georgia. A few months later, due to Sherman's advance through Georgia, he was again moved to Columbia, South Carolina. On 12 October 1864, Cooper and his comrade, Capt. Robert B. Hock, also of the 12th New York Cavalry, escaped. The pair traveled through North Carolina for eighteen days, posing as Confederate soldiers returning home. Stopping at a farmhouse to beg for food, Cooper determined to make a fraternal appeal. "I being a member of the Independent Order of Odd Fellows, gave [the farmer] some signs of that order, which he thought was a clumsily given Masonic sign, and, as he belonged to that fraternity, he tried to test me in the signs of that society. I told him I was not a Mason, but was an Odd Fellow, and he could trust me just as freely as though we both belonged to the same order."[8]

Despite the confusion, the appeal worked, and Cooper and his companion received a good breakfast and traveling directions; unfortunately, Cooper was recaptured shortly thereafter by a Confederate provost. He was exchanged for a Confederate prisoner on 20 February 1865.

Exchanges of this type—a system by which prisoners taken by each army (or navy) were repatriated—began in early 1862; by July of that year, Richmond and Washington reached a formal agreement on prisoner exchanges, and a system was devised for prisoners from either army to offset one another as they were repatriated, a zero-sum scheme. Prisoners who were released on parole were prohibited from soldiering until formal exchange notification was received. Many Freemasons benefited by this system, and non-Masons complained bitterly that Masonic warders chose Masonic prisoners as the first to be exchanged.[9]

As the war progressed, the exchange system broke down, and many men, fully aware of the miserable conditions in prison, went to extreme efforts to escape capture. The odyssey of Captain White and Lieutenant Linsley deserves mention here, not so much for the degree in which Masonry figured into their travails as for the sheer bad luck they experienced in trying to escape. Captured with their entire regiment at New Bern, North Carolina, in March 1865, Capt. George M. White of Company E, and Lt. Solomon F. Linsley of Company K, 15th Connecticut Volunteers, resolved to flee. The regiment marched, under guard, to Richmond, and during the night White and Linsley bolted and made their way to the Staunton River. The pair first contrived to steal a boat and escape by water. They crossed the river in fine style, landed safely, and prepared to make their way back to Union territory. Unfortunately, it was not until after they cast the boat adrift to prevent discovery that they realized they had landed on an island with more than half of the river left to cross. Undeterred, they made a raft and managed with some difficulty to reach the mainland where they encountered a free black man who—as fortune would have it—operated the local ferry. By inducements of money White and Linsley secured his help, and he, in turn, led them to a party of Confederate deserters who were in hiding nearby. The rebel deserters would have nothing to do with the two escapees, being convinced they were Confederate Secret Service agents posing as Union soldiers. The pair finally convinced the deserters that they were "genuine Yanks" and hatched a plan that required them to re-cross the Staunton River with the ferryman's help; they would then make their way to Unionist West Virginia.[10]

The instant the boat touched the landing, up jumped a whole company of rebel soldiers. We heard their muskets cocked and knew they were, every one of them, aimed directly into the boat, and then came the sharp, quick voice of the captain as he ordered the deserters to lay down their arms and march ashore. For half a minute, it was still as death in the boat, not a rebel or a Yankee moved. The captain repeated his command and gave them one minute to lay down their arms and come ashore, or he would give the order to fire.[11]

The deserters obeyed and filed disconsolately off the boat, but White and Linsley remained hidden. "Marse," the ferryman whispered to White, "ye's got to go ashore, de capin knows ye's hayr."

Then for the first time it dawned on me that [he] had betrayed us. My fingers fairly ached to clutch him by the throat, but I didn't do it. I whispered a selection of "cuss words" in his left ear, and they must have been heavy ones, for he at once sunk out of ear shot, and I never saw him any more. . . . Linsley and myself walked ashore. The captain had sent the deserters away under strong guard, and he now marched us off to his own quarters.

Our captor was Captain Duguid, of a North Carolina regiment . . . He gave up his own bunk to us, he being on duty all night, and had the best his stores afforded cooked for a mid-night meal for us. I shall always suppose that a part of his kindness to us was due to the discovery which he made soon after we entered the tent, that I was a brother Mason.[12]

Re-crossing the river a third time, under guard, White and Linsley were transported to Libby Prison in Richmond, where, "as a result of our effort to escape," White later recalled, "we arrived at Libby two days in advance of our regiment."[13]

Not all appeals for Masonic aid had the desired effect, however. Belle Boyd, the famous Confederate spy, issued an appeal to President Lincoln and Secretary Stanton "as a Mason's daughter" (see chapter 3) for a furlough from her confinement in Fortress Monroe to attend the funeral of her father. Lincoln was not a Freemason, but Stanton was; despite this, her request was refused.[14]

I Am Surprised You Should Ask Such a Thing

Although Belle Boyd's request for Masonic aid was ignored, a substantial number of Masons in prison were treated differently. In many cases membership in the Order was often sufficient to gain them special treatment or favor, and, regardless of other considerations, we have seen Masonic mercy overcome military duties with some frequency. Many of the witnesses cited here report that not only hostilities but also sometimes even the duties demanded of soldiers to capture and confine enemy troops were completely obviated by a Masonic plea. Although it is not possible to examine the motives of the men involved in these incidents, certain accounts do expose more explicitly the inherent conflict between Masonry and warfare. Two examples where the motivations of the participants can be more closely scrutinized invite comparison. The first involves Confederate Army surgeon Dr. John H. Claiborne who was the resident surgeon in charge of medical care at Petersburg, Virginia. During the waning days of the war, he was captured and, while waiting for transit North, he decided to try his Masonic luck with his captors.

I noticed the officer of the guard with a badge pinned on the lapel of his coat, which indicated that he was a Mason, or I thought so, and . . . I took an opportunity, the first time he came near me, to give the signal of distress. He came to me and asked what he could do for me. I asked what he was going to do with me. He said that the officers were to be sent to Fort Lafayette [a Union prison in New York Harbor]. Then I replied, "I would like to get away." He said "I will do anything for you which is not in violation of my oath as a soldier. . . . What grounds have you for asking to be released?" I said, "I am a non-combatant." He remarked, "Are you not one of the surgeons who were captured with that artillery that did such fearful execution amongst our men on Saturday night last?" I said, "Yes, but I was not at a gun—I never pulled a lanyard in my life." He smiled and said, "You were in mighty bad company, then, and you will have to take your chances with them."[15]

Dr. Claiborne was paroled a short time later, although that had less to do with Masonry than with the terms of the surrender of the Army of Northern Virginia, which had taken place only hours before.

The example of Andrew M. Benson is another case in point. At the time of his capture a captain of Company H, 1st District of Columbia Cavalry, Benson was captured during the Southside and Danville Railroad Expedition at Roanoke, Virginia, in June 1864. Initially confined in Libby Prison in Richmond, he was later transferred to Macon, Georgia, and then to the Marine Hospital in Savannah. Along with other prisoners, Benson became part of an escape plan to tunnel under the stockade. With a strap hinge and a case knife between them, Benson and his comrades dug a tunnel 120 feet long that was discovered by rebel warders at the last moment, and the would-be escapees were caught in the act.[16]

As punishment, Benson was confined to quarters. Upon his release from close arrest, he was again involved in another escape tunnel, which was likewise discovered; this time Benson was rewarded with a term of solitary confinement in the guardhouse. One morning, a Confederate officer passed by the outside of his cell and Benson made a Masonic appeal.

> I happened to think that I was a Mason, a Knight templar, but I had been one for so short a time that I really had not thought of it. This time I did, and I gave him a sign which he readily understood. He stopped and wanted to know how long I had been in there. I told him sixteen days, and informed him why I was there . . . and he told me that Colonel Wayne [the camp commander] . . . was the Grand Commander of the Knights Templars for the State of Georgia, "and" he added "should you make an application to be released, I have no doubt he will send you back to the stockade."[17]

Benson wrote an application to the Confederate officer and within a few hours, the Colonel visited Benson in his cell.

> He came down with the jailer and said to me, "You have sent for me?" I said, "Yes, Colonel, I have. I simply sent an application to you." "Well" he said, "I received it and have come here to take you out, but I find that you haven't embodied in that application all that I wish you would." I said, "Very well, Colonel, what else do you want?" "I want you to tell me now if you should see any of your comrades attempting to escape here in Savannah you will take means to let me know." "Well," I said, "Colonel, I am surprised that you should ask such a thing of an old soldier, I am surprised." He laughingly said that he didn't expect that I would consent. "But," he said, "I am going to take you out anyway."[18]

It is clear from the examples throughout this book that Masonic ties could, and did, interfere with duty. Countless reports demonstrate that Masonry stayed the soldier's hand in battle, or caused the rules of warfare to be relaxed—all contrary to customs forbidding fraternization with the enemy, and some clearly in direct violation of orders. It is not known how many pleas for Masonic favors went unheeded—almost certainly because Masons would be loathe to report such things—but these examples illustrate that although the fraternal tie could trump the demands of duty, there was a middle ground. Of those cases reported by Masons, however, these examples are rare.

Wear Silk Underclothing, Join the Masons

In some instances, surrender and captivity were the only option for Civil War soldiers, and in those cases, we again observe the taming hand of Masonry. On Christmas Day, 1864, the Masonic bond vouchsafed the surrender of a rebel detachment at Fort Fisher near Wilmington, North Carolina. Intent on surrender, a Confederate major, John M. Reese, 4th North Carolina Junior Reserves, approached elements of the 117th New York Infantry under a flag of truce. He advised their commander, Col. Rufus Daggett, that he wished to surrender his command. His troops, sent to reinforce the beleaguered garrison of the fort, were not veteran soldiers but teenage cadets, hastily assembled and sent into action. "On being farther questioned, he [Reese] identified his troops as a part of the North Carolina Junior Reserves, and that they were on the river bank, a few hundred yards distant. The Colonel, naturally enough, suspected a trick. . . . The [Confederate] Major observing this, asked the Colonel if he was a Mason. The Colonel replied, 'No, but the Captain is' (referring to Captain Stevens). The Major then stepped up to the Captain, and soon made himself known as a brother in the fraternity."[19] With this assurance, the federal officers approached the tired and hungry cadets and received their surrender without incident. Barraged with questions by the cadets about their fate—would they be killed? Stevens reassured them they "would be better off then in their own army," prompting one young rebel to remark, "We can't be any worse off, any how. We have never received a cent of pay, nor scarcely anything to eat, except what we have picked up."[20]

Given the state of prisons in both North and South, however, the optimism of Daggett's cadets was perhaps misplaced. Depending upon the camp in which a prisoner found himself, life could be tolerable or very grim indeed. New arrivals at Andersonville reportedly vomited at the odor of the compound and the sight of the inmates, and approximately 13,000 of the 45,000 federal prisoners housed there died.[21] Likewise, Southerners were outraged by conditions in Northern prisons—Alton Penitentiary, Camp Douglas, Camp Chase, Rock Island, Elmira—where inadequate housing and pestilential conditions were pointed to as examples of federal barbarity and criminal mismanagement. On both sides, inmates described wretched prison conditions, rife with disease and reeking of filth and death. "It is impossible to have any idea of the state of the skin covering bodies," wrote Surgeon William S. Ely, executive officer of the Union General Hospital at Annapolis. "In many cases I have observed, the dirt encrustation has been so thick as to require constant ablution to recover the normal condition and function . . . patients repeatedly stated that they had been unable to wash their bodies once in six months."[22]

In some camps, shelter was not provided; at many others it was the barest minimum through overcrowding and neglect of the prison authorities. Casualties rose accordingly. In one month—November 1864, for example—in Elmira, New York, 207 Confederate prisoners died, an average of nearly seven per day. In Camp Douglas in Chicago, 217 men also died in that month, most from sickness, but many from want of basic necessities.[23] At Andersonville, the very first priority for federal prisoners was finding, or constructing, a temporary hut—called "shebangs"—to keep off wind, rain, and even sun, as the prisoners were allotted no shelter of any kind, not even canvas. These rude abodes required constant repairs, and prisoners expended a great deal of effort in improving them. Clothing, too, was of immediate concern, and a great deal of effort was spent in mending, or making clothes.[24]

Food was also of paramount concern. A Union prisoner, John L. Ransom of Company A, 9th Michigan Cavalry, was captured in the autumn of 1863 in Tennessee. Interned in Belle Island prison outside Richmond, Ransom kept a diary. While there, he reported that rations were not issued on some days, and when issued often consisted of maggot-infested beans, raw rice, or cornbread made from inferior substitutes and in miniscule quantities. As winter set in, the shortages became more acute.

Dec. 30 [1863].—No rations issued yesterday to any of the prisoners and a third of all here are on the very point of starvation. Lieutenant [Virginius] Bossieux [Confederate commander of the prison camp] sympathizes with us in word but says it is impossible to help it as they have not the food for us. This is perhaps true as regards edibles but there is no excuse for our receiving such small supplies of wood. They could give us plenty of shelter, plenty of wood and conveniences we do not now get if they felt so disposed.

Dec. 31.—Still very cold and no news encouraging. Rebels very strict. . . . Man wounded by the guard shooting and ball broke his leg. Might better have shot him dead, for he will surely die. Raw rice and corn bread issued to day in small quantities.[25]

The New Year brought little relief for Ransom and his comrades; he records his fellow prisoners resorting to stealing food in order to survive.

Jan. 3 [1864]—Received a letter from Michigan. Not quite so cold but disagreeable weather. Nine men bucked and gagged at one time on the outside two of them for stealing sour beans from a swill barrel. They would get permission to pass through the gate to see the Lieutenant and instead would walk around the cook house to some barrels containing swill, scoop up their hats full and then run inside; but they were caught and are suffering a hard punishment for it.

Jan. 4.—Some ladies visited the island to see us blue coats, and laughed very much at our condition; thought it so comical and ludicrous the way the prisoners crowded the bank [a walled ditch forming a deadline that prisoners were forbidden to cross—Ed.] next the cook house, looking over at the piles of bread, and compared us to wild men and hungry dogs. A chicken belonging to the Lieutenant [Bossieux] flew up on the bank and was snatched off in short order, and to pay for it, we are not to receive a mouthful of food today, making five or six thousand suffer for one man catching a little chicken.

Jan. 15.—Everything runs along about the same. Little excitements from day to day. The weather is fair and taken all together thus far this winter has been very favorable to us as prisoners. Lieutenant Bossieux lost his dog. Some Yanks snatched him into a tent and eat him up. Bossieux very mad and is anxious to know who the guilty ones are. All he can do is to keep all our rations from us one day and he does it. Seems pretty rough when a man will eat a dog but such is the case.[26]

By late January, the food shortages at Belle Island were becoming critical. Although Ransom was not a Freemason, a comrade was, and Ransom reported that for the benefit of his messmates, that Mason approached the Confederate authorities to seek aid.

Jan. 20.—Corporal McCartin [possibly named McCarten—Ed.] is, as his name would indicate, an Irishman and his home is Louisville Ky. Is a shoemaker by trade. He is also a Mason, and I am going to write down wherein the fact of his being a Mason has brought good into the camp to-day. The boys feeling rather more hungry than usual were rather despondent, when the Corporal gets up and says "Boys, I'll go and get something to eat." Went out of the tent and in twenty minutes came back with three or four pounds of bacon and two loaves of corn bread. We were surprised and asked how he had performed the miracle. Told us then that he was a Mason as also was the Lieutenant in charge [Bossieux] from whom the food came. We decided then and there that the first opportunity that presented itself we would join the Masons.[27]

On 8 February 1864, McCartin was discovered missing. Ransom reported that he was "confident from what I have seen that he has escaped and by the help of Lieut. Bossieux. No endeavors are being made to look him up, still he offers a reward for his apprehension. They are both members of the secret craft."[28]

Later, in March of 1864, Ransom was transferred to Andersonville, where despite his increasingly failing health, he maintained his diary, which had by then grown to three notebooks comprising over a thousand pages. His own unofficial figures placed the casualty rates from disease at one in every sixteen men in April 1864—a figure he would later amend to one in three dead by November of the same year.[29]

Gravely ill with scurvy, Ransom received a transfer from Andersonville to Savannah, Georgia, and following his recovery, he was ordered to Camp Lawton in Millen, Georgia, with other federal prisoners, where he encountered Masonry one last time in prison.

Nov. 7.—A rather cold rain wets all who have not shelter. . . . A man belonging to the Masonic order need not stay here an hour. It seems as if every rebel officer was of that craft, and a prisoner has but to make himself known to be taken care of. Pretty strong secret association that will stand the fortunes of war. That is another thing I must do when I get home—join the Masons. No end of things for me to do: visit all the foreign countries that prisoners told me about . . . wear silk underclothing, join the masons.[30]

Ransom finally escaped rebel custody on 23 December 1864 after an imprisonment of nearly fourteen months. He rejoined Union forces near Savannah, Georgia, was excused from further combat duty, and was discharged shortly thereafter. True to his word, he became a Freemason on 22 February 1866, in Jackson Lodge No. 17, F. & A.M., in Jackson, Michigan.[31]

We Will Have Something to Eat Tonight

Even if he was decently fed and housed, the specter of ill health was a source of constant worry for prisoners of war. Medical facilities were rudimentary, even in well-managed camps. In poorly run stockades, the prisoners were simply left to fend for themselves, and in all camps, disease and neglect killed far more prisoners than guards and warders. At Camp Chase in the fall of 1864, smallpox, a great killer, broke out. By October "the smallpox [was] prevailing in the prisons averaging ten cases per day." A small building called the "pest house" was constructed outside of the prison walls to quarantine those with the disease. There were few survivors.[32]

Dr. Joseph Jones, a physician in the Confederate Army who worked in Andersonville, reported that from 24 February to 21 September 1864, a total of 9,479 federal prisoners—one-third of the entire prison population—died from disease. Jones reported that the prisoners, all of whom were lousy, suffered heavily from neglect and disease. "There were near five thousand seriously ill Federals in the Stockade and Confederate States Military Prison Hospital, and the deaths exceeded one hundred daily; and large numbers of the prisoners who were walking about, and who had never been entered upon the sick list, were suffering from severe and incurable diarrhœa, dysentery, and scurvy."[33]

The response of Masonic prisoners was to band together. These Masons shared rations, lived together, and held meetings, although without a charter or a dispensation from a Grand Lodge, Freemasons in prison could not operate a lodge per se. Nevertheless, Masonic prisoners associated freely and openly while incarcerated. Union Masons in Libby Prison in Richmond on at least one occasion sent a formal declaration of sympathy to the family of a Masonic comrade who died in prison.[34] At Andersonville, prisoners erected quarters known as the "Masonic Tent," which consisted of a shanty situated on the south side of the camp "but a little way from the Dead Line."[35] Through this association, which offered both physical and—

equally importantly—psychological support, individual Masons increased their chances of surviving the war.

Proof of the great influence of Masonry in the prisons comes in many instances from non-Masons who observed acts of Masonic charity while in prison and wrote about them after the war. These accounts described how Masons stuck together after capture and how Masonic prisoners on both sides received support from "enemy" Masons. John McElroy, of Company L, 16th Illinois Cavalry, was not a Mason, but he witnessed Masonry at work at Andersonville, and it occurred to him that the fraternity was one of the few humanitarian agencies inside, or outside, the prison.

> The churches of all denominations—except the solitary Catholic Priest, Father Hamilton—ignored us as wholly as if we were dumb beasts. Lay humanitarians were equally indifferent, and the only interest manifested by any Rebel in the welfare of any prisoner was by the Masonic brotherhood. The Rebel Masons interested themselves in securing details outside the Stockade in the cook-house, the commissary, and elsewhere, for the brethren among the prisoners who would accept such favors. Such as did not feel inclined to go outside on parole received frequent presents in the way of food, and especially of vegetables, which were literally beyond price. Materials were sent inside to build tents for the Masons, and I think such as made themselves known before death, received burial according to the rites of the Order.
>
> Doctor White and perhaps other Surgeons, belonged to the fraternity, and the wearing of a Masonic emblem was pretty sure to catch their eyes, and be a means of securing for the wearer the tender of their good offices, such as detail into the Hospital as nurse, wardmaster, etc.[36]

McElroy's account is corroborated by Sgt. Samuel S. Boggs, of the 21st Illinois Infantry, also incarcerated at Andersonville. Boggs agreed that Father Hamilton was the only clergyman he ever saw inside Andersonville. He also echoed McElroy's comments about Freemasonry: "Rebel Masons interested themselves in assisting their brother Masons in presents of medicine, food, tent material, reading and writing material, vegetables and in many ways not known to those not familiar with Masonry. I was neither a Catholic nor a Mason, but I do want to give credit to every merciful act shown in that hell; there were so few that it takes but little space to give them."[37]

Non-Masonic prisoners in other camps made similar reports. "I was a prisoner of war for four months, in the prison at Danville, Virginia," wrote J. L. Hinley, of Company L, 2nd Massachusetts Cavalry, in a letter dated 11 September 1914, "I was not a mason during the war, but what I saw there of masonry, induced me to join the beneficent order, and I was made a mason in 1866. I saw [at Danville] what the order did for a brother, as several of those who were masons were treated much better than others; they were taken out of prison on their word as a mason, that they would not attempt to escape—most of the Confederate officers being masons, and they faithfully observed their vows. It may be as well that I was not a mason at that time, as I escaped from the prison and safely made my way to our lines at Newbourne [New Bern], N.C."[38]

John M. Copley's experiences in prison were similar. A Confederate soldier in Company B, 49th Tennessee Infantry, Copley was captured by Union troops at the battle of Franklin (30 November 1864) and sent to the military prison at Camp Douglas, Illinois,

> Within a few weeks after being domiciled, and were becoming accustomed to our new mode of living, we were notified that this barrack must be vacated, and that we must be transferred to other barracks, to make room for those who had somewhat grown in favor with the Federal authorities, and were known to the rest of us as two classes,—one class was known as gentlemen of the "White Apron," more familiarly, as Free Masons; the other as "Loyal Men"; that is, those who petitioned for the oath of allegiance and to join the Federal army, to fight against their own blood kin and their already desolated

homes. These favored loyal gentlemen were removed to and located in the barracks which the authorities had us to vacate. All the Free Masons were stored away in barracks to themselves. They were as good Confederates as any of us, but were more highly favored on account of the order to which they belonged, and we were informed that they received much better treatment at the hands of the officials, in every particular, than the remainder of us. I did not belong to that order then; hence, I had to take the storm as it came, let it be heavy or light.[39]

"Just before we went into camp one night a citizen walked beside us for a short distance and I saw him exchange glances with Captain Hume," wrote Capt. John G. B. Adams, of the 19th Massachusetts, another non-Mason.

After he passed on Captain Hume said, "We will have something to eat to-night. That man is a mason; he says we are going into camp soon and he will come down and bring me some food." We soon after filed out of the road and into a field. The captain's brother-mason came and walked around until he saw Hume, then passed near and dropped a package containing bread and meat. Although not a mason at that time I shared the refreshments furnished by the craftsman.[40]

In some instances, the ministrations of the fraternity changed the minds of men who had previously been decidedly anti-Masonic. Capt. William A. Wash of Company I, 60th Tennessee, was captured at Big Black, Mississippi, on 17 May 1863. He was imprisoned at Johnson's Island, on Lake Erie, near Sandusky, Ohio, an officer's camp, holding three thousand Confederate prisoners. In 1870, he wrote of how his stint in prison changed his mind about Freemasonry:

From early childhood, I had imbibed a dislike to anything hidden or secret, for I imagined whatever was meritorious would not suffer by being brought out into the light. But now I take it all back, and give my testimony in behalf of Freemasonry as a good and valuable institution. During my stay in prison I had ample chance to watch its workings.

A little flock of perhaps three hundred of the Order had been gathered up from every quarter and sent to stay with us. They were regularly organized for such charitable ministering as was in their power among the fraternity. If one was sick the brotherhood were detailed to wait upon him, by day and by night, till he got well: and if he had no means, a collection was taken up from the scanty purses of his comrades to procure whatever dainties or comforts were to be had; if he died, they gave him the most decent burial possible.[41]

The local Masonic lodges in towns near the prisons also tried to help. Hosea H. Rockwell, a private in Company K, 23rd New York Volunteers, observed prison life from the outside following his discharge from the Army of the Potomac in May of 1863. A resident of Elmira, New York, he reported in 1912 that the Masonic fraternity in the town had established a benefit committee to care for rebel Masons interned there, and both lodges in Elmira, Union Lodge No. 95 and Ivy Lodge No. 397, passed resolutions to form a committee to "raise funds and ask for contributions of money and clothing, which were freely [donated] . . . to such of the prisoners as were Masons." The committee was directed to investigate and find all such cases and relieve them according to their necessities, and this continued during the entire existence of the camp at this city. The beneficiaries were rebel Masons from South Carolina, Georgia, and Mississippi.[42]

On at least two occasions the charitable work done by Union Lodge No. 95 was remarked upon in the lodge minutes:

July 18, 1864. Resolved, that the relief committee be directed to take measures for relief in the matter of clothing, delicacies, etc., for the prisoners of war now in camp in this place who are Masons.

September 20, 1864. Moved and carried that Fifty Dollars be appropriated from the funds of this Lodge for the benefit of our Southern brethren, prisoners of war in Barracks No. 3.[43]

At the September 20th meeting, the lodge also appointed a committee to erect a marker for the grave of a Confederate Mason, William B. Egerton of Company C, 12th Virginia Infantry, who died in the Elmira prison camp on 22 August 1864.[44]

In prison, as the Elmira example indicates, the benefits of the fraternity flowed to fellow members exclusively. Masons cared for Masons out of a sense of common fraternal regard and because of the obligations that each member took at his initiation to "help, aid and assist a worthy brother" in distress. However, at least some acknowledgment of the needs of non-Masonic prisoners and an attempt to care for them are recorded. Confederate Freemasons formed a Masonic Prison Association at the federal prison on Johnson's Island to ameliorate some of the privations of prison life. In an official appeal, in November 1864, Capt. Joseph J. Davis of North Carolina corresponded, as "president of the Masonic Prison Association," directly with the Union commandant to allow for Masonic contributions from outside the prison to supply not only medicines but also food, clothing, and hospital supplies to aid both Masons and non-Masons alike. "If permitted to do so," he wrote, "many of these wants can be supplied through our association, and we will not confine ourselves to the sick of our own fraternity, for (under the circumstances, I may be pardoned for saying) the diffusive charity inculcated by our order extends to all mankind and should embrace even an enemy in distress and relieve him with a hearty good will. . . . If the orders shall be so relaxed (which we respectfully ask) as to permit us to procure the class of articles alluded to, I give you the most solemn assurance that they shall be appropriated solely for the benefit of the sick."[45]

The request was approved by the prison commandant, and contributions began to accumulate. By 1865 these included $165 "from the Masons of St. Louis . . . of Nashville $165., of New York $20., and in Boston they have on hand, subject to our order, several hundred dollars. The Masons of the city of Louisville have supplied us with at least $300 worth of hospital stores and medicines, and those in St. Louis have supplied us with four boxes of hospital stores."[46]

Sometimes, however, the Masonic connection was used by captive soldiers to ward off not sickness and distress, but the ministrations of well-meaning surgeons. Capt. Isaac H. Larew, of Company E, 60th Regiment, Virginia Infantry (3rd Regiment, Wise Legion), was seriously wounded on 9 May 1864 at the Battle of Cloyd's Mountain in western Virginia. A shell struck him on the right shoulder, tearing away the shoulder blade, and Larew was captured. Initially, the doctors pronounced his wound fatal, but he survived longer than expected—several days—and a surgeon at the hospital decided that the arm should be amputated. Larew found this out and, as he was a Mason, he recruited among the federal guards several brother Masons, whom he persuaded to pledge that they would not permit the amputation. Larew survived the war and became an attorney in Pulaski City, Virginia, with his right arm intact.[47] It is interesting to note that Freemasonry traditionally required a man to be "a perfect Youth having no Maim or Defects in his Body that may render him uncapable of learning the Art of serving his Master's Lord, and of being made a Brother, and then a Fellow-Craft in due Time."[48]

In another such incident, Samuel H. Hargis, of Company D, 2nd Arkansas Mounted Rifles, was assigned as hospital orderly following the Battle of Peachtree Creek in July 1864. A federal officer spotted the Masonic pin Hargis wore, made himself known as a Mason, and appealed to Hargis to stop the amputation of his leg, which was imminent. When arguing with the surgeon failed, Hargis threatened him; the Union officer kept his leg, and Hargis, apparently, kept his job.[49] Apart from the natural abhorrence to the prospect of amputation, it is quite possible that both men's reactions arose from the Masonic stigma of such mutilations.

These and similar claims of Masonic incidents in prison may seem remarkable, but they are verifiable and many are corroborated by more than one contemporary source. Those that are not independently verifiable usually occasion little suspicion, being typical of those that are. For example, in December of 1864 an anonymous Captain J. W. C., of the 123rd Ohio Volunteers, wrote of his nine months of captivity in Libby Prison in a letter to Cornelius Moore, the editor of the *Masonic Review*. His account typifies the experiences of a Freemason in a Civil War prison and seems eminently credible, though no supporting evidence exists:

I was captured at Winchester, Va., June 15, 1863. . . . I was taken to Richmond a few days thereafter and lodged in the famous Libby Prison, of which loathsome place I was an inmate until March 21, 1864. . . . About the 1st December, our government sent some 15,000 outfits for the relief of our suffering men. The Confederate authorities appointed a committee of our officers . . . I was the only one of the number who was a Mason. Capt. D. D. Munro, 3d N.C. Regt., C.S.A., performed the same duties on the part of the rebels. He was a Scotchman, made a Mason in a Lodge in Scotland, "had passed the chair," and held a Diploma from a Lodge in Philadelphia. . . . I never asked any favors on the grounds of my being a Mason, because I do not believe it is according to the teachings of Masonry—unless I was in very destitute circumstances. This same Captain had charge of the distribution of private boxes sent to us from the North. Although they were always critically examined, mine did not have to pass such an examination, and they were always delivered to me very promptly, as well as those of a few particular friends for whom I requested the same favor. . . . This Captain used his influence with the Commandant of the prison, and had my name placed on the list [of those prisoners selected to be exchanged]. He then came up in the prison and informed me that I was to go the next day which I did. He also informed me that his life was saved at the battle of Gettysburg, by the use of a certain - - -, well known to the Craft.[50]

However, other tales, such as the account of Isaac "Ike" Hermann, are simply fantastic. Hermann was a member of Howell's Company, Georgia Light Artillery. In Davisboro, Georgia, in late 1864, he described an encounter with a Mason on a prison train bound for Andersonville. Walking along the tracks after dark, Hermann heard "the grand hailing words of distress" from an inmate in the freight car requesting food. Hermann responded by procuring food from a nearby boarding house that he delivered, along with silverware and a peculiar handmade napkin "bordered with indigo blue" to the unseen brother in the train car.[51] Incredibly, Hermann claimed that he later chanced upon this anonymous prisoner, whom he identified as one "Mr. McClucklan," a salesman, in New York City in 1868. Recognizing each other as Masons, the two men struck up a conversation that turned to Georgia, then Andersonville, and finally to the salesman's reputed appeal complete with details about the homemade napkin.[52] Clearly, the odds against such a postwar encounter strain credulity, but against the backdrop of improbable, yet verifiable, accounts of Masonic interventions elsewhere, Hermann's tale is nonetheless plausible.

Gewgaws

A discussion of Masonry in prison would not be complete without some mention of handmade Masonic jewelry. Period sources that mention Masons as prisoners of war inevitably include a description of the trinkets and charms made by soldier-inmates, many of which featured Masonic emblems. Some prisoners made ordinary jewelry and trinkets to sell or barter to guards or outsiders for food or other provisions. Other prisoners made Masonic jewelry—sometimes in large quantities—but the reason for this are unclear. It is possible that these emblems were simply made to identify members of the fraternity to one another, a common occurrence among Freemasons during the war and even today. Or perhaps these men simply found comfort in fashioning the symbols that reminded them of better, happier times.

Capt. James N. Bosang of Company C, 4th Virginia Infantry, made jewelry from soup bones to earn money for food in prison. After being wounded and captured at Spotsylvania, "he found some Masonic friends among his captors who started him on his way to a Northern Prison with a five dollar bill, which he accepted as a Masonic favor." When the five dollars ran out, Bosang, imprisoned in Fort Delaware, developed a thriving trade in making jewelry from gutta-percha buttons and resoling shoes.[53]

Col. Thomas E. Barker, formerly of Company B of the 12th New Hampshire, also earned money by making and selling trinkets in the Old Parish Prison in New Orleans and wrote that he "became quite skilled in the manufacture, from the bones in our rations, of rings, charms, Masonic emblems, etc., which were eagerly sought for and purchased by the many visitors who were allowed, on certain days of each week, to see us."[54] Federal prisoner held no monopoly on this industry; rebel captives in Elmira, New York, were similarly employed in making watch charms and other Masonic jewelry from any available material.[55]

In at least one incident, an inmate's display of a Masonic-themed trinket brought an immediate response from his captors at the prison camp in Macon, Georgia.

Lieut. Hyde of my company [Company B, 1st Vermont Cavalry][56] . . . captured at Brandy Station, Oct. 11, 1863, and about eight months a prisoner, was suffering from that usually fatal disease—in this place—diarrhoea. He was a Free Mason, and from a piece of bone I had made him a small scarf pin representing the order—the square and compass; as the poor fellow was so very destitute of anything pertaining to the comforts of life, I borrowed from him the scarf pin, and going to the gate, I handed it out to a rebel sergeant whom I had seen wearing the same symbol, I said: "The man who wears this is lying in a critical condition, and I wish you would kindly call upon him." He bowed assent, and during the day came in. Being on the watch for him, I at once guided him to where the sick man lay. He talked with him an hour or so and went out, saying he would call again. The next morning he walked hurriedly into the Lieutenant's tent, threw down a parcel, and walked out. It contained one pair of drawers, one shirt, a pair of feeting, some medicine and food.[57]

Beyond mere vanity or personally meaningful symbolism, Masonic emblems were important because they identified the wearer as a member of the Craft and unlocked what compassion there was to be had—if the circumstances permitted. For Lieutenant Hyde, however, the assistance was too little and too late, and he died a few days after this incident.[58]

Although some accounts suggest that Masonry responded to the needs of non-Masons in prison (as in Captain Davis's letter, above), documentary evidence shows that in most instances its benefits were restricted to members only. One Confederate prisoner at Elmira wrote bitterly that "I found that the worst and most worthless men could outstrip the best in a contest for the 'good places' about camp, if they were only Masons."[59] Complaints that favorable treatment was, in many cases, reserved for fellow Freemasons are almost certainly true, and the Masonic fraternity, like any other, clearly devoted its primary attention to its members before considering the needs of the public at large. The Masonic emblems worn by prisoner and guard alike reflect that fraternal bond.

Freemasonry was not practiced in the military prisons of the American Civil War; lodges did not meet nor were men initiated into the brotherhood, but its tenets were applied there. Applying those tenets provided Masons and non-Masons with an inoculation of civility in an otherwise barbaric setting. The record indicates that Freemasonry was a lifeline for many prisoners of war, transcending national and political boundaries, and in some instances even affiliation with the fraternity itself. Deprived of proper medical care, basic sanitation, suitable clothing, and even basic foodstuffs, prisoners of war in 1861−65 were forced to fend for themselves. Although soldiers made use of their Masonic credentials to gain respite, reprieve, and succor from the enemy on the battlefield, Masonry's influence in the prisons is perhaps its greatest contribution to ameliorating the suffering of the war. It is for this reason that Masonic emblems, trifling objects in ordinary times, assumed an importance far larger than mere decoration or vanity. These emblems were passports to a physical and spiritual support structure that was sorely needed in these direst of conditions. Quite simply, affiliation with the Masonic fraternity in a prison compound could literally become a matter of life and death.

1. Col. Charles L. Holbrook, a member of McClellan Army Lodge No. 6 (43rd Regiment, Massachusetts Infantry [Militia]), was also a member of Columbian Lodge in Boston in civilian life. In this undated photo, he wears a Masonic pin on his uniform. (Collection of the Grand Lodge of Masons in Massachusetts at the National Heritage Museum, GL2004.5419, photograph by David Bohl.)

2 and 3 (inset). Maj. Everett Lane, also a member of McClellan Army Lodge No. 6 (43rd Regiment, Massachusetts Infantry [Militia]), seen here wearing another Masonic device while in uniform. Masonic emblems such as this were worn in battle. (Collection of the Grand Lodge of Masons in Massachusetts at the National Heritage Museum, GL2004.5419, photograph by David Bohl.)

4. The Union ironclad USS *Baron De Kalb* (formerly USS *St. Louis*) bearing what appears to be the square and compasses between her stacks. (National Archives.)

5. "Custer's men drawing the seven fatal slips at Rectortown," by James E. Taylor, ca. 1863. The artist depicts the "lottery of death" carried out by Mosby's men in retaliation for Union treatment of Confederate prisoners and includes an unmistakable display of Masonic fellowship as indicated at right. (The Western Reserve Historical Society, Cleveland, Ohio.)

6. St. John's Lodge No. 3, A.F. & A.M., New Bern, North Carolina, ca. 1863, with Union soldiers visible in the foreground. (North Carolina Collection, University of North Carolina at Chapel Hill.)

7. St. John's Lodge No. 3, lodge-room carpet extensively decorated with Masonic symbols. (North Carolina Collection, University of North Carolina at Chapel Hill.)

8. "A Masonic Temple, commodious and a beautiful work of art, constructed of the rustic materials the Island afforded" by Masons of the 1st New York Engineer Regiment on Folly Island, South Carolina, in November 1863. The photo shows the altar (foreground), Master's chair (background), and the station of the Junior Warden at right. Note the military stores that form the pedestal for the Junior Warden. Photograph by Samuel Cooley. (Massachusetts MOLLUS Photograph Collection, U.S. Army Military History Institute, Carlisle Barracks, Pennsylvania.)

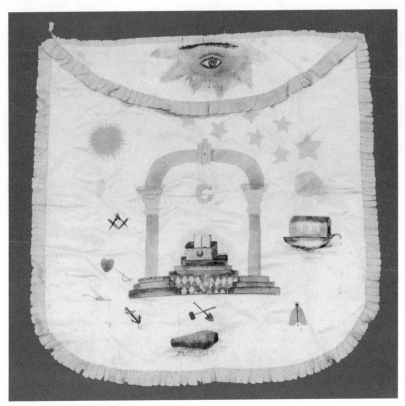

9. Hand painted, silk Masonic apron found on the battlefield of Stones River, Tennessee, (Second Battle of Murfreesboro) by Col. Hans C. Heg, 15th Wisconsin Infantry, in January 1863, and likely discarded by a Masonic soldier. (Wisconsin Veterans Museum.) Heg, who was later killed at the Battle of Chickamauga, was a member of Temple Lodge No. 96, Waterford, Wisconsin.

6

A More Decent Interment

The Masonic historian Albert G. Mackey observed, "when a Mason has reached the third degree, he becomes entitled to all the rights and privileges of Ancient Craft Masonry. . . . These are the rights of membership, of visitation, of relief, and of burial."[1] The rights of visitation and membership concern Masonic rules and customs for visiting and participating in lodges, and touch our subject only peripherally. The right of relief, and the ways in which Masonic assistance was offered during wartime, we have already explored in chapter 3. The last of these traditional Masonic rights—the right of burial—was also a part of the influence of Masonry during the Civil War, and Masonic burials figured prominently during the conflict.

In part because of the religious overtones of the fraternity, and in part because the ritual and traditions of Freemasonry focused on the transition from life to death, Masonic funeral services were popular among members in the nineteenth century, as they are today. Writing in 1855, Mackey commented that the origins of the Masonic funeral traditions were obscure, but that it was the right of every third degree (Master) Mason to be buried with Masonic honors if he desired it.

> After a very careful examination, I can find nothing in the old
> charges or General Regulations, nor in any other part of the funda-

mental law, in relation to masonic burial of deceased Brethren. It is probable that, at an early period, when the great body of the craft consisted of Entered Apprentices, the usage permitted the burial of members, of the first or second degree, with the honors of Masonry. As far back as 1754, processions for the purpose of burying Masons seemed to have been conducted . . . But the usage since then, has been greatly changed; and by universal consent, the law . . . is now adopted . . . "No Mason can be interred with the formalities of the Order, unless it be at his own special request, communicated to the Master of the Lodge of which he died a member—foreigners and sojourners excepted; nor unless he has been advanced to the third degree of Masonry, from which restriction there can be no exception. Fellow Crafts or Apprentices are not entitled to the funeral obsequies."[2]

During the Civil War, many soldiers took advantage of the right of burial. In most cases, these honors consisted of a funeral service officiated by fellow fraternity members, who assembled graveside in white aprons to give their final farewells. Period accounts list hundreds of notices of these Masonic funerals in newspapers and periodicals, and many fallen soldiers buried far from home, or who could not be transported home for interment for one reason or another, also received a Masonic ceremony if their affiliation could be discerned.[3]

Even during active campaigning, it was not uncommon for Masons to assemble and give a brief Masonic funeral service on the battlefield. At Malvern Hill, on 1 July 1862, for example, Capt. John E. Beam of Battery B, 1st New Jersey Light Artillery, was directing fire from his battery's position near the West house onto rebel batteries 1,500 yards away. The New Jersey cannoneers were effective in, "knocking these batteries to pieces" and forcing their retreat, but the tenacious Confederate gunners soon reappeared with more cannon, and a furious artillery duel developed. During this fusillade, Beam was killed. A prominent member of St. John's Lodge No. 2 in Newark, Beam was well respected by his men. While the battle was still raging, but presumably after Battery B had fended off the rebel attack, some of Beam's men took his body to "the orchard in the rear and buried him with Masonic honors, the rattle of musketry and the roar of cannon being the funeral dirge."[4]

The importance attached by Masons to funeral rites is central to understanding the nature of the fraternity. Although a Masonic burial service is not a requirement of the fraternity, many members choose to receive it, and the "lecture" given at the grave by the Master of the Lodge is emblematic of the teachings of the fraternity. Masonry, then as now, teaches its members to "circumscribe our desires and keep us in due bounds with all mankind, but more especially with a brother Mason,"[5] and the funeral service serves to reinforce those admonitions with the hope of a reward in the afterlife. Although the fraternity promotes tenets that are similar to many world religions, it lacks the component of worship of any particular deity, preferring instead to allow its members to address their prayers and hopes to a Supreme Being of their own choosing. Yet in its burial customs the fraternity comes close to religious practice.

Masonic funerals, like other fraternal ceremonies, are carefully prescribed by the Grand Lodges and despite minor differences are remarkably similar regardless of the jurisdiction. Unlike other Masonic rites they are not secret, and they disclose nothing the fraternity does not wish to expose. Masonic funeral rites were first codified in William Preston's *Illustrations of Masonry* in England in 1812. In nineteenth-century America, these rites were essentially Christian in that they included mention of a Creator and of resurrection; however, the ceremonies maintained a nondenominational tone and avoided specific reference to either Jesus Christ or the God of Abraham. In peacetime, participants would assemble at the lodge wearing white aprons to symbolize innocence and with sprigs of evergreen in their lapels to symbolize everlasting life. Thus accoutered, the Craft would normally march in procession to the funeral site.[6] Following memorial comments about the deceased, the funeral rite would be conducted. A Masonic manual written in 1855 describes the graveside service given by the Master of the lodge, which warrants inclusion here:

Let us, while in this stage of our existence, support with propriety the character of our profession, advert to the nature of our solemnities, and pursue with assiduity the sacred tenets of our Order. Then, with becoming reverence, let us supplicate the divine grace, to ensure the favor of that Eternal Being, whose goodness and power know no bounds; that, when the awful moment arrives, be it soon or late, we may be enabled to prosecute our journey, without dread or apprehension, to that far distant country whence no traveler returns.

The following invocations are then made by the Master, and the usual honours accompany each:—

Master.—May we be true and faithful; and may we live and die in love.

Answer.—So mote it be.

Master.—May we profess what is good; and always act agreeably to our profession.

Answer.—So mote it be.

Master.—May the Lord bless us, and prosper us; and may all our good intentions be crowned with success!

Answer.—So mote it be.

From time immemorial, it has been a custom among the Fraternity of Free and Accepted Masons, at the request of a brother on his death bed, to accompany his corpse to the place of interment and there to deposit his remains with the usual formalities.

In conformity to this usage, and at the special request of our deceased Brother, whose memory we revere, and whose loss we now deplore, we have assembled in the character of Masons to resign his body to the earth, whence it came, and to offer up to his memory before the world, the last tribute of our affections; thereby demonstrating the sincerity of our past esteem, and our inviolable attachment to the principles of the Order.

With proper respect to the established customs of the country in which we live, with due deference to our superiors in church and state, and with unlimited good-will towards men, we here appear, clothed as Masons, and publicly crave leave to express our submission to peace and good government, and our wish to serve the interests of mankind. Invested with the badges of innocence, we humbly bow to the Universal Parent, and implore His blessing on every zealous endeavor to promote peace and good-will, and we pray for our perseverance in the principles of piety and virtue.

The great Creator having been pleased, our of his mercy, to remove our worthy Brother from the cares and troubles of a transitory life to a state of eternal duration, and thereby to weaken the chain by which we are united, man to man, may we, who survive him, anticipate our approaching dissolution, and be more strongly cemented in the ties of union and friendship, that during the short space allotted for our present existence we may wisely and usefully employ our time; and, in reciprocal course of kind and friendly acts, mutually promote the welfare and happiness of each other.

Unto the grave we consign the body of our deceased friend, there to remain unto the general resurrection, in favorable expectation that his immortal soul may then partake of joys which have been prepared for the righteous from the beginning of the world. And may Almighty God, of his infinite goodness, at the grand tribunal of unbiased justice, extend his mercy toward him and all of us, and crown our hope with everlasting bliss in the expanded realms of a boundless eternity! This we beg, for the honour of His name, to whom be glory, now and forever. Amen.[7]

The deceased's apron would then be cast into the grave, or placed on the bier, together with the evergreen sprigs.

Masonic funeral rites in the 1860s were little changed from this example, and Civil War Masons would have emulated Preston's 1812 rite to the extent that circumstance permitted. On the battlefield, this rite might have been truncated to brief remarks, but the expressions of sympathy and commiseration, of loyalty to the brotherhood, and certainly the hope for fulfillment in the afterlife would have been commonly expressed.

Curiously, Masonic funerals in the nineteenth century were widely regarded as a benefit of membership, and many Masons who had otherwise lost interest in their lodges maintained membership for that reason alone. Aware of the tradition, expounded on by Mackey (above), Masons relied on the express promise that they were "guaranteed burial with an impressive service, which he could hope would be attended by a large number of his brethren. Even if a Mason were buried away from his home lodge, he received this tribute, for local lodges would perform the burial and send delegates to the funeral." For a culture that was as obsessed with death and mourning as the Victorians—on both sides of the Atlantic—funeral rites of this kind were no small consideration.[8]

The Men of North and South Walked Solemnly behind the Bier

It is usual enough to bury a fallen comrade in war, but as we have seen in the introduction to this book, Masons also went out of their way to bury fallen antagonists as well. Captain Wainwright's funeral, noted in the introduction, provides one example of this, but it is not an isolated case.[9]

A brief note in the regimental history of the 39th Massachusetts Infantry records the details of the interment of Lt. Isaac D. Paul who was killed at Spotsylvania on 8 May 1864, noting that "Confederate Masons carried his body to the rear and buried it with Masonic Rites."[10] Maj. James Austin Connolly of the 123rd Illinois Infantry wrote to his wife of a Masonic burial he encountered during the fighting near Atlanta. "[A] Captain who had been buried, had fallen nearer to our line than any other rebel, and he had evidently been decently interred by some Masonic brother in blue, for a headboard made of a cracker box, had been erected at his grave and inscribed with the masonic 'square and compass' and his name 'Capt. [Thomas J.] Sharp, 10th Miss., Buried by the 35th N.J. Vols. I know that he will arise again,' all written on it with a pencil, and possibly by the hand of the same soldier that killed him a few hours before."[11]

Perhaps the most famous account of a Masonic funeral during the war concerns the federal gunboat *Albatross*. Stationed on the Mississippi River in June of 1863, the *Albatross* was a screw-driven, steam-powered gunboat, fitted with three masts (just in case) and armed with rifled Parrott guns, under the command of Lt. Cmdr. John E. Hart. Hart and his crew had acquitted themselves well during the attack on Port Hudson in March 1863, but following that engagement Hart contracted yellow fever and became seriously ill. Three months later, while in action against Confederate positions at Bayou Sara near present-day St. Francisville, Louisiana, Hart, delirious with fever, shot himself in the head.[12] The log of the *Albatross* noted the following: "June 11, 1863: 4:15 p.m. The report of a pistol was heard in the captain's stateroom. The steward at once ran and found the captain lying on the floor with blood oozing from his head and a pistol near him, one barrel of which was discharged. The surgeon was at once called but life was extinct."[13]

Hart had previously mentioned that he wanted a Masonic burial, so with no other recourse to Masonic regalia on board ship, and with no one fluent in the ritual, two of Hart's shipmates contacted Confederate forces under a flag of truce and requested a Masonic service ashore. Capt. William W. Leake[14] of the Confederate army was on hand during the gunboat's attack; he also happened to be the senior warden of Feliciana Lodge No. 31, in St. Francisville. He assented to the request and the funeral was held with both Union and Confederate brethren attending.[15] After the war, Leake gave an account of the incident to the members of Feliciana Lodge No. 31.

In the spring of 1863 the United States gunboat Albatross, Lieut. Commander J. E. Hart in command, was anchored in the Mississippi River opposite Bayou Sara. Capt. Samuel White, whom I knew to be a Mason, informed me that Captain Hart had suicided, and three of the officers of the Albatross, who were Masons, had sent him to ascertain if I would bury the Captain with Masonic honors, and I consented to do so. We collected a few members of our lodge and met the procession, preceded by a flag of truce, at the top of the hill. In the procession were Brothers Benjamin F. and Samuel F. White,[16] of Bayou Sara, the surgeon and two officers of the gunboat (Masons), and a squad of marines at "trail arms." We marched in front of the corpse to Grace Church Cemetery, and buried Brother Hart in the Masonic lot. The United States surgeon and officers expressed their gratitude to the lodge and members present, and cordially invited us to accompany them on board and partake of their hospitality, but we declined to accept. The surgeon then offered to supply me with necessary family medicines if I would give him a list of what was needed. This I also declined with thanks, but he sent by Brother Samuel White a few medicines. I read the Masonic service at the grave.[17]

Captain Hart's grave remains well-tended in Grace Church Cemetery to this day, and each year the town of St. Francisville commemorates the unique circumstances of his burial with a reenactment of Hart's peculiar funeral.[18]

Less well known, the funeral of Ariel Ivers Cummings also demonstrated the transnational nature of Masonic funeral honors. Cummings, a Union surgeon attached to the 42nd Regiment of Massachusetts Infantry and a member of Washington Lodge, Roxbury, Massachusetts, died in captivity. On 10 September 1863, Union prisoners and their Confederate guards at Camp Groce near Hempstead, Texas, assembled and buried him. The preliminary arrangements for the funeral were made in the local lodge by the rebel guards, but both guards and prisoners attended the funeral.[19]

Following the funeral, the assembled Masons—Blue and Gray—met as an informal body with two Union prisoners, Lt. Col. Augustine Duganne of Metropolitan Lodge in New York City, and Henry W. Washburn of Union Lodge, New London, Connecticut, presiding. and the minutes of that meeting, expressed as a formal resolution, were sent to Washington Lodge informing them of the particulars of Cummings's burial and detailing how "lodges from the North, South, East and West are most harmoniously represented, as another illustration of the fraternal spirit which is continually adding strength to the foundation and beauty to the arches of our well-beloved Order."[20]

As I Am Not a Mason I Do Not Understand the Matter

These examples suggest the readiness of many Masons to absent themselves from the conflict—albeit briefly—and revisit the spirit of fraternalism they had known before the war. However, the lengths to which certain Masons went—such as the men of the *Albatross* requesting a temporary truce—suggests that the commitment to decently inter fellow members ran deeper than a simple nostalgia for more peaceful times. On several occasions Masons actively risked enemy fire to bury not only their fallen comrades but also to inter Masons from the enemy army. An extreme example of these peculiar sensibilities is the case of Col. Joseph Wasden of the 22nd Georgia Infantry who was killed at Gettysburg on 2 July 1863.[21]

A Union soldier opposite Wasden's Georgia troops, Augustus Woodbury, a chaplain with the 2nd Rhode Island, described what he saw.

An interesting incident occurred immediately after the battle of Gettysburg, which seems deserving of record. The Regiment was lying in the road, supporting the sharp-shooters. . . . The enemy's dead were scattered over the field. One of the men of Company C, learning, in some way, that Captain Foy was a member of the Masonic order, brought to him a diploma, bearing the name of Joseph Wasden, and issued by Franklin Lodge, Warrenton, Warren county, Georgia. It had been taken from the body of a colonel of a Georgia regiment, which was lying in the road, at a short distance from the position of the Regiment. Considering it his duty, as a Masonic brother, to see that the last rites were properly and decently performed, Captain Foy took with him Corporal [Archibald] Stalker and a detail of two or three men, proceeded to the place, carefully wrapped the body in a blanket, dug a grave in the field near by, under the sharp fire of the enemy's riflemen, and tenderly and reverently deposited the corpse of the fallen brother therein. A green leaf of corn supplied the place of the customary acacia, and the soul of the departed was commended to its God. It was a graceful and fraternal act, and was well and considerately performed.[22]

Woodbury's comrade, Elisha Hunt Rhodes, was with the regiment that day, and he also commented on Captain Foy in his diary.[23] "A Colonel of a Georgia Rebel Regiment was found dead upon the field. Capt. Thomas Foy of our Regiment discovered in some way that the Colonel was a Mason, and with the assistance of some other Masons buried him. As I am not a Mason I do not understand the matter. While the burial was going on the skirmishers were constantly firing." Wasden was buried on the grounds of the Codori farm at the "southern end" of the family's barn. On Captain Foy's orders, Corporal Stalker marked Wasden's grave himself with a wooden headboard bearing the square and compasses. Writing after the war, Foy—who was a past Master of King Solomon's Lodge No. 11, in East Greenwich, Rhode Island—also recalled the event, telling a regimental historian that he toured the interior of the barn that was occupied by wounded rebels, many of them from Wasden's regiment. He informed them of the burial and "requested them, if they lived to get home, to inform the friends of Colonel Wasden that he was decently buried, and by a Mason."[24]

The entire incident left a lasting impression on Rhodes. He received leave nine months after Gettysburg, which he used to take a furlough home. There, he petitioned Harmony Lodge No. 9, Pawtuxet, Rhode Island, for membership and was made a Mason on 29 March 1864.[25] Possessed with an understanding of Masonry's funeral customs, Rhodes later told of finding a Masonic friend dead on the field after the Third Battle of Winchester in September 1864:

I found the body of my friend Major James Q. Rice of [Company C] 2nd Conn. Heavy Artillery and had it buried by itself and shall try to send it home to his friends. He usually wore a fine Masonic pin, but someone had taken it from his coat. In fact he had been robbed of everything of value. I cut a square and compass with his name rank and Regiment upon an ammunition box cover and placed it at the head of the grave. Poor Rice, he was much older than I, but we were intimate, knowing each other as Masons and comrades.[26]

On occasion, when fighting was too intense, or sentries too trigger-happy, normal measures to recover the body of a fallen comrade were simply too hazardous. Under these circumstances, fraternal appeals to the enemy often produced the desired results. Following the Battle of Poplar Grove Church on 30 September 1864, Union troops tried to recover of the body of one of their commanders, Lt. Col. Charles Cummings of the 17th Vermont Volunteers, who had fallen just beyond the rebel line. Confederate troops in the vicinity, however, refused to honor a flag of truce, forcing a federal officer to resort to Masonry.

An officer of the 7th Rhode Island Volunteers who was a Freemason was on duty on the picket line. He watched . . . and when he saw a rebel officer he gave the sign of distress among Masons, which was immediately answered by the rebel officer, who happened to be a Mason, and a mutual agreement was made that they should meet as friends between the picket lines. Shaking hands, &c., they found each other to be Masons, and our officer communicated the earnest desire of our Vermont friends to recover the body of Col. Cummings, who was also a member of the Fraternity. The rebel officer could not respond to the request until he had seen the rebel General in command, who it is supposed was also a Mason, for the request was granted at once. The grave was found, and the body was disinterred and found in a tolerable state of preservation, and was recognized at once. He had been buried evidently by rebel Masons, for a headboard was placed over his grave with his name, rank, &c., and evidence of particular care was shown in burying him. He was raised from a dead level in the soil of old Virginia to be interred among his native Vermont hills.[27]

An Envelope of Sanity

These funeral rites were also important for other, less apparent reasons. While on active campaign, the fraternal bond was necessarily stripped away; lodges could not meet, initiate new members, or conduct business on the battlefield, but the yearning for the strong association and support of the Order remained undimmed—and in fact may have been intensified by the stressful conditions of battle and the attendant absence of normal societal bonds. These funeral rites allowed Freemasons in combat to create an envelope of fraternal sanity amid the insanity of battle.

It is certainly not unusual for soldiers to afford their brothers-in-arms a decent burial, nor is the Masonic order unique in interring the dead with special ceremony. It is, however, extraordinary to risk death to arrange a burial for a fallen enemy, or to suspend hostilities to recover a lone fallen comrade. That these acts were performed under individual initiative and not in response to orders is equally remarkable, and testifies to the depth of feeling that Masons associate with their burial rites. There are perhaps as many reasons that Masons devote such care to the interment of fallen brothers as there are incidents thereof. For some, a sense of reciprocity made such devotions obligatory—they would wish similar care had the roles been reversed. For others, the obligations that each Mason accepts upon initiation to care for a distressed worthy brother was the prime motivator. More important than individual motives, however, is that the observation of Masonic funeral rituals allowed men on both sides of the conflict to put aside their secular disagreements and return, albeit briefly, to a fraternal world in which moral men of all ranks stood equally with one another.

7

All Passions Laid Aside?

Freemasonry in the Army

After the fall of Vicksburg, there was a lull in the fighting along the Mississippi. Federal officers encamped along the river received a request from citizens of a nearby town to assist them in conducting a Masonic ritual, most of the local lodge being away in the service. The colonel summoned those officers and men he knew to be Masons in his command, and an impromptu chapter was put together to confer the degrees of Royal Arch Masonry—four degrees appendant to, but distinct from, Blue Lodge Masonry—on three men living in the town.[1] Freemasonry knows no distinction between military men and civilians, and this request was not unusual. What is noteworthy, however, is that the participants were on different sides of the conflict. Col. Jonathan B. Moore, of the 33rd Wisconsin Volunteers, had received the request from Masons at Natchez Chapter No. 1, Natchez, Mississippi, and the initiates were paroled Confederate Army officers released after the fall of Vicksburg. The ritual, it was reported, went off without a hitch.[2]

Seven hundred and fifty miles away, rebel officers reportedly returned the favor for a Union soldier known only as "L. J. Williams of the 114th New York Infantry." As the story is told in numerous Masonic circulars, Williams, captured near Savannah, Georgia, was a Fellow Craft from Downsville Lodge No. 464 in Delaware County, New York. While imprisoned he communicated with friends in New York, and allegedly his lodge there corresponded with the local lodge in Georgia, Zerubbabel Lodge No. 15 in Savannah, requesting the completion of his Masonic work. When the sought-after permission was finally granted, "he was taken from his prison and conducted to the Savannah lodge room. . . . All the chairs were occupied by Confederate officers. . . . Then and there he was made a master mason." Later that evening, Williams escaped—presumably with the assistance of Confederate Masons—although he maintained that he never knew the identity of his rescuers.[3]

Masonry in the Army

Deeply rooted in the fabric of peacetime America, Freemasonry was, as preceding chapters have clearly shown, quite prevalent among the soldiers of both armies. Although portrayed as a secret society cloaked in mystery, Masons in America were—and remain today—very visible. Army life was no different. Individual members of the fraternity identified themselves by wearing Masonic emblems—the familiar square and compasses chief among them—on their uniforms, and when associated together they coalesced in camp and bivouac. At times, this association signified nothing more than individual Freemasons banding together to share a tent, or form a mess. More elaborate expressions of Masonic solidarity were not uncommon, however. Masons in the 102nd Illinois Infantry constructed a "beautiful encampment" near Lookout Mountain in 1864, decorated with archways over the company streets formed by the long rows of tents. The arches were carved and decorated to suit the soldiers who made them, and one of these was emblazoned with the square and compasses.[4] In the camp of the 12th Indiana Infantry at Scottsboro, Alabama, the officers' tents were also decorated with verdant arches, "while in front of the Colonel's tent, a larger arch, with the Masonic emblem, all in evergreen, formed the central point of beauty."[5] These quaint symbols in the camps and bivouacs sometimes evolved into more permanent expressions of Freemasonry; given enough Masons, a regiment was sometimes justified in forming its own lodge. The officers and men of the 1st New York Engineer Regiment, famous for their skill as artificers, "erected a Masonic Temple, commodious and a beautiful work of art, constructed of the rustic materials the Island afforded" on Folly Island, South Carolina, in November 1863.[6]

The 1st New York Engineers are a typical example of the establishment of a "military lodge," that is, an actual lodge belonging to a military unit, a circumstance for which Masonry was prepared. As explained in chapter 2, a lodge of Masons must meet certain requirements before it can formally operate. First, it must have a charter or warrant—a license from a higher Masonic authority—empowering it to conduct business, initiate new members, and perform ritual work. Without such charter, granted outright or provisionally under a dispensation (known as a "Lodge UD" in Masonic parlance), the lodge would not be recognized. In Masonic terms it would be "clandestine" and Masons from regularly approved lodges would be prohibited from interacting with it. In addition to the charter, a lodge must have a "volume of sacred law," which invariably in the 1860s would have been the Holy Bible. Finally, a lodge would require some "working tools," a square, compasses, and sundry other objects of ritual significance, along with a quorum of Master Masons present to conduct business. If these three requirements were met in an army unit, a lodge might be formed.

Known as military or traveling lodges, these lodges were common during the war. Military lodges had historical precedent in America and abroad and military lodges attached to British regiments had, quite literally, exported Masonry around the globe. Despite the reluctance of some Grand Lodges to allow their formation during the Civil War, where permitted these lodges flourished. Armed with authority of the Grand Lodge of the state in which the regiment was organized these lodges functioned as satellites of the chartering Grand Lodge and were empowered to meet and conduct business just as "stationary" lodges at home.

In the Union army, a total of ninety-eight military lodges were authorized during the war, with Indiana having the most (thirty-eight). Masonic jurisdictions in the Confederate states authorized more, a total of 153 military lodges from 1861 to 1865; the Grand Lodge of Texas authorized thirty-three, Mississippi had twenty-nine, and Virginia had twenty-six.[7] Among those jurisdictions that permitted military lodges, Arkansas is typical. By war's end, the Grand Lodge of Arkansas had approved sixteen dispensations in various regiments and brigades.[8] Of these lodges, four made regular reports to the Grand Lodge: McRae Lodge of Company A, 1st (Colquitt's) Arkansas Infantry reported a total of sixty-one members; Dockery Lodge of Dockery's Brigade claimed twenty-four; Camp Bragg Lodge of the 19th Regiment, Arkansas Infantry (Dawson's) reported twenty-one members on its rolls; and Julia A. English Lodge of the 38th Arkansas Infantry stated its membership was fifteen men.[9]

Up North, the Grand Lodge of New York began granting dispensations for military lodges by resolution in 1861, but with the proviso that they were not to make Masons of men from outside New York without first obtaining the permission from the Grand Lodge of the home jurisdiction of the soldier. These jurisdictional sensitivities were at the heart of Grand Lodge concerns over military lodges nationwide.[10]

Some jurisdictions were reluctant to permit military lodges for that reason. Others such as Kansas, New Jersey, South Carolina, and Wisconsin, for instance, prohibited them out of concern that military lodges would admit the "wrong sort" of man. A committee appointed by the Wisconsin Grand Lodge to study the idea of military lodges voiced concern over the quality of men obtained through these lodges. Citing the inability of military lodges to truly know the character of the men who sought admission into the Order, it concluded that some men who petitioned a traveling lodge "would, doubtless, have been rejected if they had applied to the Lodge nearest their residence, and where they were known, and . . . others had already been rejected at home." This consideration, combined with the fact that soldiers could transfer from unit to unit with far less difficulty than civilians could move from town to town or state to state, created additional unease. A man who was rejected by a lodge in another jurisdiction could simply reapply to a military lodge with no one being the wiser, prompting the Grand Lodge committee to ask, only somewhat rhetorically, "what use is it for the fraternity of Wisconsin to labor to maintain a high standard of personal qualifications, and to sustain the dignity of the character of Free Masonry in this jurisdiction, if these unworthy and rejected applicants are to be thrust upon the Craft by other Grand Lodges, through the medium of Dispensated Lodges working outside their territorial jurisdiction?"

The answer, according to Wisconsin and Virginia, which while being at war with Wisconsin agreed with its rationale, was for the Craft to rigorously police itself, and to guard carefully, not only against unworthy candidates but also against infringing on the territory of other Grand Lodges. Virginia extended the argument, however, to include a political component as well:

> It clearly appears that these Lodges were conferring Masonic character on unworthy men, who could not obtain it at home, and initiated men who never were under the jurisdiction of their Grand Lodges. How far this evil goes, we know not; but we have reason to fear they make white men Masons who were under the jurisdiction of the Grand Lodge of Virginia. And when we see some of the Grand Lodges teaching that Masonry has politics, and her politics teach the equality of mankind and the support of the nationality of the United States, we have reason to fear that the canon of Masonry, which limits its benefits to the free-born, is through these Lodges to be set aside, and Masonry made an instrument to subvert all our social and governmental institutions.[11]

By contrast, the Select Committee on Military Lodges for the Grand Lodge of Florida was more egalitarian, concluding that it was "Masonically right and proper to authorize such Lodges, and that the practice is supported by ancient custom." Which was correct: during the Revolutionary War, there were military lodges in both American and British armies, all of which received their charters from Grand Lodges in England, Ireland, or Scotland.[12]

Acting on this report, the Florida Grand Lodge approved the formation of military lodges and adopted detailed regulations concerning their operation. Many of these restrictions echoed those placed on nonmilitary Masonic lodges and reinforced existing Masonic protocol such as requiring a minimum number of Master Masons—seven in Florida—and underscoring the importance of proper petitioning and of the secret ballot for all elections. Additional restrictions, however, defined the role that military lodges were to play within the greater Masonic framework of Florida. Only military men could associate with military lodges under the Grand Lodge dictates, and civilian membership was expressly forbidden. All military lodges in Florida regiments were also limited to a period of two years, with extensions permitted upon application, with the proviso that "if not extended within two years, then the dispensation to expire by limitation, and all acts done under such dispensation after the expiration aforesaid, and without such renewal, to be clandestine and void."[13]

These restrictions sought to reign in apprehensions about military lodges running rampant and altering the character of the institution. By excluding civilians from the military lodge process, Florida sought to maintain control over the tone of the fraternity, trusting that civilian lodges could more adequately assess the character of civilians away from the hurdy-gurdy of military life. And while those men made Masons in the army were under no stigma, the life span of the military lodges were kept artificially shortened to insure some measure of Grand Lodge control and to prevent, so far as was possible, any deleterious effects of raising new Masons so far from home. But the efforts of the Grand Lodges could only carry so far, and despite the cautionary tone of their authorization, military lodges could and did admit men from across jurisdictional lines and carry on with their own affairs largely without hindrance.

The Third Thursday of Each Month

Indeed, once armed with approval from above, soldier-Masons wasted little time in establishing lodges. The surgeon of the 39th Illinois Infantry, Charles M. Clark, reported that the men of his regiment formed a Masonic lodge even before they were sent in harm's way. "There were in the regiment quite a number of both officers and men who belonged to the Masonic fraternity, and the idea was conceived of opening a lodge in one of the many unused buildings at Fort Barnard [on the outskirts of Washington, DC]. After a dispensation had been received from the Grand Lodge of the State of Illinois, a lodge was opened and soon in working order, several of us being initiated into the mysteries of this ancient body."[14] The 43rd Massachusetts Volunteers also established a lodge while in bivouac—at Camp Rogers, near New Bern, North Carolina, 30 December 1862, and held twice-weekly meetings under canvas. Using all the ingenuity that soldiers possess, the men "provided a stove, and fitted up certain desks and benches, all covered with a dark red cambric, giving the whole tent a very homelike and inviting appearance."[15]

Sometimes no other purpose than sheer boredom prompted the organization of a regimental lodge. The 46th Indiana Infantry, encamped along the Mississippi during the spring of 1864, formed a lodge in one of the plantation homes in Osceola, Arkansas, on a request for dispensation by the regimental surgeon, Horace Coleman. With permission granted, Masonic jewels were fabricated from sheet metal scrounged at a steamboat repair shop, and the lodge held regular meetings that "helped to break the monotony of the situation." The regimental history is silent, however, on how long the boredom, or the lodge, lasted.[16]

A more dynamic lodge traveled with the 39th Massachusetts Infantry. Putnam Army Lodge (UD) No. 8, was authorized by a special dispensation of the Grand Lodge of Massachusetts, dated 13 November 1862, and it began operating seven days later. By that date six other lodges had already been formed by Massachusetts regiments (for the 2nd, 3rd, 16th, 17th, 25th, and 48th), and the members of Putnam Army Lodge lost no time in electing officers and initiating candidates. The first meeting was presided over by Colonel Davis, but military rank had no bearing on status within the lodge itself, and the lodge officers were comprised of a mix of officers and enlisted men.[17] "By-laws for the proper management of the lodge along with blank forms for application for membership were adopted and, though the Third Thursday of each month was named as the regular meeting date there were far more special than regular assemblings. . . . Applications for membership came in rapidly and the record for the remainder of calendar year was twenty-three candidates admitted and seventeen meeting, $580 being received for dues and degrees."[18]

The regimental history suggests that the lodge preferred to meet indoors, as opposed to meeting under canvas. At Mitchell's Station, Virginia, near Culpepper, the members met in a Methodist chapel. While encamped at Poolesville, Maryland, the lodge used the local schoolhouse, with guards posted to ensure secrecy. A soldier of the regiment, John S. Beck, of Company C, noted in his diary on 14 March 1864, "in the evening, [I] took the Second Degree in Army Lodge, No. 8 . . . Free and Accepted Masons." Two nights later, he took his third degree. By war's end, "more than fifty" men were initiated into Putnam No. 8, and of those, thirty-nine took all three degrees.[19]

Military lodges were yet another expression of Masons' invariable tendency to coalesce for the betterment of the group, and the army lodges focused on taking care of its own. Unlike civilian lodges, wounds and death were a common feature of military life, and the lodges coped as best they could with the attrition of death and disease. One regimental history detailed how battle casualties had denuded the lodge of the 39th Illinois Infantry of nearly all its officers. "After leaving this camp our lodge was broken up, for active operations in the field commenced, and during the succeeding months at the front the majority of the officers of our lodge were either killed or wounded—Captain Chauncey Williams, Company H, our Worthy Master, being killed in action August 16th, 1864; and two other officers of the lodge, Captain Leroy A. Barker, Company A, and Lieutenant Norman C. Warner, Company E, were each so seriously wounded at the same time that amputation of their legs became necessary, and they were discharged."[20]

Putnam Army Lodge No. 8 was also decimated in combat; "during the activities in the field, the Master, [Senior Deacon], [Junior Steward] and Marshall were killed, the Treasurer and Secretary were captured."[21] When Col. Phineas Stearns Davis, the Master of the lodge, was killed on 11 July 1864, the lodge voted to bear the expense of sending the colonel's body back to Massachusetts with an escort. At the final meeting of the lodge at the State House in Boston on 29 January 1866 fourteen members attended. There they voted to remit the $198 on hand in the treasury to the charitable relief of the disabled members of the lodge and to the widows and orphans of the regiment. A final tribute was paid to the lodge founder, with $50 voted to commission a portrait of Colonel Davis.[22]

Another very active traveling lodge was the National Zouave Lodge (UD), F. & A. M., of the 10th Regiment of New York Volunteer Infantry. Like Putnam Lodge, they also conducted regular meetings subject to the requirements of the service. Among the first granted a dispensation in June 1861 by the Grand Lodge of New York, the National Zouave Lodge was active until 25 May 1863. A frontline unit, the lodge held its meetings twice monthly when in camp, but active campaigning prevented a more regular routine. According to Pvt. Charles H. Ludwig, of Company A,

the brethren procured the necessary working tools and paraphernalia, which were so constructed that all could be packed in a small space and carried with the regiment. But no opportunity presented for opening the Lodge until the regiment arrived in Virginia, where the first communication was held in a tent in Camp Hamilton.

After the regiment was removed to Fort Monroe, the Lodge met regularly, when the exigencies of military service would permit, in a double casemate on the western face of the Fort, and these communications were attended by brethren from all the regiments in the vicinity. Characterized as these gatherings were by the warlike surroundings, they were invested with a charm that has fixed its impress in the memory of every brother who was so fortunate as to attend them. The . . . casemates were often so thronged with visitors that it was almost impossible to proceed with the work of the ritual. Here all passion was laid aside, and with us frequently met the gray-clad solider from the South, a prisoner within our military lines, but a brother within our Masonic limits. Without our crowded walls the private soldier and the general officer met on the level of equality, to part when the lodge was closed on the square of discipline. Here the beautiful tenets of our institution tempered the rough and rugged life of the soldier.[23]

Ludwig claimed that members of his lodge were among those Union Masons who assisted in the rescue of Confederate Masonic property from St. Tammany Lodge No. 5, of Hampton, Virginia, when that lodge was burned and later plundered (see chapter 3).[24] Notwithstanding that gesture of fraternal goodwill, a request made shortly after to Confederate Masons to allow National Zouave Lodge to use the lodge in occupied Norfolk, Virginia, was not viewed favorably. The request was denied, according to the regiment's biographer, "on the grounds that the Grand Lodge of Virginia had severed her connection with the Grand Lodge of New York. But this unfraternal treatment did not prevent the brethren of National Zouave Lodge from assisting the half-starved families of their brethren of the Virginia jurisdiction with both money and their surplus rations—thus demonstrating that the principles of our institution know neither geographical lines nor political differences. A tent was fitted up, and here the Lodge met until the regiment was ordered to join the Army of the Potomac."[25]

"We Take the New York Papers Regular"

Whether or not a regiment formed a military lodge, Masons found a way to socialize with fellow members of the Craft, sometimes benefiting themselves and their comrades in the process. Food was an item of considerable interest both in camp and in the field; for the common soldier, something better than army fare could only be had by scrounging, and for some soldiers foraging became not only a way of life but also an art form. One Mason in Company K, 24th Kentucky Infantry (U.S.), Jarret C. Redman, boasted to his messmates of his prowess as a forager. In his expeditions from camp, Redman would invariably procure some desirable and highly sought-after comestible, but his comrades remained mystified as to how he accomplished these feats of legerdemain. Finally it was discovered that Redman's modus operandi was to quietly leave camp and visit the nearest town, where he would make himself known as a member of the fraternity; he would then return loaded with the benefits of brotherhood in edible form, regardless of whether he was in Union or Confederate territory.[26]

As we have seen, brothers on opposite sides would frequently assist one another when wounded or captured, but overt fraternization with the enemy—involving Masons and non-Masons alike and often with the approval of officers in charge—was also remarked upon during the war, and documentary evidence is replete with examples of soldiers communicating with men in the enemy ranks.[27] As old as history itself, the natural curiosity of a soldier about his enemy was a powerful motivational factor. Near Port Hudson in July of 1863, Union Corp. James K. Hosmer of Company D, 52nd Massachusetts Infantry, who was not a Freemason, determined to meet some of his opposite numbers and was willing to travel to their positions to do it. During a lull in the fighting, Hosmer made up his mind to cross the front lines and see a "live reb" in order to decide for himself what manner of men they were. "Several were free-masons; and there was mysterious clasping and mighty fraternizing with the brethren on our side. . . . I came back at last to our covert, took a drink of rebel water out of [a rebel sniper's] canteen, and found my hostility to these fellows much mitigated. I could see why commanders generally frown on this sort of communication. It is likely to establish relations altogether too brotherly for the purposes of war. The great principle involved is liable to sink out of sight before the personal friendship."[28]

Nor was Hosmer's experience an isolated one; fraternizations during the war were very common, and Masonic fraternization was also frequent. After the battle of James Island off Charleston, South Carolina, on 16 June 1862, Henry T. Sisson, the paymaster of the 1st Rhode Island Infantry approached the Confederate positions under a flag of truce, accompanied by three officers, all of them Freemasons.

> The rebel officer that came down to meet them happened to be a Mason also. Maj. Sissons [sic] remarked, "I suppose by *the tools you*

carry I have the honor of meeting a Craftsman, as well as an enemy in war?" The rebel officer replied, "You do, and I am happy to meet you as such, and regret that circumstances compel us to meet in any other manner than the former—but such are the fortunes of war."

While they were awaiting an answer the rebel officer sent after some more Masons, they cracked a bottle of wine and drank "to the health of the craftsman, whether in *peace* or in war." The rebel officers remarked: "*We take the New York papers regular,* and should we find your names down as prisoners we will remember you—and should your names escape our notice, please send us your cards." Major S. thanked them for their kindness, but jokingly informed them they were "reckoning prisoners in the wrong column" and assured them *that they, when taken,* should be dealt as kindly with as they have promised to do.[29]

Indulging in fraternal revelry could sometimes have unintended consequences, however, as Confederate troops discovered at the Battle of Hoover's Gap, Tennessee, on 24 June 1863. Part of Rosecrans's Tullahoma campaign, a brigade of Union mounted infantry under the command of Col. John T. Wilder consisting of the 17th and 72nd Indiana and the 92nd, 98th, and 123rd Illinois, surprised Confederate troops who were temporarily leaderless. Armed with Spencer repeating carbines, the Union forces devastated them, discovering later that the rebel officers were at a nearby spring, attending a Masonic picnic commemorating St. John's day.[30]

Despite the risks attendant in such dereliction of duty, the degree to which Masons actively disregarded hostilities to simply exchange pleasantries is nonetheless noteworthy. Remarkable as it may seem that Confederate Masons would risk themselves to aid their federal brothers and vice versa, as we have seen in chapters 3–5, the casual fraternization and indulgence in fraternal activities described above is almost more so. The former may be ascribed to the natural human tendency to help another in distress, but the latter can only be ascribed to the strength of the Masonic bond superseding—if only temporarily—other oaths and loyalties, and perhaps to the yearning of all soldiers for an end to war and the resumption of normal life.

Invisible Freemasons

Throughout the war, as we have seen, Masonry was prominent among the soldiers and sailors of both sides, but one component of the fraternity remained invisible. By the eve of the Civil War, some 500,000 free blacks resided in the United States with nearly 50 percent living in the free states of the North.[31] Between 1861 and 1865, nearly 200,000 free black men served as laborers, cooks, carpenters, nurses, teamsters, and scouts for the Union army. As fraternal organizations helped white males enter society and thrive, black men also benefited from fraternalism, but less visibly.

In early 1863 the enlistment of black troops in the Union forces became a reality when the war department authorized Massachusetts to raise a regiment of black soldiers for combat service. The black population of Massachusetts being too small to fill the requirements of a whole regiment, a committee was formed to solicit black volunteers from across the loyal states. The result was three regiments: the 5th Massachusetts (Colored) Cavalry Regiment and the 54th and 55th Massachusetts (Colored) Infantry Regiments, the first officially sanctioned black regiments to enter service. By mid-1863 and into 1864, several more black regiments were raised, and by 20 October 1864 there were 140 black regiments in the Union army comprising over 100,000 troops. They participated in every major campaign with the exception of Sherman's invasion of Georgia.[32]

That the Union army permitted black troops to enlist and fight should not be interpreted as integration of the military. Largely due to racial stereotyping, black troops in the federal army were led by white officers; interactions between black Union soldiers and their officers thus mirrored the familiar societal architecture of white superiors and black subordinates. Although many black troops enlisted in furtherance of the cause of freedom, the expectations of black soldiers and those of their white officers were not always congruent. Clearly some white officers were determined to end slavery, and they volunteered to lead black troops as a demonstration of their total commitment to the struggle. These "nigger officers," as they were derisively called, typically shared their men's commitment to the abolition of slavery, but not all white officers were so similarly inclined, and indeed some accepted positions in black regiments for purely mercenary motives. These men surely cared little for the ideology of racial equality, and many may have despised their men even more because of the stigma they bore in serving with black soldiers, particularly if their motivation was to attain rapid advancement by any means.[33]

But, as the army wrestled with racial questions, Freemasonry also struggled with the concept of race, and indeed still struggles. Not until the end of the twentieth century did Masonry begin the process of breaking down racial barriers that had existed since the antebellum period. At that time lodges were segregated by race, and in some American jurisdictions that remains the case even today. Segregation did not, however, prevent black men from joining the ranks of the fraternity and—though largely unseen, or at least unnoticed—the effect of their membership was and remains far reaching.[34]

Although Masonry in white America served many functions both culturally and socially, African American Masonry arguably contributed much more, helping to shape the African American identity. Masonry, for the black man, became not only a social force but also a social safety net, reinforcing brotherhood and community solidarity and protecting members against misfortunes, economic or otherwise. Despite these high achievements, the black Masonic experience was not an untroubled one.[35]

Black lodges were not officially recognized by the mainstream fraternity, and as a general rule black men were turned away from mainstream Masonry. A few exceptions do exist, however; the earliest record of a black man belonging to a white lodge in the United States dates from 1844, and at least one record implies that a black Freemason was initiated into an otherwise all-white lodge in 1821. The minutes of St. John's Lodge No. 55 in Newark, New Jersey, on 4 September 1838 show that a black Mason was accepted into a regular lodge meeting, stating, "John Williams, a colored man, having been announced as a visitor, was, after examination, admitted." Similarly, there is a record that a black man was a member and an officer in St. John's Lodge in New Bern, North Carolina. The Proceedings of the Grand Lodge of North Carolina show Brother William H. Hancock, a free black man, as Tyler of that lodge from 1849 to 1852 and as a member for several years afterward.[36]

Black Freemasons, however, were not deterred by the exclusionary tendencies of mainstream Masonry. Nearly a century earlier, African, or Prince Hall, Masonry had evolved as a subset of the fraternity peculiar to America, though it began in a British regiment. In 1775 a free black man, Prince Hall, and fourteen other freedmen were initiated into Lodge No. 441, a military lodge in the British army—the 38th Regiment of Foot—stationed in Boston. When the British evacuated Boston in 1776, Prince Hall was granted a dispensation to form an entirely new lodge. African Lodge No. 1 (UD) was constituted under British Masonic authority for the limited purpose "to go in procession on St. John's Day, and as a Lodge to bury their dead," but they could not actually confer degrees or initiate new members. On 2 March 1784, Prince Hall, acting as Master of African Lodge No. 1, petitioned the Grand Lodge of England for official sanction as a regular lodge.[37] His request was granted in May 1784, and African Lodge No. 459 of Boston became the flagship of Prince Hall Affiliation (PHA) Masonry—Masonry by and for American black men. Under the authority of the charter of African Lodge No. 459, Prince Hall established lodges in Philadelphia and Providence, Rhode Island, on 25 June 1797, with the original African Lodge of Boston becoming the "Mother Lodge" of the PHA hierarchy.[38]

White Freemasons, however, did not recognize these Prince Hall Affiliation (PHA) lodges as genuine and labeled them "clandestine" in part over an argument within the fraternity on whether or not the first Prince Hall lodge was validly chartered, an argument that continues to be voiced to this day. This split between black and white Masons in the United States mirrored the social separateness that occurred within the army and, arguably, that still characterizes contemporary black-white relations in America. Still, by 1860 PHA lodges were found in eighteen states and in Canada. Prince Hall jurisdictions included most of the Atlantic coastal states as far south as Virginia, and many midwestern states. In the South, however, only Maryland, Virginia, and Louisiana saw Prince Hall Masonry before 1860. The scarcity of PHA Masonry in Southern states arose from the prohibition on people of color being allowed to assemble under various state laws and from ancient Masonic tradition barring slaves or former slaves from Masonic membership. Prince Hall Masonry did not challenge that requirement of the fraternity, and its presence in the three Southern states mentioned above was largely due to their being centers of free black population. During the war, there is some evidence—largely anecdotal—of the expansion of black Masonry into areas of the Confederacy occupied by Union troops, although no serious scholarship exists that disproves the assertion that the African American arm of the fraternity was not widespread in the South until after the war. By 1868, however, Prince Hall Masonry was found in every state of the former Confederacy and it remains an integral part of black communities today.[39]

Records of black military lodges during the war are scare, but at least one regiment, the famed 54th Massachusetts, did have a traveling lodge. It was formulated in September 1863 when 1st Sgt. William H. W. Gray of Company C, received a Masonic charter from "the Prince Hall Lodge of Boston" and organized a lodge on Morris Island, South Carolina, during a lull in the fighting around Charleston. "The meeting place was a dry spot in the marsh near our camp, where boards were set up to shelter the members." Later, the Lodge met, with Gray as its Master, in the third story of a house opposite the Citadel. Reportedly the lodge had a membership of twenty to thirty soldiers.[40]

The Civil War and the participation of black men in the defeat of slavery brought with it an anticipation that a more liberal attitude in Freemasonry would result. However, in some Masonic jurisdictions, this looked-for liberality was not forthcoming. Instead, more prohibitive legislation was passed in many Grand Jurisdictions, and Masonry—at least mainstream Masonry—was still regarded as the province of white men only.[41] Recognition of Prince Hall Lodges and Masonic desegregation was therefore admittedly slow in coming. However, the purpose of Masonry was not social activism but fellowship, and in this the Prince Hall Lodges, both civilian and military, succeeded fully as well as their white counterparts, and their swift growth throughout the South in the five years following the war demonstrates this amply. By the end of the nineteenth century, the gains were even more widespread, with Prince Hall lodges at the center of the black business and professional community.[42]

Although contrary to current norms concerning diversity and inclusiveness, it is quite possible that at least in the immediate postwar period, separate lodges may have been a positive development in the fraternity as a whole. Certainly this view, carried to its ultimate conclusion, would constitute a de facto justification for continuing segregationist policies (both in the fraternity and elsewhere in society), but it is worth considering the distinct possibility that the growth and subsequent flourishing of separate black fraternal institutions in America was beneficial during the postwar period, and indeed throughout the civil rights era. One historian has suggested that Freemasonry provided a "road to self-hood" for black men in America.[43] This road was, however, multifaceted. Initially, Prince Hall Masonry helped to shape African American cultural identity through the rituals of Freemasonry. At the same time, the bonds of brotherhood offered at least a certain measure of social support and, although Masonry is not a benefit society, limited protection against economic misfortunes. However, the isolation that allowed PHA Masonry to develop and flourish without interference from white culture also provided an institutional bulwark against integration of the fraternity as a whole, a situation that continues to bedevil American Freemasonry.

Despite the racial segregation that characterized Masonry during the war, we must consider that the experience of Masonry seems to have been universally positive for soldiers regardless of whether their lodge was all black or all white. And, it is clear that Masonry fulfilled the same function for all soldiers, regardless of race: camaraderie, solidarity, and support. This prompts the question of whether black and white Masons ever interacted during the war? The answer hinges on Masonic recognition. Because white Grand Lodges did not recognize Prince Hall Masonry at that time, PHA Masons were considered "clandestine" by white Masons, and, hence, could not be deemed Masons at all. This would have effectively forbid any Masonic intercourse between black and white members. Still, one wonders if in the dark of night, that perhaps Masonic words were exchanged, or a dim Masonic sign seen, that broke the color bar at least momentarily. Although it is distinctly possible, there is no evidence to suggest that it did.

The Gentle Touch of Masonry

> Numberless stories are told, of how the gentle touch of Masonry softened the rigors of war.
> —Ralph J. Pollard, *Freemasonry in Maine, 1762–1945*[44]

Whether the experience of active campaigning was worse than the tedium of camp life is perhaps debatable, but certainly Freemasonry served as an aid in ameliorating the hardships of both, the latter directly and the former indirectly. Although the fraternity could not force men to lay all passions aside, still it gave its members useful activity in camp, from meetings to initiation of new members to arbor building. The comfort drawn from comradeship during periods of inactivity may also have made it easier for soldiers to withstand and recover from the stresses of combat. Military lodges allowed soldiers to transport their peacetime Masonic experience to far-flung bivouacs and to the edge of battle, allowing access, however briefly, to the trappings of civility. In sum, the wartime lodges were like enough to the lodge the soldier left behind him, some solidly built and appointed, others open to the sky, but all provided for a spiritual experience, comradeship, aid, and succor and supplied a conduit for his energies and thoughts from the brutal business at hand to less sanguinary activities.

Although Freemasonry made no epic contributions to end the war or stem the flow of blood, or treasure, its numberless small and quiet agencies were possessed of a power greater than even the Grand Lodges supposed, which allowed individual soldier-Masons to improve their lot and mitigate the sufferings and deprivations of their fellows.

Afterword

Official records make no mention of the part which Masonry played
in the history of the war, but it crops out here and there in personal
reminiscences. If all the deeds of kindness done on the field of battle,
in the hospitals, and prison camps, and in fact anywhere that soldiers
were found could be recorded they would fill hundreds of volumes
and reveal some of the most pathetic stories imaginable, touching both
Blue and Gray.

—Clay W. Holmes, *The Elmira Prison Camp: A History of the Military
Prison at Elmira, N.Y., July 6, 1864, to July 10, 1865*

Before he became a Freemason, Benjamin Franklin famously quipped of
the fraternity: "Their Grand Secret is, That they have no Secret at all, and
when once a man is entered, he finds himself obligated, *se defendo,* to carry
on the Jest with as solemn a Face as the rest."[1] Although Franklin later re-
pudiated those words by joining the Order, eventually rising to the position of Grand Master of Pennsylvania, he was not alone in characteriz-
ing the supposedly trivial character of the Masonic fraternity. Another
titan of American social and political thought, John Quincy Adams, the
sixth president of the United States and a vociferous Anti-Mason, likewise
labeled Masonry as not only meaningless but dishonest as well.

> The secrets, to the keeping of which the Entered Apprentice is sworn,
> are *indefinite.* In genuine Masonry, when revealed to him, he finds
> them *frivolous.* . . . So must it be with every reflecting, intelligent
> man; nor is it conceivable that any such Entered Apprentice, on leav-
> ing the lodge after his admission, should fail to have observed, with
> pain and mortification, the contrast between the awful solemnity of
> the oath which he has taken, and the extreme insignificance of the

secrets revealed to him. It is to meet this unavoidable impression, that the institution is graduated. The lure of curiosity is still held out, and its attractive power is sinewed, by the very disappointment which the apprentice has experienced. He takes the degrees of Fellow Craft and Master Mason, and still finds disappointment—still finds himself bound by tremendous oaths to keep trifling and frivolous secrets. The practice of the institution is deceptive and fraudulent. It holds out to him a promise of which it never performs. Its promise is light—its performance is darkness.[2]

Yet the influence of Freemasonry in the American Civil War belies both Franklin's satire and Adams's poison pen. The examples in this volume make the case that Masonry was by no means a light and trifling boys' club; the organization transformed itself *sua sponte* from social club to a transcendent force on the battlefield. Equally remarkably, it achieved this prominence based on individual actions totally lacking in centralized organization.

It is not easily discovered, however, why Freemasons so religiously adhered to their fraternal allegiances in situations where they could have easily ignored them and looked the other way, with no one but themselves the wiser. Although precise reasons why individual Masons reacted the way they did during battle is impossible to determine, one can assign general motivations to these accounts by recalling the importance of both the Masonic oath and the prescribed modes of recognition among Masons, as well as the psychological strength of Masonry's tribal bonds.

The Oaths

Blue Lodge Masons are bound by three oaths, invariably—during the Civil War—taken on a Bible, each more intricate than the preceding and each requiring more of the Mason in terms of obligation to his fellows. By these oaths, the Mason bound himself to, inter alia, relieve distressed worthy brothers, and their widows and orphans. The nature of the semiliterate society of the nineteenth century made oaths far more prevalent and more weighty than today, and they served a wider purpose. In antebellum America, oaths served the function that written contracts fulfill today, and were used in many transactions of middle- and lower-class life.[3] When used in a social context and requiring an ongoing duty, whether of military service or of obligations and duty toward fellow Masons, they would have constituted a magnetic tug on the consciences of those who swore them. To be sure, some oaths were broken, but the evidence indicates that they were not disregarded lightly. A study that examined the mutiny of the Bengal Europeans in India in 1859 concluded that soldiers in India—contemporaries of Union and Confederate troops—viewed oaths as very serious undertakings, not to be lightly disregarded. An English gunner quoted in that study declared that "I should have considered I was committing a mortal sin had I taken a wrong oath, and I remember what oath I took." Others viewed oaths as the sole reason for their military service, binding to the point that they declined to seek discharge due to injury or illness.[4]

Although Anti-Masons criticized Masonic oaths as "annihilating" other oaths taken in the course of civic duty and rendering the oath-taker subject to the thrall of Freemasonry, the experience of Masonic soldiers does not lend credence to that assertion.[5] In practice, the Masonic oath did not pervert the duty of the soldier against achieving ultimate victory; but it did compel that compassion and forbearance would not be forgotten in wartime.

Masonic Recognition

Once the oaths were taken, Masons were taught how to recognize another Mason in public. In peacetime, the signs and signals might have appeared as boyish affairs, quaint gestures given little thought by the participants. But, as we have seen, in wartime they assumed an importance altogether greater. Traditional to the fraternity, this requirement of recognition is ancient, and its origins remain subject to speculation even today. Regardless of their antiquity, we can note the requirement in the 1723 *Constitutions*. Charge VI of that document provides an express instruction concerning the treatment of strangers who purport to be Brothers:

You are cautiously to examine him, in such a Method as Prudence shall direct you, that you may not be impos'd upon by an ignorant, false Pretender, whom you are to reject with Contempt and Derision, and beware of giving him any Hints of Knowledge.

But if you discover him to be a true and genuine *Brother,* you are to respect him accordingly; and if he is in want, you must relieve him if you can, or else direct him how he may be reliev'd: you must employ him some days, or else recommend him to be employ'd. But you are not charged to do beyond your Ability.[6]

The examples included in this volume tell of Masons using signs and gestures to ascertain membership of one another, and—with very few exceptions—those reports show that once membership status was verified, Masonic aid of some kind was dispensed.

Charge VI of the Freemason's Constitutions, was, and remains, a central tenet of the fraternity. Imposed on all Master Masons, this duty to care for a fraternity brother extended not only to instances in which charitable relief was requested but also when a Mason was in peril.

Far from being a closely held secret, this fraternal requirement was widely known even outside the brotherhood. Lodges frequently warned of imposters or charlatans who passed themselves off as Masons in order to benefit from Masonic charity, and indeed the fraternity even came under attack for its compulsion to help other Masons. During the furor of Anti-Masonry, this intramural loyalty was among the chief complaints of the Freemasonry's detractors, who branded Masonic self-preservation as the worst sort of cronyism. They particularly objected to the Masonic practice of signaling distress—the Grand Hailing Sign—and sought to denigrate it at every opportunity. In 1828, an Anti-Mason tract republished William Morgan's version of the Masonic oath, including the portion that concerns the Masonic "distress call."

"Whenever I see the grand hailing sign of distress given, or hear the words accompanying that sign, and the person who gives it appears to be in distress, I will fly to his relief at the risk of my life, should there be a greater probability of saving his life than losing my own." This oath is revealed by [William] Morgan . . . it is universal in American Freemasonry.[7]

By 1860 Anti-Masonry's force was spent, and membership in the fraternity increased. Yet the requirements of the fraternity had not changed. Each newly made Mason bound himself to the same obligations as Masons in years gone by, and each was taught how to recognize other Masons. Like caches hidden by frontier explorers, the duties contained within the obligation lay dormant until needed. When Masonic recognition occurred and Masonic aid was requested, the oath was triggered. And for the Civil War Mason, the oath itself was a powerful mechanism; the honor accruing to its fulfillment was little compared to the disgrace brought about by its violation.

The Masonic Bond

With the question of why Masons adhered to their fraternal allegiances at least theoretically answered, another question emerges. Civil War soldiers took some oaths that they later broke when circumstances changed or when they came under duress. The officer corps of Confederate armed forces, many of whom had been in federal service, disregarded their oaths as their state governments seceded. Paroled prisoners, too, on both sides, were often lukewarm in adhering to the conditions of their paroles. In one well-known example Union troops discovered that thousands of Confederates captured at Chattanooga had been previously paroled at Vicksburg and had never been exchanged. Federal officers voiced outrage at the breaking of the parole promise; the Confederacy argued that the paroles were irregular and not binding, giving official sanction to the parolees.[8] If these oaths could be broken on the grounds of nationality, extreme changes in circumstance, or reversal of fortune, the question then must be asked, why were Masonic oaths important enough to observe almost universally?

The answer lies in Masonic solidarity. A comment in the Masonic constitution of Kentucky, published in 1818, makes it clear that the Masonic duty "to relieve the distressed is a duty incumbent on all men, but particularly on masons, who are linked together by an indissoluble chain of sincere affection. . . . If a brother be in want, every heart is moved; when he is hungry, we feed him; when he is naked, we clothe him; when he is in trouble, we fly to his relief. Thus we confirm the propriety of the title we bear, and convince the world at large, that BROTHER among masons is something more than a name."[9] Echoing this theme later in the century, a Masonic commentator observed that the "most important object of the Order is solidarity among its members, and the uniformity of Masonic action for the benefit of the children of the widow and all mankind."[10] Although the war fractured the ties among the Grand Lodges, individual Masons would, and did, see other Masons as reflections of themselves, and they reacted accordingly. They recognized that these Masons were formed by the same experiences as themselves, and extended to them the benefits of comradeship regardless of the circumstances and without much inquiry. Masonry had done their vetting for them. These commonalities allowed Masons to see their counterparts as belonging to the same identity, bestowing on them the esteem sometimes denied their non-Masonic comrades in arms. We see this assertion borne out by the proclivity of Masons to form their own lodges in camp, to tent or mess together even in prison, and to participate in the (at first glance) outlandish practice of "visiting" foreign lodges in enemy territory. This latter activity particularly seems preposterous—yet it occurred.

Such was the strength of these bonds that men who had never entertained a thought for Masonry were changed by observing them. Elisha H. Rhodes, for example, saw the fraternal solidarity firsthand at Gettysburg (see chapter 3); within the year, he had become a Freemason. Nor was Rhodes alone. Thousands of soldiers witnessed the devotion of men to other men whom they had never met and were impressed by it. Although no studies exist on why men joined the fraternity in the 1860s, Freemasonry's reputation in battle was certainly a factor.

These Masonic interventions occurred in an age without modern communications, and incidents in one theater or at one battlefield would not have reached other Masons quickly, or even at all—certainly not as instantaneous communication reaches us today. Masons in prison would have been even more isolated. Because of this, we can rightly assume that this phenomenon was not perpetuated by a wave of enthusiasm or the result of a coordinated effort, rather that it was inherent in the fraternity. Although there can be no definitive answer to the question of why Masons decided that their Masonic oaths outweighed other military obligations, Masonic solidarity witnessed on the battlefield and in the prison camps must have reinforced Masons' sense of identity and thus contributed to perpetuating Masonic acts of mercy.

Conclusion

The examples we have seen of Masonic fraternization and intervention might lead to speculation that Masonry was a subversive element during the war, or that it required soldiers to set aside their national differences and work toward a common Masonic political aim, whatever that might be. It is clear however that there was no common Masonic political ambition whatsoever; partly this is because Masonry eschews politics entirely, but also it must be remembered that there was no centralized Masonic government then or now. Just as each state was politically self-determining in 1860, with some opting for secession and others demanding that the Union be preserved, this fracture was also present in Freemasonry. Members of the Order who came under the auspices of, for example, the Grand Lodge of Virginia would perforce conform to the pro-secession views of the state of Virginia, and the evidence shows that Virginia Masons did exactly that. Likewise the Masons of New York upheld, or at least conformed to, the opposite political view. Both groups donned uniforms, shouldered weapons, and marched to war as their state required, with Masonry very much in the background. But when the political speeches yielded to the din of musketry the equation somehow changed. Although Masons and non-Masons alike extended mercy to enemy combatants or civilians absent any fraternal obligations, the fact that Masons made these gestures during the war and regularly extended mercy to their Masonic counterparts—sometimes under fire and in opposition to what purely political allegiance might demand—reinforces the interpretation that the fraternal bond transcended nationality.

Without knowing it, thousands of Civil War Masons disproved Ben Franklin's jest. By actions, not words, they demonstrated the practical benefits of Freemasonry under the harshest circumstances, when and where other social associations, status, wealth, or honors counted for nothing. And in silent rebuttal to John Adams, Civil War Freemasons made the case that Masonry could *and did* deliver on a great promise, transforming itself from a peacetime social preoccupation to a universal currency of compassion based on individual actions. That it did so without any centralized control is evidence of the profound degree to which it inspired its members.

Notes

Introduction

1. The *Harriet Lane* was a side-wheeled gunboat of 619 tons, with a crew of one hundred. She was armed with three 32-pounders and four 24-pounder howitzers. See United States Naval War Records Office, *Official Records of the Union and Confederate Navies in the War of the Rebellion,* series I, vol. 5, p. 704, hereafter cited as *ORN;* see also John Thomas Scharf, *History of the Confederate States Navy from Its Organization to the Surrender of Its Last Vessel,* 2nd ed. (Albany, NY: J. McDonough, 1894), 505–7.

2. United States War Department, *The War of the Rebellion: A Compilation of the Official Records of the Union and Confederate Armies,* series 1, vol. 15, chap. 27, "Recapture of Galveston, Tex.," 218–19, hereinafter cited as *OR.*

3. Allen E. Roberts, *House Undivided, the Story of Freemasonry and the Civil War,* 2nd ed. (Richmond, VA: Macoy Publishing and Masonic Supply Co., 1990), 145–46. Also buried that day was Wainwright's second in command, Lt. Edward Lea, who was killed in the boarding action. In one of the war's many ironies, among the boarders of the *Harriet Lane* was Confederate army officer Maj. Albert Miller Lea—Lt. Edward Lea's father. His son died in his arms. See W. T. Block, "A Towering East Texas Pioneer: A Biographical Sketch of Colonel Albert Miller Lea," *East Texas Historical Journal* 32, no. 2 (1993): 23–33, at 23.

4. Frank P. Graves, *The Burial Customs of the Ancient Greeks* (Brooklyn, NY: Columbia College, 1891), 10.

5. Charles Mills, *The History of the Crusades for Recovery and Possession of the Holy Lands* (Philadelphia: Lea and Blanchard, 1844), 52.

6. Mark C. Carnes, *Secret Ritual and Manhood in Victorian America* (New Haven, CT: Yale University Press, 1989), 1.

7. U.S. Bureau of the Census, *The Eighth Census [1860]* (Washington, DC: U.S. Government Printing Office, 1864), 15. For Georgia Masonic membership numbers, see William Henry Rosier and Fred L. Pearson Jr., *Grand Lodge of Georgia, 1786–1980* (Macon, GA: Educational and Historical Commission, Grand Lodge of Georgia, 1983).

Prologue

1. For accounts detailing the supposed meeting of Hancock and Armistead behind the lines at Gettysburg, see Matthew Page Andrews, *The Women of the South in War Times* (Baltimore: Norman, Remington, 1920), footnote, p. 224; H. F. Lewis, "General Armistead at Gettysburg," *Confederate Veteran* 27, no. 11 (1920): 406.

2. Wayne E. Motts, *Trust in God and Fear Nothing: Gen. Lewis A. Armistead, CSA* (Gettysburg, PA: Farnsworth House, 1994), 8–10, 12–13.

3. Robert K. Krick, "Armistead and Garnett: The Parallel Lives of Two Virginia Soldiers," in *The Third Day at Gettysburg and Beyond,* ed. Gary W. Gallagher (Chapel Hill: University of North Carolina Press, 1994), 112–13. See also Motts, *Trust in God,* 36–37; "Did General Armistead Fight on the Federal Side at First Manassas or Confess When Dying at Gettysburg That He Had Been Engaged in an 'Unholy Cause'?" *Southern Historical Society Papers* 10 (August–September 1882): 424–28; and *Confederate Veteran* 15, no. 12 (1907): 552.

4. Jeffrey G. Burcham, Master of Winchester Hiram Lodge No. 21, A.F. & A.M, Winchester, Virginia, "Letter to Most Worshipful Donald M. Robey, July 24, 1993," a copy of which is in the author's possession (courtesy Wayne E. Motts).

5. Paul M. Bessel, "Letter to Wayne E. Motts, December 21, 1994," with enclosed manuscript of Donald M. Robey, Past Grand Master of Virginia, a copy of which is in the author's possession (courtesy Wayne E. Motts).

6. *History of Union Lodge No. 7, Junction City, Kansas, 1857–1976.* Undated, pp. 13–14.

7. Interview with W. Ron McKenzie Sr., Secretary, Union Lodge No. 7, Junction City, Kansas, 18 May 2007.

8. See Motts, *Trust in God,* 16.

9. Earl J. Hess, *Pickett's Charge—The Last Attack at Gettysburg* (Chapel Hill: University of North Carolina Press, 2001), 40; Stephen W. Sears, *Gettysburg* (New York: Mariner, 2004), 52.

10. Arthur J. L. Fremantle, *The Fremantle Diary* (Short Hills, NJ: Burford Books, 1954), 210.

11. Richard Rollins, ed., *Pickett's Charge: Eyewitness Accounts of the Battle of Gettysburg* (Mechanicsburg, PA: Stackpole, 2005), 11.

12. Ibid., 10.

13. It is interesting to note that Armistead's forlorn hope was not the only penetration of the Union lines that day. A few hundred yards south of the copse of trees, the line held by Hall's 59th New York was also broken, albeit briefly, by men of Kemper's brigade. See also Carol Reardon, "'I Think the Union Army Had Something to Do with It': The Pickett's Charge Nobody Knows," in *The Gettysburg Nobody Knows,* ed. Gabor S. Boritt (New York: Oxford University Press, 1997), 133.

14. J. H. Stine, *History of the Army of the Potomac,* 2nd ed. (Washington, DC: Gibson Bros., 1893), 538.

15. Ibid., 540.

16. Ibid., 539. This "red barn" is probably the Codori barn, which although painted white at the time of the battle was later rebuilt and painted red in 1882. R. A. Bright, in his correspondence with Stine, may simply have referenced the barn in its contemporary color.

17. Hess, *Pickett's Charge,* 261–65 and 438n33. See also Sears, *Gettysburg,* 449.

18. Stine, *History of the Army of the Potomac,* 531.

19. Hess, *Pickett's Charge,* 438; see also the account of Capt. A. N. Jones of the 7th Virginia, Kemper's brigade, published in Rollins, *Pickett's Charge,* 190.

20. Thomas C. Holland, "What Did We Fight For?" *Confederate Veteran* 31 (November 1923): 423.

21. Kathy Georg Harrison and John W. Busey, *Nothing but Glory: Pickett's Division at Gettysburg* (Gettysburg, PA: Thomas Publications, 1993), 107–8.

22. James T. Carter, "Flag of the Fifty-Third Va. Regiment," *Confederate Veteran* 10 (June 1902): 263.

23. Harrison and Busey, *Nothing but Glory,* 113.

24. Rollins, *Pickett's Charge,* 213–14.

25. Harrison and Busey, *Nothing but Glory,* 114, 319, 399. See also Thomas C. Holland, "With Armistead at Gettysburg," *Confederate Veteran* 29 (February 1921): 62.

26. Milton Harding, "Where General Armistead Fell," *Confederate Veteran* 19 (August 1911): 371; see also Harrison and Busey, *Nothing but Glory,* 354.

27. D. B. Easley, "With Armistead When He Was Killed," *Confederate Veteran* 20 (September 1912): 379, reprinted in Rollins, *Pickett's Charge,* 203–4.

28. Ibid.

29. Harrison and Busey, *Nothing but Glory,* 374. Grand Lodge of Virginia Proceedings shows Easley on the rosters of South Boston (Virginia) Lodge No. 91 in 1885 along with other family members or members with the same last name through 1903.

In 1904, he affiliated with Shepherd Lodge No. 99 in South Boston, Virginia, and was on the rosters until 1907 when he withdrew. He affiliated with Hurt Lodge No. 26, Scottsburg, Virginia, in 1907 and withdrew in 1920 and reaffiliated with South Boston Lodge No. 91. Information courtesy Marie Barnett, librarian, Grand Lodge of Virginia, in a letter to the author dated 23 May 2007.

30. "Letter to Howard Townsend, July 24, 1913," D. B. Easley Papers, U.S. Military History Institute, Carlisle Barracks, Pennsylvania, reprinted in Rollins, *Pickett's Charge*, 205–6.

31. William Morgan, *Illustrations of Masonry by One of the Fraternity* (Batavia, NY: David C. Miller, 1827), 74–76.

32. Hess, *Pickett's Charge*, 285–87.

33. Sears, *Gettysburg*, 449.

34. Albert A. Nofi and David G. Martin, *The Gettysburg Campaign, June–July 1863*, 3rd ed. (Conshohocken, PA: Combined Publishing, 1997), 200.

35. Testimony of Frederick Fuger, Supreme Court of Pennsylvania, reprinted in Rollins, *Pickett's Charge*, 346.

36. "Letter of Lt. Anthony W. McDermott," in *The Bachelder Papers: Gettysburg in Their Own Words*, vol. 3, ed. David Ladd and Audrey Ladd (Dayton, OH: Morningside, 1994), 1412–13.

37. Charles H. Banes, *History of the Philadelphia Brigade: Sixty-Ninth, Seventy-First, Seventy-Second, and One Hundred and Sixth Pennsylvania Volunteers* (Philadelphia: J. B. Lippincott, 1876), 192.

38. Morgan, *Illustrations of Masonry*, 84.

39. "Testimony of Charles H. Banes," *Reed et al. v. The Gettysburg Battle-Field Memorial Association, et al.*, Supreme Court of Pennsylvania, Middle District, No. 30, May Term, 1891, p. 275. For the complete transcript of the Banes testimony, see also "Testimony of Col. Charles H. Banes, Taken before the Commissioners at the Office of W. W. Ker, Esq. on Thursday, April 24, 1890," in Ladd and Ladd, eds., *The Bachelder Papers*, 3:1700–19.

40. "Letter of Capt. John C. Brown—July 1st 1887," in Ladd and Ladd, eds., *The Bachelder Papers*, 3:1494–95.

41. Ibid., 1496–97.

42. *OR*, series 1, vol. 27, chap. 39, "Report of Winfield S. Hancock," 1889, p. 376.

43. Bingham was a member of Chartiers Lodge No. 297, in Canonsburg, and had been initiated on 24 February 1862. He received his Fellow Craft degree on 14 April 1862 and became a Master Mason on 12 May 1862, just over a year before the battle. Grand Lodge of Pennsylvania membership records indicate that he "resigned" from

Chartiers Lodge on 23 June 1862, but that he reaffiliated with Union Lodge No. 121, Philadelphia, on 10 September 1868, and was a Life member there. See Grand Lodge of Pennsylvania, *Membership Records,* vol. 3-2, p. 118, and vol. 4-1, p. 132. (Information courtesy Cathy Giaimo, assistant librarian, Grand Lodge of Pennsylvania, "Letter to Michael Halleran—May 2, 2007," in possession of the author.) As captain of Company G, 140th Pennsylvania Infantry, he was awarded a Congressional Medal of Honor for his actions during the Battle of the Wilderness in May 1864. He mustered out of the army as a brevet brigadier general. He was elected to Congress as a Republican in 1878 and served as a representative for Pennsylvania for thirty-three years until his death in 1912.

44. See Nofi and Martin, *The Gettysburg Campaign,* 200–201. Bingham had no formal medical training whatever. He did however hold a law degree from Washington and Jefferson College in Washington, Pennsylvania.

45. "Letter of Capt. & Judge Advocate Henry H. Bingham," in *The Bachelder Papers,* vol. 1, *Morningside,* ed. Ladd and Ladd, 351–52. Although beyond the scope of this work, Bingham's comments about Armistead's "regret" were later publicized and bastardized by Union Gen. Abner Doubleday. Doubleday made the spurious assertions that Armistead had fought for the Union in 1861 and later switched sides, and that Armistead acknowledged to Bingham at Gettysburg that he had fought for an "unholy cause." Doubleday's claims are patently false. Armistead was clearly west of the Mississippi during the time Doubleday claims he fought for the federal army. Although Armistead's statement to Bingham concerning his regrets about doing "him [Hancock] and you all an injury" is somewhat nebulous, clearly it alludes to his feelings at fighting his former friends and colleagues; he did not cast aspersions on the Confederate cause. Doubleday's remarks in his 1882 book *Chancellorsville and Gettysburg* ignited a storm of indignation in the South. See, for example, "Did General Armistead Fight on the Federal Side at First Manassas?" 424–28. See also *Confederate Veteran* 15, no. 12 (1907).

46. Hancock was a member of Charity Lodge No. 190, Norristown, Pennsylvania. He received all three degrees of the Blue Lodge on 31 October 1860 by special dispensation. S.v. Winfield Scott Hancock in William R. Denslow and Harry S. Truman, Missouri Lodge of Research, *10,000 Famous Freemasons,* vols. 1–4 (Richmond, VA: Macoy Publishing and Masonic Supply Co., 1957–61).

47. Brinton was classically educated, graduating from Yale University in 1858, and he studied medicine in America and Europe. Following his involvement at Gettysburg, he was surgeon-in-charge of the U.S. Army hospital at Quincy, Illinois. After the war, Brinton returned to Pennsylvania and was in private practice in Westchester, Pennsylvania. He was professor of ethnology and archaeology for the Academy of

Natural Sciences in Philadelphia in 1884, and taught archaeology and linguistics at the University of Pennsylvania from 1886 until his death in 1899. S.v., Encyclopaedia Britannica, 11th ed., vol. 4, part 3, 1911.

48. "Letter of Dr. Daniel G. Brinton," in Ladd and Ladd, eds., *The Bachelder Papers*, 1:358–59. It is possible, as some accounts have claimed, that Armistead received an additional wound in the abdomen that was neither noted nor recalled by Dr. Brinton.

49. Glenn Tucker, *High Tide at Gettysburg* (Old Saybrook, CT: Konecky and Konecky, 1993), 431n53.

Chapter 1

1. Margaret C. Jacob, *Living the Enlightenment: Freemasonry and Politics in Eighteenth-Century Europe* (New York: Oxford University Press, 1991), 34.

2. David Stevenson, *The Origins of Freemasonry: Scotland's Century, 1590 to 1710* (Cambridge: Cambridge University Press, 1988), 5–6.

3. Arturo de Hoyos and S. Brent Morris, *Freemasonry in Context: History, Ritual, Controversy* (Lexington, MA: Lexington Books, 2004), 1.

4. Jacob, *Living the Enlightenment*, 35.

5. David T. Beito, *From Mutual Aid to the Welfare State: Fraternal Societies and Civil Services, 1890–1967* (Chapel Hill: University of North Carolina Press, 2000), 5.

6. Jacob, *Living the Enlightenment*, 25.

7. Albert G. Mackey, *The Mystic Tie; or, Facts and Opinions Illustrative of the Character and Tendency of Freemasonry*, 10th ed. (New York: Masonic Publishing and Manufacturing Co., 1867), 1–2.

8. Ibid., 3–4.

9. Ibid.

10. Joe W. Trotter, "African American Fraternal Organizations in American History: An Introduction," *Social Science History* 28, no. 3 (2004): 355–66, at 357.

11. Charles W. Heckethorn, *The Secret Societies of All Ages and Countries*, vol. 1 (London: Geo. Redway, 1897), 318.

12. Noel P. Gist, "Secret Societies: A Cultural Study of Fraternalism in the United States," *University of Missouri Studies Quarterly* 15, no. 4 (1940): 1–184, at 24.

13. Lynn Dumenil, *Freemasonry and American Culture, 1880–1930* (Princeton, NJ: Princeton University Press, 1984), xi–xii.

14. Beito, *From Mutual Aid to the Welfare State*, 10.

15. Mark C. Carnes, *Secret Ritual and Manhood in Victorian America* (New Haven, CT: Yale University Press, 1989), 4–5.

16. Ibid., 25.

17. Lorman Ratner, *Anti Masonry: The Crusade and the Party* (Englewood Cliffs, NJ: Prentice-Hall, 1969), 86–87. See also de Hoyos and Morris, *Freemasonry in Context,* 247; and Jacob H. Tatsch, "An American Masonic Crisis—the Morgan Incident of 1826 and Its Aftermath," *Ars Quatuor Coronatorum* 34 (1921): 196–209.

18. Edward L. Glaeser and Claudia D. Goldin, *Corruption and Reform: Lessons from America's Economic History* (Chicago: University of Chicago Press, 2006), 246–47.

19. Dumenil, *Freemasonry and American Culture,* 7–8. Masonic membership figures found at *Proceedings, Grand Lodge of Indiana* (Indianapolis: Elder and Harkness, 1860), 84–86. U.S. population figures from *The Eighth Census [1860],* 15.

20. Dumenil, *Freemasonry and American Culture,* 33–42.

21. Carnes, *Secret Ritual and Manhood in Victorian America,* 54.

22. Avery Allyn, *A Ritual of Freemasonry Illustrated by Numerous Engravings, to Which Is Added a Key to the Phi Beta Kappa, The Orange, and Odd Fellows Societies with Notes and Remarks* (New York: William Gowans, 1853), 265.

23. Ibid.

24. Ralph P. Lester, *Look to the East! A Ritual of the First Three Degrees of Freemasonry* (Whitefish, MT: Kessinger Publishing, 2004), as published in Joshua Gunn, "The Two Rhetorics of Freemasonry; or, On the Function and Necessity of Masonic Secrecy," *Heredom* 15 (2007): 1–34, at 12.

25. Ibid.

26. Allyn, *A Ritual of Freemasonry,* 268–69.

27. See *Proceedings, Grand Lodge of Louisiana, February 14, 1859* (New Orleans: Bulletin Book and Job Office, 1859), 212–15; *Proceedings, Grand Lodge of Georgia 1857* (Macon: S. Rose, 1857), 175; *Proceedings, Grand Lodge of Massachusetts, March 10–December 27, 1858* (Boston: Hugh H. Tuttle, 1859), 78–81.

28. For specifics about Masonic officers, see, generally, Albert G. Mackey, *An Encyclopedia of Freemasonry and Its Kindred Sciences,* vols. 1–2 (New York: Masonic History Co., 1919).

29. Henry Wilson Coil, *Coil's Masonic Encyclopedia* (New York: Macoy Publishing, 1961), 272.

30. E.g., the description of the 1830–50 era Waterbury Connecticut lodge, in Sarah J. Prichard, *The Town and City of Waterbury, Connecticut,* vol. 3 (New Haven, CT: Price and Lee, 1896), 1123–24.

31. E.g., J. U. Green, "Prison Life and Escape of Col. Green," *Confederate Veteran* 7 (February 1899): 57.

32. Clarence H. Poe and Betsy Seymour, eds., *True Tales of the South at War: How*

Soldiers Fought and Families Lived, 1861–1865 (New York: Courier Dover Publications, 1995), 8.

33. *Masonic Review* 30, no. 3, (1865), 98.

34. Allyn, *A Ritual of Freemasonry*, vi.

35. Gist, "Secret Societies," 137.

36. Carnes, *Secret Ritual and Manhood in Victorian America*, 4–5.

37. Jason A. Kaufman, *For the Common Good? American Civil Life and the Golden Age of Fraternity* (New York: Oxford University Press, 2002), 40.

38. Carnes, *Secret Ritual and Manhood in Victorian America*, 28–29 and 31.

Chapter 2

1. William R. Denslow and Harry S. Truman, Missouri Lodge of Research, *10,000 Famous Freemasons*, vol. 1 (Richmond, VA: Macoy Publishing and Masonic Supply Co., 1957), 73.

2. Ibid., 23. Major Anderson (later general) was also an honorary member of Pacific Lodge No. 233 in New York City, and became a Templar at Columbian Commandery No. 1 in that same city. It is interesting to note that Beauregard and Anderson were well acquainted. Anderson taught gunnery at West Point and Beauregard was his protégé there.

3. See, generally, Denslow and Truman, *10,000 Famous Freemasons*, vols. 1–4.

4. Concerning the details of the surrender at Appomattox, see Joshua L. Chamberlain, *The Passing of the Armies* (New York: Bantam Books, 1993), 195–96. Col. (later Major General) Joshua Chamberlain was a Medal of Honor recipient, professor of grammar and rhetoric, later president at Bowdoin College, Maine, and governor of that state from 1866 to 1871. His Masonic biography may be found in Denslow and Truman, *10,000 Famous Freemasons*, 1:196.

5. Gordon's lodge membership has been variously attributed to Gate City Lodge No. 2 in Atlanta, Georgia, and Atlanta Lodge No. 59. Denslow records Gordon being a visitor to Cherokee Lodge No. 66, Rome, Georgia, on two occasions; see Denslow and Truman, *10,000 Famous Freemasons*, 2:129. Long the subject of speculation, recent scholarship by Gordon's Masonic biographer, David L. Canaday, Past Master of the Georgia Lodge of Research, reports that John B. Gordon appears on the records of Atlanta Lodge No. 59, demonstrating his affiliation, in the microfilm records of the Grand Lodge of Georgia (Disk No. 222 for 1892, 1893), although the dates of his progress through the Masonic degrees remains unknown. It is therefore possible that Gordon was not a Mason during the war. Letter from David L. Canaday, 8 October 2008, in possession of the author. See also Thomas C. McDonald, *Freemasonry and Its*

Progress in Atlanta and Fulton County, Georgia: With Brief History of the Grand Lodge F. & A.M. of Georgia, 1786–1925 (N.p., 1925), 13.

6. John C. Palmer, *The Morgan Affair and Anti-Masonry* (Whitefish, MT: R. A. Kessinger, 2006), 109–10. See also Rob Morris, "Honors to the Faithful Who Upheld the Banners of Masonry during the Season of Political Anti-Masonry, 1826 to 1836 in Western New York," *Voice of Masonry* 2, no. 6 (1864): 241–43; Theda Skocpol et al., "How Americans Became Civic," in *Civic Engagement in American Democracy*, ed. Theda Skocpol and Morris P. Fiorina (Washington, DC: Brookings Institution Press, 1999), 40.

7. Masonic membership figures found in *Proceedings, Grand Lodge of Indiana*, 84–86. U.S. population figures from U.S. Bureau of the Census, *The Eighth Census [1860]*, 15.

8. Theodore A. Ross, *Odd Fellowship, Its History and Manual* (New York: M. H. Hazen, 1888), 14, 606.

9. James A. Mowris, *A History of the One Hundred and Seventeenth Regiment, N.Y. Volunteers from the Date of Its Organization, August, 1862, till That of Its Muster Out, June, 1865* (Hartford, CT: Case, Lockwood, 1866), 206–7.

10. Charge II, "Of the Civil Magistrate Supreme and Subordinate," *The Constitutions of the Free-Masons. Containing the History, Charges, Regulations, &c. of that most Ancient and Right Worshipful Fraternity. For the Use of the Lodges* (London, 1723). According to historian Margaret Jacob, "the compilation of the text and preface is universally attributed to James Anderson." See Margaret C. Jacob, *Living the Enlightenment: Freemasonry and Politics in Eighteenth-Century Europe* (New York: Oxford University Press, 1991), 233n37.

11. Albert G. Mackey, "Freemasonry in the Civil War," *The Builder* (December 1922): 370.

12. Allen E. Roberts, *House Undivided, the Story of Freemasonry and the Civil War*, 2nd ed. (Richmond, VA: Macoy Publishing and Masonic Supply Co., 1990), 18.

13. *Transactions of the Grand Royal Arch Chapter of Michigan* (N.p., 1907), 169.

14. Grand Lodge of Pennsylvania, *Minutes of the Right Worshipful Grand Lodge of the Most Ancient and Honorable Fraternity of Free and Accepted Masons of Pennsylvania (1859–1864)*, vol. 10 (N.p., 1906), 171.

15. Roberts, *House Undivided*, 21.

16. *Masonic Review* 27, no. 4 (1862): 279.

17. *Masonic Review* 23, no. 4 (1860): 45.

18. *Masonic Review* 27, no 4 (1862): 280.

19. *Proceedings, Grand Lodge of Virginia* (Richmond: Grand Lodge of Virginia, 1861), 7.

20. Cf. Grand Lodge of Virginia, *Free Masonry and the War: Report of the Commit-*

tee under the Resolutions of 1862, Grand Lodge of Virginia (Richmond: Chas. H. Wynne, Printer, 1865).

21. Ibid., 12.

22. Calvin Smith, *The Autobiography of Calvin Smith of Smithville* (Philadelphia: Sanford H. Robison, 1907), 55–56.

23. Ross, *Odd Fellowship*, 601.

24. Skocpol, "How Americans Became Civic," 55.

25. Michael A. Dreese, *The 151st Pennsylvania Volunteers at Gettysburg: Like Ripe Apples in a Storm* (Jefferson, NC: McFarland, 2000), 63. Government records indicate that Private Miller may have been a member of Company I, not Company J, of the same regiment.

26. Ibid., 63.

27. John H. Worsham, *One of Jackson's Foot Cavalry, His Experience and What He Saw during the War 1861–1865, Including a History of "F Company," Richmond, Va., 21st Regiment Virginia Infantry, Second Brigade, Jackson's Division, Second Corps, A. N. Va.* (New York: Neale Publishing, 1912), 128–29.

Chapter 3

1. Marion Morrison, *A History of the Ninth Regiment, Illinois Volunteer Infantry* (Monmouth, IL: John S. Clark, 1864), 69–70.

2. W. P. McGuire, "An Incident of Masonic Power," *Confederate Veteran* 30 (October 1922): 396.

3. Charles W. Moore, *The Freemason's Monthly Magazine*, vol. 18 (Boston: Hugh Tuttle, 1859), 53.

4. Foster Pratt, ed., *The Michigan Freemason*, vol. 6 (Kalamazoo, MI: 1875), 164.

5. Albert G. Mackey, *The Principles of Masonic Law* (New York: J. W. Leonard, 1856), 205–6.

6. Charles W. Moore, *The Freemason's Monthly Magazine*, vol. 21 (Boston: Hugh Tuttle, 1862), 51.

7. Joseph F. Newton, "Albert Pike's Masonic Library: A Civil War Incident," *Master Mason* 2, no. 5 (1925): 410–11. See also *Transactions of the Supreme Council of the 33d Degree for the Southern Jurisdiction*, October 1895, 127. Col. Thomas H. Benton Jr. was a nephew of the famous Missouri Senator of the same name.

8. *OR*, series 1, vol. 15, chap. 28, 1886, p. 289. Very probably the federal officer in question is Lt. Col. Abel Smith Jr., the battalion commander. It is also possible that the identity of the Confederate commander is Horace H. Miller, formerly of the 20th Mississippi. Another account of the parley between colonels Miller and

Smith, which does not mention the handoff of Masonic regalia, is found in Frank Moore, *The Rebellion Record: A Diary of American Events* (New York: G. P. Putnam, 1863), 472.

9. Jim Bradshaw, "Chrétien Point Remembers Plantation Days, Civil War," *Lafayette (LA) Daily Advertiser*, 30 September 1997, 17.

10. Roberts, *House Undivided*, 153–54.

11. Ibid. Forrest himself was a Freemason—a member of Angerona Lodge No. 168 in present-day Memphis, Tennessee. See Denslow and Truman, *10,000 Famous Freemasons*, 1:63. It appears that Forrest withdrew from the Craft in 1868 following his affiliation with the Ku Klux Klan. See Roberts, *House Undivided*, 320.

12. 19 September 1864, also known as the Battle of Opequon.

13. William H. Armstrong, *Major McKinley: William McKinley and the Civil War* (Kent, OH: Kent State University Press, 2000), 101.

14. Ibid. See also Grand Lodge of Pennsylvania, at http://www.pagrandlodge. org/mlam/presidents/mckinley.html, accessed 11 May 2007. McKinley later affiliated with Canton Lodge No. 60, Canton, Ohio, on 21 August 1867; he demitted from Canton Lodge No. 60, and was a charter member of Eagle Lodge No. 431, also in Canton. Following his assassination, Eagle Lodge changed its name to William McKinley Lodge on 24 October 1901.

15. David Craft, *History of the One Hundred Forty-First Regiment, Pennsylvania Volunteers, 1862–1865* (Towanda, PA: Reporter-Journal Printing Co., 1885), 83.

16. Charles Tuttle, *An Illustrated History of the State of Wisconsin* (Boston: B. B. Russell, 1875), 429.

17. Richard M. Devens, *Reminiscences of the Blue and Gray '61–'65 by Frazar Kirkland* [pseud.] (Philadelphia: Hartford Publishing, 1867), 480–81.

18. Ibid.

19. 16 May 1863.

20. Charles A. Dana, *Recollections of the Civil War: With the Leaders at Washington and in the Field in the Sixties* (New York: D. Appleton, 1899), 54–55. Rawlins was a member of Miners Lodge No. 273 of Galena, Illinois. He was promoted to brigadier general in August of 1863 and later served as secretary of war in the Grant administration, from March 1869 until his death on 9 September 1869. Grand Lodge of Illinois records confirm Rawlins's membership, and the lodge returns indicated that he was raised in Miners Lodge, possibly in the previous year. *Proceedings of the Most Worshipful Grand Lodge, Ancient Free and Accepted Masons, State of Illinois*, 25th Grand Annual Communication, 3–4 October 1865 (A.L. 5865) (Springfield: 1865), 239. See Rawlin's Masonic biography in Denslow and Truman, *10,000 Famous Freemasons*, 4:13.

21. Robert R. Mackey, *The Uncivil War: Irregular Warfare in the Upper South, 1861–1865* (Norman: University of Oklahoma Press, 2004), 40.

22. "Remarks of the Master, St. John's Lodge No. 47, January 10, 1863," St. James Lodge No. 47 (Baton Rouge, LA) Records, Mss. 2860, Louisiana and Lower Mississippi Valley Collections, LSU Libraries, Baton Rouge, Louisiana.

23. Bendix was one of the founding members of Mecca Temple, in New York City—the first temple of the Nobles of the Mystic Shrine. See William B. Melish, *History of the Imperial Council Ancient Arabic Order Nobles of the Mystic Shrine 1872–1921,* 2nd ed. (Cincinnati, OH: Abingdon Press, 1921), 41.

24. Peter Ross, *A Standard History of Freemasonry in New York* (New York: Lewis Publishing, 1899), 498.

25. Butler was a member of Pentucket Lodge, Lowell, Massachusetts. See Denslow and Truman, *10,000 Famous Freemasons,* 1:162–63.

26. *Masonic Review* 28, no. 9 (1863): 266–67.

27. Ibid., 268. St. Tammany Lodge No. 5 of Hampton, Virginia, was chartered in 1759 and remains in operation as of this writing. The lodge Web site may be found at http://no5.vamason.org/.

28. News and Courier (Charleston, SC). *"Our Women in the War": The Lives They Lived; the Deaths They Died* (Charleston, SC: News and Courier Book Presses, 1885), 195.

29. Charles W. Moore, *The Freemason's Monthly Magazine,* vol. 22 (Boston: Hugh Tuttle, 1863), 323–24. Hinds identified himself as "S. Warden 'United Brethren' Army Lodge No. 3."

30. The Grand Lodge of North Carolina states that Conoho Lodge No. 131 was chartered on 3 December 1850, not December 5th, but that could be a difference in penmanship. Grand Lodge records indicate that the lodge was arrested in 1884. It is no longer an active lodge in that state. See http://www.grandlodge-nc.org/education/history/LodgeHistoryVi.PDF, accessed 29 May 2007.

31. Moore, *The Freemason's Monthly Magazine,* vol. 22, p. 324.

32. Ibid.

33. The historical record is silent as to the name and number of this lodge, although it is probably Orr Lodge No. 104, of Washington, North Carolina, established in 1838. The lodge appears to have been closed from 1861 to 1868, perhaps due to the wartime service of its members and its later destruction. See Past Masters of Orr Lodge No. 104, at http://www.masonicsites.org/orr104/OrrPastMasters.html, accessed 5 June 2006.

34. *OR,* series 1, vol. 335, 1891, p. 310.

35. Ibid., 311.

36. Frances H. Casstevens, *The Civil War and Yadkin County, North Carolina* (Jefferson, NC: McFarland, 1999), 98.

37. Benjamin Butler and Jessie Ames Marshall, *Private and Official Correspondence of Gen. Benjamin F. Butler: During the Period of the Civil War*, vol. 3 (Norwood, MA: Plimpton Press, 1917), 538. This order is described in Denslow and Truman, *10,000 Famous Freemasons*, 1:163, as "Order No. 38 which had to do with Confederate Masonic property at New Bern."

38. Ibid., 4:39.

39. *OR*, series 1, vol. 39 (part 3), 1892, pp. 713–14. See also William T. Sherman, *Memoirs of General William T. Sherman, By Himself*, vol. 2 (New York: D. Appleton, 1875), 175–76.

40. Albert G. Mackey, "Freemasonry in the War—A Series of Sketches," *The Key-Stone* 2, no. 4 (1866): 178–81.

41. Ibid.

42. Ibid.

43. Leviticus 19:18, 19:34; Matthew 7:12; Luke 6:27–36.

Chapter 4

1. Emory Speer, *Lincoln, Grant, and Other Biographical Addresses* (New York: Neale Publishing, 1909), 239.

2. The story of "Colonel" Raynor is commonly found in present-day Masonic articles and on the Internet. Raynor was actually a subaltern when this incident occurred, and following it he escaped from Libby Prison in Richmond where he rejoined his regiment at that rank. He was later promoted to lieutenant colonel of the 56th Ohio Volunteers. At war's end, he received a promotion to brigadier general by brevet "for distinguished and gallant services" effective from 13 March 1865. See U.S. Congress, *Journal of the Executive Proceedings of the Senate of the United States of America* 15 (13 February 1866 to 28 July 1866): 924.

3. John S. C. Abbott, "Heroic Deeds of Heroic Men. XVI.—The Capture, Imprisonment, and Escape," *Harper's New Monthly Magazine* 34, no. 200 (1867): 154.

4. *Masonic Review* 26, no. 6 (1862): 373–74.

5. Colonel Radford, with six companies of Virginia Cavalry, was ordered by General Johnston to cross Bull Run and attack the enemy from the direction of Lewis's house during the afternoon of the battle. See "Report of General G. T. Beauregard [sic], C. S. Army, and Resulting Correspondence." *OR*, series 1, vol. 2, 1880, chap. 9, p. 484.

6. Abbott, "Heroic Deeds of Heroic Men," 155.

7. Charles Lanman, *The Red Book Of Michigan; Civil, Military, and Biographical History* (Detroit: E. B. Smith, 1871), 360.

8. *Masonic Review* 26, no. 6 (1862): 373.

9. Samuel P. Bates, *History of Pennsylvania Volunteers—1861–5,* vol. 1 (Harrisburg, PA: B. Singerly, State Printer, 1869), 670–71.

10. William Horatio Barnes, *The Fortieth Congress of the United States: Historical and Biographical,* vol. 2 (New York: George F. Perine, 1870), 243. A Republican representative for Florida in the 40th and 41st Congresses, 1868–71, Hamilton's middle name was, curiously, "Memorial."

11. Jacob Jewell, *Heroic Deeds of Noble Master Masons during the Civil War from 1861 to 1865 in the U.S.A.* (Pueblo, CO: Privately published, 1916), 38–40. Jewell misnamed this source, calling him "W. H. Morgan." Grand Lodge of Kansas records indicate that William A. Morgan was initiated in the lodge at Cottonwood Falls on 26 January 1872, passed 1 March, and was raised 17 May 1872. He served as an officer in various capacities in that lodge, including Secretary in 1874, Junior Warden in 1876, and two stints as Tyler—1874 and 1886. He died on 24 March 1917. Information provided by Chuck Hoffmeister, Grand Lodge of Kansas, 4 June 2007.

12. "Letter of Capt. Asa W. Bartlett," in *The Bachelder Papers: Gettysburg in Their Own Words,* vol. 3, ed. David Ladd and Audrey Ladd (Dayton, OH: Morningside, 1994), 1484. See also Asa A. Bartlett, *History of the Twelfth Regiment: New Hampshire Volunteers in the War of the Rebellion* (Concord, NH: Ira C. Evans, 1897), 516.

13. Information on file with Grand Lodge of New Hampshire, courtesy of Ruth Marden, 1 May 2007.

14. Mary Genevie Green Brainard, *Campaigns of the One Hundred and Forty-Sixth Regiment, New York State Volunteers* (New York: G. P. Putnam's Sons, 1915), 76.

15. Jewell, *Heroic Deeds,* 40–41. Harris was initiated on 2 September 1887, passed 4 November, and raised 2 December 1887. He served as Junior Steward for Emporia Lodge No. 12 in 1889 and was lodge Secretary from 1906 to 1909. He died 28 January 1920. Information provided by Chuck Hoffmeister, Grand Lodge of Kansas, 4 June 2007.

16. Jewell, *Heroic Deeds,* 27. Jewell's original text indicated that the name of the correspondent was S. H. Culpepper of Company B and identified the wounded man as J. C. Allen. This information is surely incorrect. There is no S. H. Culpepper listed in the roster of the 8th Georgia, although J. C. Allen does appear. National Archive records indicate that a J. C. Allen, also known as a C. J. Allen, was a member of Company B of the 8th Georgia. A roster of Company D of the regiment indicates that Clement Jeremiah Allen was wounded at the Wilderness and lost his eyesight during that battle. The company roster also contains the same of Simon F. Culpepper. See

"Muster Roll of Co. D." at http://home.earthlink.net/~larsrbl/CoD8thGARoster. htm, See also the Civil War Soldiers and Sailors database located at http://www.itd .nps.gov/cwss/soldiers.cfm.

17. Frank Moore, "A Masonic Incident," in *The Civil War in Song and Story, 1860– 1865* (New York: P. F. Collier, 1899), 299–300. See also *Masonic Review* 28, no. 5 (1863): 157–58. The names of the participants are not accurately reflected in Moore's recounting of this incident, and the actual identities of the soldiers are found in Daniel N. Rolph, *My Brother's Keeper: Union and Confederate Soldiers' Acts of Mercy during the Civil War* (Mechanicsburg, PA: Stackpole, 2002), 20, 121n4.

18. Newton Martin Curtis, *From Bull Run to Chancellorsville: The Story of the Sixteenth New York Infantry Together with Personal Reminiscences* (New York: G. P. Putnam's Sons, 1906), 193.

19. Ibid., 97.

20. Jewell, *Heroic Deeds,* 28. In his letter to Jewell, Bynum alludes to his military rank as major. The roster of the 2nd Mississippi does include a George Washington Bynum as a member of Company A "Tishomingo Rifles," 2nd Mississippi Infantry, but his rank is listed as private. It is possible that he earned greater military rank in either another unit, or in the U.S. Army post-1865.

21. Mackey, *The Uncivil War,* 27.

22. Ibid., 35

23. *Masonic Review* 30, no. 7 (1865): 220

24. Ibid. Mathew J. Borland appears in the roster of the 10th OVC as a lieutenant. See *Official Roster of the Soldiers of the State of Ohio,* vol. 11 (Akron, OH: Werner Co., 1891), 515.

25. George S. Burkhardt, *Confederate Rage, Yankee Wrath: No Quarter in the Civil War* (Carbondale: Southern Illinois University Press, 2007), 212–13.

26. Born in Cincinnati, Ohio, in 1839, Taylor was a sergeant in Company B, 10th New York Volunteers, until 1862 when he joined the staff of *Leslie's Illustrated* newspaper as an artist and war correspondent. Although Taylor's sketch betrays an intimate knowledge of Masonry, it is not known if he was a member of the Order.

27. *Masonic Review* 30, no. 1 (1865): 20–21. See also Linus Pierpont Brockett, *The Camp, the Battle Field, and the Hospital; or, Lights and Shadows of the Great Rebellion* (Philadelphia: National Publishing, 1866), 419–24, for a version of a similar story—it may well be the same event—where the author claims Mosby gave a Masonic handshake before sparing his life and returning a Masonic pin.

28. J. Marshall Crawford, *Mosby and His Men: A Record of the Adventures of That Renowned Partisan Ranger, John S. Mosby* (New York: G. W. Carleton, 1867), 289–90. See also J[ohn] Stevens Mason, "Retaliation by Col. John S. Mosby," *Confederate Vet-*

eran 14, no. 2 (1906): 68. A similar tale about Mosby appears in John Truesdale, *The Blue Coats, and How They Lived, Fought, and Died for the Union* (Philadelphia: Jones Bros., 1867), 371–72.

29. Kevin H. Siepel, *Rebel: The Life and Times of John Singleton Mosby* (New York: St. Martin's Press, 1983), 129.

30. Robert G. Evans, ed., *The 16th Mississippi Infantry: War Letters and Reminiscences* (Jackson: University Press of Mississippi, 2002), 303.

31. Henry W. Graber, *A Terry Texas Ranger: The Life Record of H. W. Graber* (Austin, TX: State House Press, 1987), 206.

32. Graber became a Master Mason on 12 September 1868. Letter from Bruce Mercer, Assistant Librarian, Grand Lodge of Texas, 8 June 2006, in possession of the author.

33. Rolph, *My Brother's Keeper: Union and Confederate Soldiers' Acts of Mercy,* 25–26.

34. In naval parlance, a "cutting-out expedition" generally involves sending a small detachment of sailors and marines to storm a moored or docked enemy ship, capture her, and sail her out of port. *Archer,* a fishing schooner, was captured on 24 June 1863 off Portland, Maine, by the bark *Tacony* under Lt. C. W. Read, C.S.N. Realizing that the U.S. Navy was carrying on an intensive search for his raiding ship, Lieutenant Read, in order to elude his pursuers, transferred his force to *Archer* and burned *Tacony.* See *Dictionary of American Naval Fighting Ships,* Department of the Navy, Naval Historical Center, at http://www.history.navy.mil/danfs/index.html, accessed 8 May 2007.

35. *ORN,* series I, vol. 2, 1895, pp. 322–25. See also Robert Alun Jones, *Confederate Corsair: The Life of Lt. Charles W. "Savez" Read* (Mechanicsburg, PA: Stackpole, 2000); David W. Shaw, *Sea Wolf of the Confederacy: The Daring Civil War Raids of Naval Lt. Charles W. Read* (Dobbs Ferry, NY: Sheridan House, 2005), 200–201.

36. Ibid., 325.

37. Ibid., 326.

38. Charles W. Cowtan, *Services of the Tenth New York Volunteers (National Zouaves), in the War of the Rebellion* (New York: Charles H. Ludwig, 1882), 136–37.

39. Bettie M. Wehland, "My Hardy County, West Virginia Ancestors: The Barr Band," at http://wvgenweb.org/hardy/barrband.htm, accessed 29 September 2008.

40. Grand Lodge of Virginia records show that a Hugh Barr of Moorefield, West Virginia, was initiated, passed, and raised into Moorefield Lodge No. 29 in the 1870 returns to the Grand Lodge of Virginia, and that he held the office of Tyler. Information courtesy of Marie Barnett, Librarian, Grand Lodge of Virginia, in a letter to the author dated 9 January 2008. It should be noted that at that time, Moorefield Lodge had not transferred to West Virginia Grand Lodge jurisdiction and, additionally, that West Virginia Grand Lodge reports no information on Hugh Barr.

41. "The Blue and the Gray," *Confederate Veteran* 1, no. 3 (1893): 75.

42. Ibid., 75–76.

43. Ibid.

Chapter 5

1. Benjamin Gregory Cloyd, "Civil War Prisons in American Memory" (PhD diss., Louisiana State University, 2005), 1.

2. Homer B. Sprague, *Lights and Shadows in Confederate Prisons: A Personal Experience, 1864–5* (New York: G. P. Putnam's Sons, 1915), 38–39.

3. DeWitt B. Stone Jr., ed., *Wandering to Glory: Confederate Veterans Remember Evans' Brigade* (Columbia: University of South Carolina Press, 2002), 210.

4. Albert Theodore Goodloe, *Confederate Echoes: A Voice from the South in the Days of Secession and of the Southern Confederacy* (Nashville: Smith and Lamar, 1907), 284–85.

5. Jenny Goellnitz, "Stonewall's Surgeon: A Biographical Website Devoted to Dr. Hunter Holmes McGuire, M.D.," at http://www.huntermcguire.goellnitz.org/, accessed 9 June 2006. It was McGuire who amputated Jackson's arm after his wounding at Chancellorsville on 2 May 1863.

6. Dewitt C. Gallaher, "Diary of DeWitt Clinton Gallaher," 1 March 1865 (notes), *The Valley of the Shadow: Two Communities in the American Civil War,* University of Virginia, spring 1998, at http://jefferson.village.virginia.edu/vshadow2/, accessed 7 June 2006.

7. William Walter Scott, *Annals of Caldwell County (North Carolina)* (Lenoir, NC: News-Topic Print, 1930), 140. See also John Preston Arthur, *Western North Carolina: A History 1730–1913* (Raleigh, NC: Edwards and Broughton, 1914).

8. Alonzo Cooper, *In and Out of Rebel Prisons* (Oswego, NY: R. J. Oliphant, 1888), 174.

9. E.g., the story of Captain Henry Buist of the 1st Battalion, South Carolina Sharpshooters, as found in McHenry Howard, *Recollections of a Maryland Confederate Soldier and Staff Officer under Johnston, Jackson and Lee* (Baltimore: Williams and Wilkins, 1914), 320–26.

10. Sheldon B. Thorpe, *The History of the Fifteenth Connecticut Volunteers in the War for the Defense of the Union, 1861–1865* (New Haven, CT: Price, Lee and Adkins, 1893), 206–8.

11. Ibid., 208.

12. Ibid., 209.

13. Ibid., 211.

14. Belle Boyd, *Belle Boyd in Camp and Prison* (London: Saunders, Otley and Co., 1865), 25. Stanton was a member of Steubenville Lodge No. 45, Steubenville, Ohio.

On moving to Pittsburgh, Pennsylvania, he became a charter member of Washington Lodge No. 253 in that city in 1851. He resigned his membership on 29 November 1859.

15. George S. Bernard, ed., *War Talks of Confederate Veterans* (Petersburg, VA: Fenn and Owen, 1892), 263.

16. Andrew M. Benson, "My Capture, Prison Life and Escape," *Civil War Papers,* (Boston, 1900), 113.

17. Ibid., 116.

18. Ibid., 116–17.

19. James A. Mowris, *A History of the One Hundred and Seventeenth Regiment, N.Y. Volunteers from the Date of Its Organization, August, 1862, till That of Its Muster Out, June, 1865* (Hartford, CT: Case, Lockwood, 1866), 154.

20. Ibid., 156.

21. Cloyd, "Civil War Prisons in American Memory," 45.

22. Lonnie R. Speer, *Portals to Hell: The Military Prisons of the Civil War* (Mechanicsburg, PA: Stackpole, 1997), 7. See also Cloyd, "Civil War Prisons in American Memory," 60–62.

23. Michael Horigan, *Elmira: Death Camp of the North* (Mechanicsburg, PA: Stackpole, 2002), 127.

24. Ovid Futch, "Prison Life in Andersonville," in *Civil War Prisons,* by William B. Hesseltine (Kent, OH: Kent State University Press, 1972), 9.

25. John L. Ransom, *Andersonville Diary, Escape and List of Dead* (Philadelphia: Douglass Brothers, 1883), 28.

26. Ibid., 30, 33.

27. Ibid., 33–34.

28. Ibid., 40.

29. Ibid., 183.

30. Ibid., 112.

31. Information on file at the Grand Lodge of Michigan. Accessed via telephone conversation with Jennifer Lazarov, Grand Lodge of Michigan, 17 December 2007.

32. For an example of the privations endured by rebel prisoners in Camp Chase, see George C. Osborne, ed., "A Confederate Prisoner at Camp Chase—Letters and a Diary of Private James W. Anderson," *Ohio State Archeological and Historical Society Quarterly* 59 (December 1950): 45–57; Robert E. Miller, "War within Walls: Camp Chase and the Search for Administrative Reform," *Ohio State Archeological and Historical Society Quarterly* 96 (Winter–Spring 1987): 33–56, at 53.

33. United States Sanitary Commission, *Sanitary Memoirs of the War of the Rebellion* (New York: Hurd and Houghton, 1867), 508, 511, 516.

34. W. H. Merrell, *Five Months in Rebeldom; or, Notes from the Diary of a Bull Run*

Prisoner at Richmond (Rochester, NY: Adams and Dabney, 1862), 45. For a description of the same incident, see also Alfred Ely and Charles Lanman, *Journal of Alfred Ely, a Prisoner of War in Richmond* (New York: D. Appleton, 1867), 180–81.

35. John McElroy, *Andersonville: A Story of Rebel Military Prisons, Fifteen Months a Guest of the So-Called Southern Confederacy* (Toledo, OH: D. R. Locke, 1879), 633.

36. Ibid., 377.

37. Samuel S. Boggs, *Eighteen Months a Prisoner under the Rebel Flag: A Condensed Pen-Picture of Belle Isle, Danville, Andersonville, Charleston, Florence and Libby Prisons, from Actual Experience* (Lovington, IL: Privately published, 1889), 46.

38. Jacob Jewell, *Heroic Deeds of Noble Master Masons during the Civil War from 1861 to 1865 in the U.S.A.* (Pueblo, CO: Privately published, 1916), 28–29.

39. John M. Copely, *A Sketch of the Battle of Franklin, Tenn.; with Reminiscences of Camp Douglas* (Austin, TX: Eugene von Boeckmann, 1893), 147–48.

40. John Gregory Bishop Adams, *Reminiscences of the Nineteenth Massachusetts Regiment* (Boston: Wright, Potter Printing Company, 1899), 113.

41. William A. Wash, *Camp, Field and Prison Life: Containing Sketches of Service in the South, and the Experience, Incidents and Observations Connected with Almost Two Years' Imprisonment at Johnson's Island, Ohio* (St. Louis: Southwestern Book and Publishing, 1870), 190–91.

42. Clay W. Holmes, *The Elmira Prison Camp: A History of the Military Prison at Elmira, N.Y., July 6, 1864, to July 10, 1865* (New York: G. P. Putnam's Sons, 1912), 67–68. Holmes became a member of Ivy Lodge No. 397 in Elmira, New York, in 1869, "because of the kindness received by [his] father at the hands of a 'Rebel Mason' during the battle of Fredericksburg."

43. Ibid., 267.

44. Ibid. Holmes writes that Private Egerton was a member of Company B although government documents indicate that he was on the muster rolls of the 12th Virginia in C Company.

45. *OR*, series 2, vol. 7, 1899, p. 1168.

46. Allen E. Roberts, *House Undivided, the Story of Freemasonry and the Civil War*, 2nd ed. (Richmond, VA: Macoy Publishing and Masonic Supply Co., 1990), 242.

47. S. A. Cunningham, "A Model U.C.V. Camp," *Confederate Veteran* 7 (April 1899): 167. Cunningham, or the editorial staff of the *Confederate Veteran*, has misidentified Isaac Larew as "J. H. Larew," an error almost certainly attributable to penmanship.

48. Charge IV, "Of MASTERS, WARDENS, FELLOWS and APPRENTICES," *The Constitutions of the Free-Masons: Containing the History, Charges, Regulations, &c. of that Most Ancient and Right Worshipful Fraternity. For the Use of the Lodges* (London, 1723).

49. Jewell, *Heroic Deeds*, 41–42.

50. *Masonic Review* 30, no. 1 (1865): 20–21.

51. Isaac Hermann, *Memoirs of a Veteran Who Served as a Private in the 60's in the War between the States: Personal Incidents, Experiences and Observations* (Atlanta: Byrd Printing, 1911), 175–76. Hermann also served in the 1st Georgia Infantry (Ramsey's). See Robert N. Rosen, *The Jewish Confederates* (Columbia: University of South Carolina Press, 2000), 14, 52, 175.

52. Hermann, *Memoirs of a Veteran Who Served as a Private*, 264–66.

53. Lyon G. Tyler, ed., *Encyclopedia of Virginia Biography*, vol. 4 (New York: Lewis Historical Publishing, 1915), 493.

54. Asa A. Bartlett, *History of the Twelfth Regiment: New Hampshire Volunteers in the War of the Rebellion* (Concord, NH: Ira C. Evans, 1897), 440–41.

55. Holmes, *The Elmira Prison Camp*, 353.

56. Very probably this man is 1st Lt. Horace A. Hyde of Swanton, Vermont.

57. S. M. Dufur, *Over the Dead Line; or, Tracked by Blood-Hounds* (Burlington, VT: Free Press Association, 1902), 98–99.

58. Ibid., 99.

59. Anthony M. Keiley, *In Vinculis; or, The Prisoner of War, Being the Experience of a Rebel in Two Federal Pens* (New York: Blelock, 1866), 187.

Chapter 6

1. Albert G. Mackey, *The Principles of Masonic Law* (New York: J. W. Leonard, 1856), 191.

2. Ibid., 208.

3. E.g., the wartime funeral of Capt. James H. Weatherell on 26 June 1864, as found in Joseph K. Newell, *Ours: Annals of the Tenth Regiment, Massachusetts Volunteer Infantry in the Rebellion* (Springfield, MA: C. A. Nichols, 1875), 323–24. A typical diary entry of wartime funerals is found in Kate Stone, *Brokenburn: The Journal of Kate Stone, 1861–1868* (Baton Rouge: Louisiana State University Press, 1955), 48.

4. Michael Hanifen, *History of Battery B, First New Jersey Artillery* (Ottawa, IL: Republican-Times Printers, 1905), 26–77. See also the brief account of the Masonic burial of "Captain Hayes" of the 1st Tennessee Cavalry in *OR*, series. 1, vol. 31 (part 1), 1890, p. 692.

5. Avery Allyn, *A Ritual of Freemasonry Illustrated by Numerous Engravings, to Which Is Added a Key to the Phi Beta Kappa, The Orange, and Odd Fellows Societies with Notes and Remarks* (New York: William Gowans, 1853), 42.

6. Lynn Dumenil, *Freemasonry and American Culture, 1880–1930* (Princeton, NJ: Princeton University Press, 1984), 40–41.

7. Jonathan Ashe, *The Masonic Manual; or, Lectures on Freemasonry, Containing the*

Instructions, Document, and Discipline of the Masonic Economy (New York: J. W. Leonard, American Masonic Agency, 1855), 175–76. See also James Hardie, *The New Free-Mason's Monitor; or, Masonic Guide for the Direction of Members of That Ancient and Honourable Fraternity* (New York: George Long, 1818).

8. Mark C. Carnes, *Secret Ritual and Manhood in Victorian America* (New Haven, CT: Yale University Press, 1989), 57; Dumenil, *Freemasonry and American Culture,* 40; Dorothy A. Lipson, *Freemasonry in Federalist Connecticut* (Princeton, NJ: Princeton University Press, 1977), 172.

9. E.g., J. A. Scarborough, "Joe Cothern's Capture of a Cannon," *Confederate Veteran* 12 (January 1904): 29.

10. Alfred S. Roe, *The Thirty-Ninth Regiment Massachusetts Volunteers, 1862–1865* (Worcester, MA: Regimental Veteran Association, 1914), 402.

11. James A. Connolly, Diary of Major James Austin Connolly, "Letter to Wife—Before Atlanta, July 31, 1864," *Illinois State Historical Society* 35 (1899): 354. The soldier in question is very probably Capt. Thomas J. Sharp of Company E of the 10th Mississippi.

12. *ORN,* series I, vol. 19: West Gulf Blockading Squadron (15 July 1862–14 March 1863), 710; series I, vol. 20: West Gulf Blockading Squadron (15 March 1863–31 December 1863), 36, 46–47; William R. Denslow and Harry S. Truman, Missouri Lodge of Research, *10,000 Famous Freemasons,* vols. 1–4 (Richmond, VA: Macoy Publishing and Masonic Supply Co., 1957–61), 1:192.

13. "Yankee Grave Dixie Decorates," *Times-Picayune* (New Orleans), 24 October 1937.

14. Leake was captain of Company C, 1st Louisiana Cavalry in May of 1862, where he was involved in a flap with his commanding general, Beauregard. See *OR,* series 1, vol. 10 (part 2), chap. 22, pp. 543–44. There is anecdotal evidence that during the time of the *Albatross* incident, Leake was an officer in Company B, Cochrane's battalion. See *Times-Picayune* (New Orleans), 24 October 1937.

15. Denslow and Truman, *10,000 Famous Freemasons,* 1:192. See also Samuel R. Irwin, "Unusual Funeral Recalled in St. Francisville," *The Advocate* (Baton Rouge), 18 June 2006, 20A.

16. This reference very probably refers to Pvt. Samuel F. White of Company I, 28th (Gray's) Louisiana Infantry. It is not possible to determine the exact service record of his brother from government records.

17. "Masonic Burial by an Enemy," *Confederate Veteran* 14 (September 1906): 408.

18. Irwin, "Unusual Funeral Recalled in St. Francisville," 20A.

19. Augustine J. H. Duganne, *Camps and Prisons: Twenty Months in the Department of the Gulf,* 2nd ed. (New York: J. P. Robens, 1865), 269. See also Charles P. Bossom,

History of the Forty-Second Regiment Infantry: Massachusetts Volunteers, 1862, 1863, 1864 (Boston: Mills, Knight, 1886), 427.

20. Duganne, *Camps and Prisons,* 269–70. Augustine J. H. Duganne was a member of the 176th New York Infantry, mustering out as a lieutenant colonel. Henry W. Washburn was very probably a sergeant in the 6th Vermont Infantry.

21. George Sheldon, *When the Smoke Cleared at Gettysburg: The Tragic Aftermath of the Bloodiest Battle of the Civil War* (Nashville: Cumberland House, 2003), 161–62.

22. Augustus Woodbury, *The Second Rhode Island Regiment: A Narrative of Military Operations in Which the Regiment Was Engaged from the Beginning to the End of the War for the Union* (Providence, RI: Valpey, Angell, 1875), 425. See also Lillian Henderson, *Roster of the Confederate Soldiers of Georgia, 1861–1865,* vol. 2, p. 934. Cf. Stewart Sifakis, *Compendium of the Confederate Armies: South Carolina and Georgia* (New York: Facts on File, 1995), 225–26. Wasden's Masonic record is verified in returns to the Grand Lodge of Georgia from 1855 to 1859. See *Proceedings of the Most Worshipful Grand Lodge of Georgia,* (Macon, GA: S. Rose and Co. Printers, 1859), 121.

23. Rhodes enlisted in the 2nd Rhode Island Volunteer Infantry Regiment as a private in 1861 and by 1865 had been promoted to lieutenant colonel. In his extraordinary diary, he records being present at nearly every major engagement in the Eastern theater, seeing combat from First Manassas to Appomattox. He received renewed national interest following the broadcast of Ken Burn's television documentary *The Civil War* (1990); he retired from military life as a brigadier general and died 14 January 1917.

24. Robert Hunt Rhodes, ed., *All for the Union: The Civil War Diary and Letters of Elisha Hunt Rhodes* (New York: Vintage Books, 1992), 111. Foy's remarks are found in Horatio Rogers, *Record of the Rhode Island Excursion to Gettysburg, October 11–16, 1886* (Providence: E. L. Freeman and Son, State Printers, 1887), 22–23. See also George Sheldon, *When the Smoke Cleared at Gettysburg: The Tragic Aftermath of the Bloodiest Battle of the Civil War* (Nashville: Cumberland House, 2003), 161–62.

25. Rhodes, ed., *All for the Union,* 247. After the war, Rhodes became Master of that lodge in 1886. See ibid., xvi.

26. Ibid., 177–78.

27. As reprinted in *Masonic Review* 30, no. 4 (1865): 106.

Chapter 7

1. For a detailed explanation of the Royal Arch, or Capitular Rite, see Henry Wilson Coil, *Coil's Masonic Encyclopedia,* (New York: Macoy Publishing, 1961), 578–86.

2. John E. Mason, "A Masonic Incident as Told by Sir Knight John Edwin Mason," *Knight Templar* 21, no. 3 (1975): 24.

3. Jacob Jewell, *Heroic Deeds of Noble Master Masons during the Civil War from 1861 to 1865 in the U.S.A.* (Pueblo, CO: Privately published, 1916), 14–15. It should be noted that New York Masonic records cannot be located that show any correspondence between New York and Georgia concerning this individual, and further, that the regimental history of the 114th New York Volunteers contains no reference to an "L. J. Williams" as a member of that unit. See generally Elias P. Pellet, *History of the 114th Regiment, New York State Volunteers: Containing a Perfect Record of Its Services, Embracing All Its Marches, Campaigns, Battles, Sieges and Sea-voyages, with a Biographical Sketch of Each Officer, and a Complete Register of the Regiment* (Norwich, NY: Telegraph and Chronicle Power Press Print, 1868).

4. Stephen F. Fleharty, *Our Regiment: A History of the 102d Illinois Infantry Volunteers, with Sketches of the Atlanta Campaign, the Georgia Raid, and the Campaign of the Carolinas* (Chicago: Brewster and Hanscom, 1865), 49. See also Bell I. Wiley, *The Life of Johnny Reb* (Baton Rogue: Louisiana State University Press, 1999), 168.

5. Moses D. Gage, *From Vicksburg to Raleigh; or, A Complete History of the Twelfth Regiment Indiana Volunteer Infantry* (Chicago: Clarke, 1865), 172.

6. William L. Hyde, *History of the One Hundred and Twelfth Regiment, N.Y. Volunteers* (Fredonia, NY: W. McKinstry, 1866), 61.

7. John B. Vrooman and Allen E. Roberts, "Sword and Trowel: The Story of Traveling and Military Lodges," *Transactions of the Missouri Lodge of Research* 21 (1964): 42.

8. Ibid., 47–48.

9. Ibid., 48.

10. Peter. Ross, *A Standard History of Freemasonry in New York* (New York: Lewis Publishing, 1899), 496.

11. Grand Lodge of Virginia, *Free Masonry and the War*, 22–23.

12. Vrooman and Roberts, "Sword and Trowel," 51.

13. Ibid., 51–52.

14. Charles M. Clark, *The History of the Thirty-Ninth Regiment Illinois Volunteer Veteran Infantry (Yates Phalanx) in the War of the Rebellion, 1861–1865* (Chicago: Privately published, 1889), 174.

15. Edward Henry Rogers, *Reminiscences of Military Service in the Forty-Third Regiment, Massachusetts Infantry during the Great Civil War, 1862–1863* (Boston: Franklin Press/Rand Avery, 1883), 105.

16. Thomas H. Bringhurst and Frank Swigart, eds., *History of the Forty-Sixth Regiment, Indiana Volunteer Infantry, September, 1861–September, 1865* (Logansport, IN: Wilson, Humphrey's, 1888), 25.

17. Alfred S. Roe, *The Thirty-Ninth Regiment Massachusetts Volunteers, 1862–1865* (Worcester, MA: Regimental Veteran Association, 1914), 144.

18. Ibid., 145.

19. Ibid, 152.

20. Clark, *The History of the Thirty-Ninth Regiment Illinois Volunteer Veteran Infantry*, 174.

21. Roe, *The Thirty-Ninth Regiment Massachusetts Volunteers*, 146.

22. Ibid., 152.

23. Charles W. Cowtan, *Services of the Tenth New York Volunteers (National Zouaves), in the War of the Rebellion* (New York: Charles H. Ludwig, 1882), 440–41.

24. Ibid, 442.

25. Ibid.

26. Jewell, *Heroic Deeds,* 41–42. Jewell identifies the solider in question as "Garrett Redman"; government records indicate the name originally cited as the primary name and list "Garret C. Redman" as an alias.

27. E.g., Jewell, *Heroic Deeds,* 16, which tells of a Union officer having attended a meeting across enemy lines in Louisiana in 1864.

28. James K. Hosmer, *The Color Guard—Being a Corporal's Notes of Military Service in the Nineteenth Army Corps* (Boston: Walker, Wise, 1864), 218–19, 221.

29. Charles W. Moore, *The Freemasons' Monthly Magazine,* vol. 21 (Boston: Hugh Tuttle, 1862), 312–13. In addition to misspelling his name, Moore incorrectly lists Sisson as a major in the 3rd Rhode Island.

30. Peter Cozzens, *This Terrible Sound: The Battle of Chickamauga* (Urbana: University of Illinois Press, 1996), 18.

31. Joe W. Trotter, "African American Fraternal Organizations in American History: An Introduction," *Social Science History* 28, no. 3 (2004): 362.

32. James M. McPherson, *The Negro's Civil War: How American Blacks Felt and Acted during the War for the Union* (New York: Vintage Books, 1991), 145, 175, 211, 227.

33. Ira Berlin, Joseph Patrick Reidy, and Leslie S. Rowland, eds., *Freedom's Soldiers: The Black Military Experience in the Civil War* (Cambridge: Cambridge University Press, 1998), 31.

34. In 1989 the Grand Lodge of Connecticut passed a resolution formally recognizing black Masons. Since that time the two Masonic bodies officially recognize each other in thirty-nine states and the District of Columbia, with members free to intermingle and attend each other's meetings. But the states of the former Confederacy (minus Virginia and North Carolina and plus West Virginia) still do not, as of this writing, maintain relations with Prince Hall Affiliated Masons, nor do Prince Hall Masons recognize them. See Jay Reeves, "Masons in South Struggling with Racial Separation," *Decatur (Alabama) Daily News,* 22 October 2006.

35. Trotter, "African American Fraternal Organizations in American History," 356.

36. Harold V. Voorhis, *Negro Masonry in the United States* (Whitefish, MT: Kessinger Publishing, 1995), 76–77.

37. George W. Crawford, *Prince Hall and His Followers: Being a Monograph on the Legitimacy of Negro Masonry* (New York: Crisis, 1914), 17.

38. Edward N. Palmer, "Negro Secret Societies," *Social Forces* 23, no. 2 (1944): 207–12, at 208. See also William H. Upton, "Prince Hall's Letter Book," *Ars Quatuor Coronatorum* 13 (1900): 54–61, at 54–55.

39. Ibid.

40. Luis F. Emilio, *A Brave Black Regiment: The History of the Fifty-Fourth Regiment of Massachusetts Volunteer Infantry, 1863–1865.* (Boston: Boston Book Company, 1894), 129, 313.

41. Voorhis, *Negro Masonry in the United States,* 77.

42. Booker T. Washington, *The Story of the Negro: The Rise of the Race from Slavery,* vol. 2 (New York: Doubleday, 1909), 157–58, 170.

43. Donald R. Shaffer, *After the Glory: The Struggle of Black Civil War Veterans* (Lawrence: University Press of Kansas, 2004), 2.

44. Ralph J. Pollard, *Freemasonry in Maine, 1762–1945* (Portland: Grand Lodge of Maine, n.d.), 79.

Afterword

1. Grand Lodge of Pennsylvania, *F & A. M. Memorial Volume, Franklin Bi-Centenary Celebration* (Lancaster, PA: New Era Printing, 1906), 60.

2. John Quincy Adams, *Letters on the Masonic Institution* (Boston: T. R. Marvin, 1847), 70–71.

3. Peter Stanley, "Military Culture and Military Protest: The Bengal Europeans and the 'White Mutiny' of 1859," in *Rebellion, Repression, Reinvention: Mutiny in Comparative Perspective,* ed. Jane Hathaway and Geoffrey Parker (Westport, CT: Praeger, 2001), 114.

4. Ibid.

5. *Proceeding of the United States Anti-Masonic Convention, September 11, 1830* (Philadelphia: J. P. Trimble, 1830), 7–8.

6. Charge VI, "Behaviour Towards a Strange Brother," *The Constitutions of the Free-Masons. Containing the History, Charges, Regulations, &c. of that most Ancient and Right Worshipful Fraternity. For the Use of the Lodges* (London, 1723).

7. Henry Dana Ward, *The Anti-Masonic Review, and Monthly Magazine,* vol. 1, no. 8 (New York: Vanderpool and Cole, 1828), 232.

8. Gary D. Brown, "Prisoner of War Parole: Ancient Concept, Modern Utility," *Military Law Review* 156 (June 1998): 200–223, at 206–7. See also *OR,* series 2, vols. 5 and 6, 1899.

9. James Moore and Cary L. Clarke, *Masonic Constitutions; or, Illustrations of Masonry: Compiled by the Direction of the Grand Lodge of Kentucky* (Lexington, KY: Worsley and Smith, 1818), 84–86.

10. *Proceedings of the Supreme Council of the Sovereign Grand Inspectors General of the Thirty-Third and Last Degree, Ancient Accepted Scottish Rite for the Northern Masonic Jurisdiction of the United States of America* (Binghamton, NY: Binghamton Republican Printers, 1899), 145–46.

Glossary

1. F. R. Worts, "The Apron and Its Symbolism," *Ars Quatuor Coronatorum* 74 (1961): 133–37.

2. Robert Macoy, *General History, Cyclopedia, and Dictionary of Freemasonry* (New York: Masonic Publishing Co., 1870), 88.

3. Albert G. Mackey, *An Encyclopedia of Freemasonry and Its Kindred Sciences,* vols. 1–2 (New York: Masonic History Co.), 1:126.

4. S. Brent Morris, *The Complete Idiot's Guide to Freemasonry* (New York: Alpha Books, 2006), 278.

5. Henry Wilson Coil, *Coil's Masonic Encyclopedia,* (New York: Macoy Publishing, 1961), 312.

6. Morris, *The Complete Idiot's Guide to Freemasonry,* 279.

7. Macoy, *General History, Cyclopedia, and Dictionary of Freemasonry,* 120.

8. Mackey, *Encyclopedia,* 1:261.

9. Ibid., 419.

10. Noel P. Gist, "Secret Societies: A Cultural Study of Fraternalism in the United States," *University of Missouri Studies Quarterly* 15, no. 4 (1940): 95.

11. Mackey, *Encyclopedia,* 2:691.

12. Ibid., 690.

13. Ibid., 789.

14. Gist, "Secret Societies," 126.

15. Charles C. Torrey, "Concerning Hiram ('Huram-abi'), the Phoenician Craftsman," *Journal of Biblical Literature* 31, no. 4 (1912): 154.

Glossary of Masonic Terms

Acacia—A genus of deciduous, hardwood shrubs and trees of the subfamily Mimosoideae of the family Fabaceae. One subspecies, *Acacia seyal,* holds significance to Freemasons as being the Shittah tree mentioned in the book of Exodus (25–28), the wood of which was used to construct the Arc of the Covenant. In addition, the foliage of the acacia appears in Masonic ritual as a ceremonial marker on the grave of Hiram, *the Widow's Son,* and is symbolic of eternal life and to a certain extent resurrection. The evergreen sprigs used in Masonic funeral ceremonies are evocative of the acacia.

Apron—A white apron, often made of leather, is one of the most important symbols of Freemasonry. It is evocative of the garment worn by operative stonemasons. The earliest representations of the Masonic apron occurs in an English portrait of Antony Sayer (1717), the first modern English Grand Master, and on the frontispiece illustration to Anderson's first *Book of Constitutions* (1723). This evidence suggests they were quite large, reaching to the knees and made of leather with long tie strings. By the late eighteenth century, the size of aprons began to diminish and by the nineteenth century uniformity and regularity produced a British apron that was 14 to 16 inches wide and 12 to 14 inches deep, plain white for Entered Apprentices, and decorated with blue designs for Fellow Crafts and Master Masons.[1] Macoy, writing in 1870, stated that the American *Blue Lodge* "Apron is a pure white lambskin, 15 inches wide and 13 inches deep, with a flap of triangular shape about 5 inches deep at the point, square at the bottom . . . the trimmings are blue, and in the Royal Arch degree the trimmings are scarlet, or blue and scarlet."[2] Often referred to as a lambskin in and of itself, the garment is worn about the waist at Masonic meetings. American Masons are taught that the apron symbolizes purity of life and rectitude of conduct. A new member is presented with a white apron at his admission into the fraternity, and with any advance in the fraternity he is entitled to wear other aprons of varying types.

Blue Lodges—Also called *Craft Lodges* in Great Britain and Ireland, refers to Masonic lodges that perform the first three Masonic *Degrees* (see below), as opposed to appendant Masonic orders such as the *Scottish Rite* or the *York Rite*. The appellation "Blue Lodge" is reputed to refer to the traditional color of Masonic regalia in lodges chartered under English or Irish Freemasonry. See *Apron,* above.

Cable Tow—A rope or line for drawing or leading, and a Masonic allusion to the ties that bind men to the fraternity. According to Mackey, "'every brother must attend his Lodge if he is within the length of his cable tow.' The old writers define the length of a cable tow, which they sometimes called, 'a cable's length,' to be three miles for an Entered Apprentice. But the expression is really symbolic and, as it was defined by the Baltimore Convention in 1842, means the scope of a man's reasonable ability."[3]

Certificate—See *Diploma*.

Charter—An official document issued by a Grand Lodge to a certain number of members, empowering them to organize a lodge and confer degrees. A Charter must be physically present in a lodge before a meeting can be convened, and it is an ancient and long-established right that any individual Mason may demand to view the Charter personally before he enters the lodge. Also known as a *Warrant*.

Communication—A meeting of the lodge. Regular or stated communications of lodges occur at preordained times known to the members (e.g., the first and third Mondays of each month). Special and emergency communications are meetings called by the order of the Master of the lodge.

Compasses—A technical drawing instrument that can be used for inscribing circles or arcs, the compasses (always plural to differentiate this tool from the navigational compass) are an allegorical symbol to Freemasons illustrating the boundaries of morality beyond which a man should never transgress. Apart from mere symbolism, however, the compasses are also part of the *furniture of the Lodge,* and even the most rudimentary lodge will be supplied with a pair of compasses, which in many lodges are quite ornate. Symbolically combined with the square (see below) the two symbols form the interlocking symbol of the fraternity.

Cowan—An ancient word, meaning one who works as a mason without having served a regular apprenticeship. Among Freemasons, the term means someone who pretends to be a Mason without having been regularly initiated. According to Morris, "the 1647 records of Kilwinning Lodge explain that a cowan is a 'Mason without the Word,' which is a skilled craftsman who didn't belong to a lodge. In contemporary union terms, this would be a 'scab worker.' The dictionary definition is 'a dry stone dyker,' someone who builds without mortar."[4]

Craft—Collectively the members of a trade, or mechanical occupation. In Freemasonry it connotes the entire Masonic fraternity.

Degrees—A step or advancement in Freemasonry. Traditional Masonry consisted of three degrees: Entered Apprentice, Fellow Craft, and Master Mason. In the early nineteenth century, Freemasons in France, as well as in Europe and America, developed additional degrees within the umbrella of Masonry that comprise appendant bodies to the fraternity. The Entered Apprentice degree is the threshold of Masonry. As the Entered Apprentice absorbs and comprehends certain catechisms and acquires more fluency in fraternal custom, he progresses to the second degree—*Fellow Craft.* The third degree, *Master Mason,* the culmination of the *Blue Lodge* experience, confers full Masonic membership. Each stage of Masonry has with it concomitant gestures and phrases that serve as authentication of the level obtained. Beyond Blue Lodge, a Mason may receive additional degrees through a number of concordant bodies, the Scottish Rite and the York Rite being common examples. Often termed "higher" degrees, this progression is confusing to both layman and Masons alike. Coil tells us that "in the United States, various terms have been applied to the high degrees, such as appendant, appurtenant, concordant, supplementary, allied, associated, and finally, one that is descriptive but inconvenient: degrees for which the degree of Master Mason is a prerequisite. Some oppose the term high degrees, because they dislike the implication that the Master's degree is not the highest, but the name is simple and convenient and its long usage would seem to preclude any possibility of avoiding it."[5] According to Morris, a "high degree is any Masonic degree after 3° Master Mason, for example the Royal Arch Degree of the York Rite or the 32° Master of the Royal Secret of the Scottish Rite. 'High Degree Masons' only have authority in the organization that gave them the high degree."[6] An aid to understanding this complicated structure is that the third degree of Masonry is the passport to the degrees offered by other Masonic bodies, without which, those rites are inaccessible.

Demit—A withdrawal from the fraternity. A Mason may demit from his lodge at his pleasure and remain in good standing as a Mason. The term originates from the French reflective verb *se demettre,* meaning "to resign [an employment]."

Deputy—An officer appointed by the Grand Master of a Masonic jurisdiction to represent him. Deputies may be responsible for Masonic Districts (District Deputy Grand Master), or a conglomeration of districts known as an Area (Area Deputy Grand Master).

Diploma—In the nineteenth century, Masons would receive a formal certificate from their lodge indicating membership in the fraternity. Presentation of this certificate when visiting other lodges where the member was not known would ease admission. However, custom required, and still requires, with the membership cards of today, a *Ne Varietur* (a legal warning that the certificate may not be altered or changed and that any changes rendered the document invalid) and a requirement that the member sign the certificate personally, which allows comparison of his handwriting as a precautionary measure. Macoy writes, "in Freemasonry this would designate a certificate of membership, and of good standing, issued by a Lodge to its members, to be used by them when traveling among strangers. These documents have been in vogue since 1663, and in some jurisdictions traveling brothers, who are strangers, are not permitted to visit Lodges, if they are not provided with one."[7] Also called *Certificate*.

Dispensation—An official instrument permitting an act or ceremony, such as forming a new lodge, or conducting business without a charter. Dispensations are issued by the *Grand Lodge*.

Entered Apprentice—The first degree of Freemasonry. Upon his admission as an Entered Apprentice, a new member symbolically serves an apprenticeship in the fraternity, which, while entitling him to certain benefits of the fraternity, does not expose him to the full scope of membership. Nineteenth-century American Entered Apprentices were required to memorize Masonic catechisms and demonstrate their proficiency before being allowed to progress to the degree of Fellow Craft.

Fellow Craft—The second degree of Freemasonry. According to Mackey, "the Second Degree of Freemasonry in all the Rites is that of the *Fellow Craft*. In the French it is called *Compagno;* in Spanish, *Compañero;* in Italian, *Compagno;* and in German, *Gesell;* in all of which the . . . meaning of the word is a fellow workman, thus showing the origin of the title from an operative institution."[8] The Fellow Craft degree retains the preparatory character of the Entered Apprentice degree, exposing more of the fraternity to the participant, but reserving full membership until suitable proficiency has been demonstrated.

Furniture of the Lodge—Objects of ritual significance without which a lodge cannot be opened, a "Volume of Sacred Law," which can be the Christian Bible, the Tanakh (Hebrew Bible), Qur'an, or any other holy book, a Square, and Compasses. These objects must be placed in the center of the lodge before the meeting may be convened.

Grand Lodge—The supreme Masonic governing body within a certain jurisdiction over which presides the Grand Master and consisting in membership of all Masters and Wardens of all lodges within its territory and such past Masters as may be elected to it. American and Canadian Grand jurisdictions are organized along state or provincial lines (e.g., the Grand

Lodge of Kansas). Masonic jurisdictions elsewhere are generally organized along national lines (e.g., the United Grand Lodge of England). Local Blue Lodges are directly subordinate to the Grand Master and his deputies in matters Masonic.

Jewels—Representative symbols of rank and authority in the lodge. Often metal ornaments suspended on chains or cords, these jewels are badges of office and may be simple or ornate according to the resources of the lodge. A builder's square is the badge of the Worshipful Master; a stylized level, that of the Senior Warden; and the stylized plumb-rule is the insignia of the Junior Warden. The jewels of office are typically worn on the person during meetings.

Labor—A Masonic term indicating the members are engaged in ritual work. According to Mackey, "when the Lodge is engaged in reading petitions, hearing reports, debating financial matters, etc., it is said to be occupied in *business;* but when it is engaged in the form and ceremony of initiation into any of the Degrees, it is said to be at *work.* Initiation is Masonic labor."[9]

Lecture—Each Masonic degree contains oral instruction in the form of lectures that set forth the ceremonies, traditions, secrets, and customs, as well as providing moral instruction to the participant.

Lodge—Masons meet *as* a lodge, not *in* a lodge; thus, this term refers both to an aggregation of working Masons and to the premises wherein Masons meet (which are also often called Temples). Although there are no formal rules, the lodge premises will generally be laid out on an east–west line.

Master Mason—The third degree of Freemasonry. Essentially unchanged from 1717 to the present, the ritual represents the penultimate Masonic experience. Upon reaching the degree of Master Mason, a member of the fraternity is entitled to vote and hold office within the Order.

Minutes—The records of a lodge as kept by the lodge secretary, which comprise the official history of an individual lodge.

Monitors—Published manuals of ceremonies and rituals. The first Masonic monitor, William Preston's *Illustrations of Masonry,* was published in

London in 1772. It contained examples of rules and regulations, prayers for opening and closing lodges, and Masonic lectures. Since that time, Masonic ritualists have continued Preston's tradition of publishing monitors to the ceremonies. Contemporary Masonic monitors present the reader with ritual work—much of it in coded form—to assist Masons in learning the ceremonial and ritualistic speaking parts, while maintaining the Masonic requirement of secrecy. Monitors differ from exposés largely because of this deference to secrecy, yet Masons (then and now) found both monitors and exposés as useful aids in committing the extensive speaking parts to memory.

Oath—Every candidate for Freemasonry, before being admitted to the fraternity, is required to make a solemn oath pledging secrecy and agreeing to conform to the obligations of Freemasonry and agreeing to a penalty for noncompliance. Gist comments that "one of the familiar aspects of the fraternal oath is the self-threat, a device ostensibly used to impress upon the candidate the seriousness of the obligation and the necessity of observing it. In order to produce the proper psychological effects some obligations have included as part of the oath, threats that are terrifying and revolting, at least to the candidate who is more credulous than critical."[10] This oath pledging secrecy prevented Civil War Masons, when relating their wartime experiences, from divulging details about the fraternity except in the most general terms.

Obligation—The promise made by a Freemason upon his admission into a degree of Masonry in which he indicates his submission to the requirements of the fraternity. As a member progresses through each degree, the obligations become more substantial.

Officers—The principle officers of a Masonic lodge are the Worshipful Master who acts as president, the Senior Warden (vice president), Junior Warden (2nd vice president), Senior and Junior Deacons, Secretary, Treasurer, and Tyler, who is charged with guarding the outer door of the lodge and preventing unauthorized entry. In addition to the officers listed above, lodges may have other officers including Stewards, Masters of Ceremony, Historians, and Musicians.

Raised—A Masonic term meaning the reception of the candidate into the third degree of Masonry.

Recognition—Masonic recognition is the acknowledgment and acceptance of other Masonic bodies without the jurisdiction in question. A Masonic body would formally recognize only those Masonic organizations that are "regular" and "well governed." Recognition allows mutual visiting by members and is essential for the universality of the fraternity. See *Visit, Right of.*

Royal Arch Masonry—Royal Arch Masonry consists of four degrees: Mark Master, Past Master, Most Excellent Master, and Royal Arch Mason and form part of the York Rite (see below).

Scottish Rite—A product of French Freemasonry, the Ancient and Accepted Scottish Rite is an appendant body of Masonry that confers higher degrees on its members. The Scottish Rite of 1802 comprised a total of thirty-three degrees inclusive of the three degrees of *Blue Lodge.* See also *Degrees.*

Secretary—An officer of the lodge who is charged with keeping the lodge records and with attending to correspondence to or from the lodge. The Secretary must be a Master Mason.

Sign of Distress—A gesture used by Masons to indicate dire peril and to request assistance. Mackey states, "this is probably one of the original modes of recognition adopted. . . . It is to be found in the earliest ceremonies extant of the [eighteenth] century, and its connection with the Third Degree makes it evident that it probably belongs to that Degree. To Freemasons of the Nineteenth Century, it is called the *Grand Hailing Sign,* to indicate its use in hailing or calling a Brother whose assistance may be needed. . . . It is impossible to be explicit; but it may be remarked, that looking to its traditional origin, the sign is a defensive one, first made in the hour of attack, to give protection to the person. This is perfectly represented by the European and English form, but utterly misrepresented by the American."[11]

Signs and Tokens—Gestures that act as passwords and recognition symbols to members of the Craft. "It is evident that every secret society," Mackey writes, "must have some conventional mode of distinguishing strangers from those of its members, and Masonry, in this respect, must have followed the universal custom of adopting such modes of recognition. . . . Signs, in fact, belong to all secret associations, and are no more peculiar to Masonry than is a system of initiation. The forms differ, but the principle is always the same"[12] In describing tokens, he writes, "In Masonry, the grip of recognition is called a token, because it is an outward sign of the covenant of friendship and fellowship entered into between the members of the Fraternity, and is to be considered as a memorial of that covenant."[13]

Gist comments that "most secret societies have as one of their recognition sign the fraternal handclasp. Some orders even have a special grip for each of the degrees. Like titles and passwords, they are symbolic in character. Since it is difficult to have any considerable number of different handclasps it would appear that many of the grips of various societies are so similar as to be confusing. . . . Quite as common among the usages of secret orders are the symbolic signs—'working signs' or 'due guards' as they are sometimes referred to. . . . Some . . . have signs for each degree or rank as well as special signs of recognition, salutation, distress, and the like."[14]

Silence and Circumspection—One of the cardinal virtues of Masonry expressed by the Latin phrase *Audi, Vide, Tace* (see, hear, be silent), which is the motto of the United Grand Lodge of England.

UD, Under Dispensation—A lodge that has not yet received its official charter from the Grand Lodge. Lodges under dispensation may be allowed to conduct all business and work as a regular lodge, or may be restricted to performing only certain functions at the discretion of the Grand Lodge.

Visit, Right of—A Freemason in good standing has a right to visit any lodge, wherever situated, under Masonic law. This Right of Visit has been long recognized as one of the most important of Masonic privileges, which contributes to the universality of the fraternity. A Mason visiting a foreign lodge is, however, required to submit to an examination to prove that he is a member if no one in attendance is able to vouch for him. The examination may be relatively brief or lengthy at the will of the examining brethren and may include questions on Masonic words, gestures, or ritual work.

Warrant—See *Charter*.

Widow's Son—Hiram (חִירָם), the architect of the Temple of Solomon, first appears in I Kings (7:14), a "a widow's son of the tribe of Naphtali." A skilled craftsman in the employ of Hiram, King of Tyre, he was sent to aid King Solomon in the construction of the temple. He is later mentioned by the Chronicler in (II Chron. 2:12) as the "son of a woman of the daughters of Dan, and his father was a man of Tyre, skilful to work in gold, and in silver, in brass, in iron, in stone, and in timber, in purple, in blue, and in fine linen, and in crimson; also to grave any manner of graving, and to find out every device which shall be put to him."[15] An archetype of the Freemasons, and a prominent figure in Masonic ritual, a "widow's son" is an appellation often used by Masons when identifying themselves, or a member of the Order.

Working Tools—In each of the ritual degrees of Freemasonry, tools of the building trade are used as symbols of the lessons of the fraternity. Mackey lists them as the Twenty-Four-Inch Gage, Common Gavel, Square, Level, Plumb, Skirret, Compasses, Pencil, Trowel, Mallet, Pickax, Crow, and Shovel, although there are subtle variations by jurisdiction worldwide. Each tool is emblematic of a certain lesson or desirable characteristic.

Worshipful Master—The leader of the lodge. Distinguished from a Master Mason by the title Worshipful, the Master of the Lodge is elected by the voting members and presides over the lodge as its chief executive.

York Rite—The oldest American "high degree," the York Rite is comprised of three distinct bodies, the Chapter of Royal Arch Masons, the Cryptic Masons Councils, and the Knight Templar Commanderies. Its door are open to Master Masons.

Bibliography

Regimental Histories, Diaries, and Personal Recollections

Adams, John Gregory Bishop. *Reminiscences of the Nineteenth Massachusetts Regiment.* Boston: Wright, Potter Printing, 1899.

Baker, Levi W. *History of the Ninth Mass. Battery.* South Framingham, MA: J. C. Clark Printing, 1888.

Banes, Charles H. *History of the Philadelphia Brigade: Sixty-Ninth, Seventy-First, Seventy-Second and One Hundred and Sixth Pennsylvania Volunteers.* Philadelphia: J. B. Lippincott, 1876.

Bates, Samuel P. *History of Pennsylvania Volunteers—1861–5.* Vol. 1. Harrisburg, PA: B. Singerly, State Printer, 1869.

Bartlett, Asa A. *History of the Twelfth Regiment: New Hampshire Volunteers in the War of the Rebellion.* Concord, NH: Ira C. Evans, 1897.

Baxter, William. *Pea Ridge and Prairie Grove; or, Scenes and Incidents of the War in Arkansas.* 1864. Reprint, with an introduction by William Shea, Fayetteville: University of Arkansas Press, 2000.

Benson, Andrew M. "My Capture, Prison Life and Escape," *Civil War Papers* 1, Boston (1900): 109–38.

Bernard, George S., ed. *War Talks of Confederate Veterans.* Petersburg, VA: Fenn and Owen, 1892.

Bishop, Judson W. *The Story of a Regiment: Being a Narrative of the Service of the Second Regiment, Minnesota Veteran Volunteer Infantry, in the Civil War of 1861–1865.* St. Paul: Privately published, 1890.

Boggs, Samuel S. *Eighteen Months a Prisoner under the Rebel Flag: A Condensed Pen-Picture of Belle Isle, Danville, Andersonville, Charleston, Florence and Libby Prisons, from Actual Experience.* Lovington, IL: Privately published, 1889.

Bossom, Charles P. *History of the Forty-Second Regiment Infantry: Massachusetts Volunteers, 1862, 1863, 1864.* Boston: Mills, Knight, 1886.

Boyd, Belle. *Belle Boyd in Camp and Prison.* London: Saunders, Otley, 1865.

Brainard, Mary Genevie Green. *Campaigns of the One Hundred and Forty-Sixth Regiment, New York State Volunteers.* New York: G. P. Putnam's Sons, 1915.

Brewerton, G. Douglas. *The War in Kansas: A Rough Trip to the Border, among New Homes and a Strange People.* New York: Derby and Jackson, 1856.

Bringhurst, Thomas H., and Frank Swigart, eds. *History of the Forty-Sixth Regiment, Indiana Volunteer Infantry, September, 1861–September, 1865.* Logansport, IN: Wilson, Humphrey's, 1888.

Britton, Wiley. *Memoirs of the Rebellion on the Border, 1863.* Chicago: Cushing, Thomas, 1882.

———. *The Union Indian Brigade in the Civil War.* Kansas City, MO: Franklin Hudson Publishing, 1922.

Brockett, Linus Pierpont. *The Camp, the Battle Field, and the Hospital; or, Lights and Shadows of the Great Rebellion.* Philadelphia: National Publishing, 1866.

Browne, Junius Henri. *Four Years in Secessia: Adventures within and beyond the Union Lines: Embracing a Great Variety of Facts, Incidents, and Romance of the War.* Chicago: O. D. Case, 1865.

Butler, Benjamin, and Jessie Ames Marshall. *Private and Official Correspondence of Gen. Benjamin F. Butler: During the Period of the Civil War.* Vols. 1–5. Norwood, MA: Plimpton Press, 1917.

Chamberlain, Joshua L. *The Passing of the Armies.* New York: Bantam Books, 1993.

Clark, Champ. *My Quarter Century of American Politics.* Vol. 1. New York: Harper and Brothers, 1920.

Clark, Charles M. *The History of the Thirty-Ninth Regiment Illinois Volunteer Veteran Infantry (Yates Phalanx) in the War of the Rebellion, 1861–1865.* Chicago: Privately published, 1889.

Cooper, Alonzo. *In and Out of Rebel Prisons.* Oswego, NY: R. J. Oliphant, 1888.

Copley, John M. *A Sketch of the Battle of Franklin, Tenn.; with Reminiscences of Camp Douglas.* Austin, TX: Eugene von Boeckmann, 1893.

Cowtan, Charles W. *Services of the Tenth New York Volunteers (National Zouaves), in the War of the Rebellion.* New York: Charles H. Ludwig, 1882.

Craft, David. *History of the One Hundred Forty-First Regiment, Pennsylvania Volunteers, 1862–1865.* Towanda, PA: Reporter-Journal Printing, 1885.

Curtis, Newton Martin. *From Bull Run to Chancellorsville: The Story of the Sixteenth New*

York Infantry Together with Personal Reminiscences. New York: G. P. Putnam's Sons, 1906.

Dana, Charles A. *Recollections of the Civil War: With the Leaders at Washington and in the Field in the Sixties.* New York: D. Appleton, 1899.

Dreese, Michael A. *The 151st Pennsylvania Volunteers at Gettysburg: Like Ripe Apples in a Storm.* Jefferson, NC: McFarland, 2000.

Dufur, S[imon]. M[iltimore]. *Over the Dead Line; or, Tracked by Blood-Hounds.* Burlington, VT: Free Press Association, 1902.

Duganne, Augustine J. H. *Camps and Prisons: Twenty Months in the Department of the Gulf,* 2nd ed. New York: J. P. Robens, 1865.

Eddy, Richard. *History of the Sixtieth Regiment New York State Volunteers.* Philadelphia: Privately published, 1864.

Ely, Alfred, and Charles Lanman. *Journal of Alfred Ely, a Prisoner of War in Richmond.* New York: D. Appleton, 1867.

Emilio, Luis F. *A Brave Black Regiment: The History of the Fifty-Fourth Regiment of Massachusetts Volunteer Infantry, 1863–1865.* Boston: Boston Book Company, 1894.

Evans, Robert G., ed. *The 16th Mississippi Infantry: War Letters and Reminiscences.* Jackson: University Press of Mississippi, 2002.

Fleharty, Stephen F. *Our Regiment: A History of the 102d Illinois Infantry Volunteers, with Sketches of the Atlanta Campaign, the Georgia Raid, and the Campaign of the Carolinas.* Chicago: Brewster and Hanscom, 1865.

Fremantle, Arthur J. L. *The Fremantle Diary.* Short Hills, NJ: Burford Books, 1954.

Futch, Ovid. "Prison Life in Andersonville." In *Civil War Prisons,* by William B. Hesseltine, 9–31. Kent, OH: Kent State University Press, 1972.

Gage, Moses D. *From Vicksburg to Raleigh; or, A Complete History of the Twelfth Regiment Indiana Volunteer Infantry.* Chicago: Clarke, 1865.

Gallaher, Dewitt C. "Diary of DeWitt Clinton Gallaher." Spring 1998. *The Valley of the Shadow: Two Communities in the American Civil War,* University of Virginia, at http://jefferson.village.virginia.edu/ vshadow2/.

Galwey, Thomas F. *The Valiant Hours: Narrative of "Captain Brevet," an Irish-American in the Army of the Potomac.* Harrisburg, PA: Stackpole, 1961.

Glazier, Willard W. *The Capture, the Prison Pen and the Escape: Giving a Complete History of Prison Life in the South.* Hartford, CT: H. E. Goodwin, 1868.

———. *Three Years in the Federal Cavalry.* New York: R. H. Ferguson, 1874.

Goodloe, Albert Theodore. *Confederate Echoes: A Voice from the South in the Days of Secession and of the Southern Confederacy.* Nashville: Smith and Lamar, 1907.

Goss, Warren Lee. *The Soldier's Story of His Captivity at Andersonville, Belle Isle, and Other Rebel Prisons.* Boston: Lee and Shepard, 1867.

Graber, Henry W. *A Terry Texas Ranger: The Life Record of H. W. Graber*. Austin, TX: State House Press, 1987.

Grigsby, Melvin. *The Smoked Yank*. Sioux Falls, SD: Dakota Bell Publishing, 1888.

Hanifen, Michael. *History of Battery B, First New Jersey Artillery*. Ottawa, IL: Republican-Times Printers, 1905.

Harrold, John. *Libby, Andersonville, Florence: The Capture, Imprisonment, Escape and Rescue of John Harrold, a Union Soldier in the War of the Rebellion with a Description of Prison Life among the Rebels—the Treatment of Union Prisoners—Their Privations and Sufferings*. Philadelphia: W. B. Selheimer, 1870.

Hermann, Isaac. *Memoirs of a Veteran Who Served as a Private in the 60's in the War between the States: Personal Incidents, Experiences and Observations*. Atlanta: Byrd Printing, 1911.

Hitchcock, George A. *From Ashby to Andersonville: The Civil War Diary and Reminiscences of George A. Hitchcock, Private, Company A, 21st Massachusetts Regiment: August 1862–January 1865*. Edited by Ronald G. Watson. Mason City, IA: Savas Publishing, 1997.

Holmes, Clay W. *The Elmira Prison Camp: A History of the Military Prison at Elmira, N.Y., July 6, 1864, to July 10, 1865*. New York: G. P. Putnam's Sons, 1912.

Hosmer, Francis J. *A Glimpse of Andersonville and Other Writings*. Springfield, MA: Loring and Axtell, 1896.

Hosmer, James K. *The Color Guard—Being A Corporal's Notes of Military Service in the Nineteenth Army Corps*. Boston: Walker, Wise, 1864.

Howard, McHenry. *Recollections of a Maryland Confederate Soldier and Staff Officer under Johnston, Jackson and Lee*. Baltimore: Williams and Wilkins, 1914.

Hyde, William L. *History of the One Hundred and Twelfth Regiment, N.Y. Volunteers*. Fredonia, NY: W. McKinstry, 1866.

Isham, Asa B., Henry M. Davidson, and Henry B. Furness. *Prisoners of War and Military Prisons; Personal Narratives of Experience in the Prisons at Richmond, Danville, Macon, Andersonville, Savannah, Millen, Charleston, and Columbia . . . with a List of Officers Who Were Prisoners of War from January 1, 1864*. Cincinnati: Lyman and Cushing, 1890.

Keiley, Anthony M. *In Vinculis; or, The Prisoner of War, Being the Experience of a Rebel in Two Federal Pens*. New York: Blelock, 1866.

Kelley, Daniel George. *What I Saw and Suffered in Rebel Prisons*. Buffalo, NY: Matthews and Warren, 1866.

Kellogg, Robert H. *Life and Death in Rebel Prisons: Giving a Complete History of the Inhuman and Barbarous Treatment of Our Brave Soldiers by Rebel Authorities, Inflicting Terrible Suffering and Frightful Mortality, Principally at Andersonville, Ga., and Florence, S.C.* Hartford, CT: L. Stebbins, 1866.

Lewis, John H. *Recollections from 1860 to 1865*. Washington, DC: Peake, 1895.

Long, Lessel. *Twelve Months in Andersonville: On the March—in the Battle—in the Rebel Prison Pens, and at Last in God's Country.* Huntington, IN: Thad and Mark Butler, 1886.

McElroy, John. *Andersonville: A Story of Rebel Military Prisons, Fifteen Months a Guest of the So-Called Southern Confederacy.* Toledo, OH: D. R. Locke, 1879.

McMorries, Edward Y. *History of the First Regiment Alabama Volunteer Infantry C.S.A.* Montgomery, AL: Brown Printing, 1904.

Merrell, W. H. *Five Months in Rebeldom; or, Notes from the Diary of a Bull Run Prisoner at Richmond.* Rochester, NY: Adams and Dabney, 1862.

Morrison, Marion. *A History of the Ninth Regiment, Illinois Volunteer Infantry.* Monmouth, IL: John S. Clark, 1864.

Mott, Smith B. *The Campaigns of the Fifty-Second Regiment, Pennsylvania Volunteer Infantry, First Known as "The Luzerne Regiment," Being the Record of Nearly Four Years' Continuous Service, from October 7, 1861, to July 12, 1865, in the War for the Suppression of the Rebellion.* Philadelphia: J. B. Lippincott, 1911.

Mowris, James A. *A History of the One Hundred and Seventeenth Regiment, N.Y. Volunteers from the Date of Its Organization, August, 1862, till That of Its Muster Out, June, 1865.* Hartford, CT: Case, Lockwood, 1866.

Newell, Joseph K. *Ours: Annals of the Tenth Regiment, Massachusetts Volunteer Infantry in the Rebellion.* Springfield, MA: C. A. Nichols, 1875.

News and Courier (Charleston, SC). *"Our Women in the War": The Lives They Lived; the Deaths They Died.* Charleston, SC: News and Courier Book Presses, 1885.

Northrop, John Worrell. *Chronicles from the Diary of a War Prisoner in Andersonville and Other Military Prisons of the South in 1864: An Appendix Containing Statement of a Confederate Physician and Officer Relative to Prison Condition and Management.* Wichita, KS: Privately published, 1904.

Pellet, Elias P. *History of the 114th Regiment, New York State Volunteers: Containing a Perfect Record of Its Services, Embracing All Its Marches, Campaigns, Battles, Sieges and Sea-voyages, with a Biographical Sketch of Each Officer, and a Complete Register of the Regiment.* Norwich, NY: Telegraph and Chronicle Power Press Print, 1868.

Perry, Henry Fales. *History of the Thirty-Eighth Regiment Indiana Volunteers Infantry, One of the Three Hundred Fighting Regiments of the Union Army in the War of the Rebellion, 1861–1865.* Palo Alto, CA: F. A. Stuart, 1906.

Putnam, George H. *A Prisoner of War in Virginia, 1864–5.* New York: G. P. Putnam's Sons, 1912.

Ransom, John L. *Andersonville Diary: Escape and List of Dead.* Philadelphia: Douglass Brothers, 1883.

Rhodes, Robert Hunt, ed. *All for the Union, the Civil War Diary and Letters of Elisha Hunt Rhodes.* New York: Vintage Books, 1992.

Roe, Alfred S. *The Thirty-Ninth Regiment Massachusetts Volunteers, 1862–1865.* Worcester, MA: Regimental Veteran Association, 1914.

Rogers, Edward Henry. *Reminiscences of Military Service in the Forty-Third Regiment, Massachusetts Infantry during the Great Civil War, 1862–1863.* Boston: Franklin Press/ Rand Avery, 1883.

Sherman, William T. *Memoirs of General William T. Sherman, By Himself.* Vol. 2. New York: D. Appleton, 1875.

Smith, Calvin. *The Autobiography of Calvin Smith of Smithville.* Philadelphia: Sanford H. Robison, 1907.

Sorrel, Gilbert Moxley. *Recollections of a Confederate Staff Officer.* New York: Neale Publishing, 1905.

Sprague, Homer B. *Lights and Shadows in Confederate Prisons: A Personal Experience, 1864–5.* New York: G. P. Putnam's Sons, 1915.

Stone, DeWitt B., Jr., ed. *Wandering to Glory: Confederate Veterans Remember Evans' Brigade.* Columbia: University of South Carolina Press, 2002.

Stone, Kate. *Brokenburn: The Journal of Kate Stone, 1861–1868.* Baton Rouge: Louisiana State University Press, 1955.

Thorpe, Sheldon B. *The History of the Fifteenth Connecticut Volunteers in the War for the Defense of the Union, 1861–1865.* New Haven, CT: Price, Lee and Adkins, 1893.

Wash, William A. *Camp, Field and Prison Life: Containing Sketches of Service in the South, and the Experience, Incidents and Observations Connected with Almost Two Years' Imprisonment at Johnson's Island, Ohio.* St. Louis: Southwestern Book and Publishing, 1870.

Woodbury, Augustus. *The Second Rhode Island Regiment: A Narrative of Military Operations in Which the Regiment Was Engaged from the Beginning to the End of the War for the Union.* Providence, RI: Valpey, Angell, 1875.

Worsham, John H. *One of Jackson's Foot Cavalry, His Experience and What He Saw during the War 1861–1865, Including a History of "F Company," Richmond, Va., 21st Regiment Virginia Infantry, Second Brigade, Jackson's Division, Second Corps, A. N. Va.* New York: Neale Publishing, 1912.

Monographs

Andrews, Matthew Page. *The Women of the South in War Times.* Baltimore: Norman Remington, 1920.

Armstrong, William H. *Major McKinley: William McKinley and the Civil War.* Kent, OH: Kent State University Press, 2000.

Arthur, John Preston. *Western North Carolina: A History, 1730–1913.* Raleigh, NC: Edwards and Broughton, 1914.

Barnes, William Horatio. *The Fortieth Congress of the United States: Historical and Biographical.* Vol. 2. New York: George F. Perine, 1870.

Barton, Oswald Swinney. *Three Years with Quantrill: A True Story Told By His Scout John McCorkle.* Norman: University of Oklahoma Press, 1992.

Bearss, Edwin C. *Hardluck Ironclad: The Sinking and Salvage of the Cairo, Being a First-Hand Account of the Discovery of the Torpedoed Union Gunboat and of Operations to Raise Her from the Bottom of the Yazoo . . . Including a History of the Western Flotilla of Which She Was a Part.* Baton Rouge: Louisiana State University Press, 1966.

Beito, David T. *From Mutual Aid to the Welfare State: Fraternal Societies and Civil Services, 1890–1967.* Chapel Hill: University of North Carolina Press, 2000.

Berlin, Ira, Joseph Patrick Reidy, and Leslie S. Rowland, eds. *Freedom's Soldiers: The Black Military Experience in the Civil War.* Cambridge: Cambridge University Press, 1998.

Billings, John Davis. *Hardtack and Coffee.* Boston: G. M. Smith, 1888.

The Border Ruffian Code in Kansas. New York: Tribune Office, 1856.

Boritt, Gabor S., ed. *The Gettysburg Nobody Knows.* New York: Oxford University Press, 1997.

Britton, Wiley. *The Civil War on the Border.* 2 vols. New York: G. P. Putnam's Sons, 1898.

Brownlee, Richard S. *Gray Ghosts of the Confederacy: Guerrilla Warfare in the West, 1861–1865.* Baton Rouge: Louisiana State University Press, 1984.

Burkhardt, George S. *Confederate Rage, Yankee Wrath: No Quarter in the Civil War.* Carbondale: Southern Illinois University Press, 2007.

Carnes, Mark C. *Secret Ritual and Manhood in Victorian America.* New Haven, CT: Yale University Press, 1989.

Casstevens, Frances H. *The Civil War and Yadkin County, North Carolina.* Jefferson, NC: McFarland, 1999.

Cloyd, Benjamin Gregory. "Civil War Prisons in American Memory." Ph.D. diss., Louisiana State University, 2005.

Coddington, Edwin B. *The Gettysburg Campaign.* New York: Charles Scribner's Sons, 1984.

Coffin, Charles Carleton. *Marching to Victory.* New York: Harpers and Brothers, 1889.

Commager, Henry Steele, ed. *The Blue and the Gray: The Story of the Civil War as Told by Participants.* Vols. 1 and 2. New York: Fairfax Press, 1982.

Cornish, Dudley Taylor. *The Sable Arm: Black Troops in the Union Army, 1861–1865.* Lawrence: University Press of Kansas, 1987.

Cozzens, Peter. *This Terrible Sound: The Battle of Chickamauga.* Urbana: University of Illinois Press, 1996.

Crawford, J. Marshall. *Mosby and His Men: A Record of the Adventures of That Renowned Partisan Ranger, John S. Mosby.* New York: G. W. Carleton, 1867.

Crow, Fred J. W. *What Is Freemasonry?* London: Gale and Polden, 1919.

Cutler, William G. *History of the State of Kansas.* Chicago: A. T. Andreas, 1883.

Devens, Richard M. *Reminiscences of the Blue and Gray '61–'65 by Frazar Kirkland* [pseud.]. Philadelphia: Hartford Publishing, 1867.

Dodge, Grenville M. *The Battle of Atlanta and Other Campaigns, Addresses, Etc.* Council Bluffs, IA: Monarch, 1910.

Dowdey, Clifford. *Lee and His Men at Gettysburg.* Lincoln: University of Nebraska Press, 1999.

Dumenil, Lynn. *Freemasonry and American Culture, 1880–1930,* Princeton, NJ: Princeton University Press, 1984.

Duncan, Robert L. *Reluctant General: The Life and Times of Albert Pike.* New York: E. P. Dutton, 1961.

Fahey, David M. *Temperance and Racism: John Bull, Johnny Reb, and the Good Templars.* Lexington: University Press of Kentucky, 1996.

Foote, Shelby. *Stars in Their Courses: The Gettysburg Campaign, June–July 1863.* New York: Modern Library, 1994.

Fox, William Freeman. *Regimental Losses in the American Civil War, 1861–1865.* Albany, NY: Albany Publishing, 1889.

Gallagher, Gary W., ed. *The Third Day at Gettysburg and Beyond.* Chapel Hill: University of North Carolina Press, 1994.

Georg Harrison, Kathy, and John W. Busey. *Nothing but Glory: Pickett's Division at Gettysburg.* Gettysburg, PA: Thomas Publications, 1993.

Glaeser, Edward L., and Claudia D. Goldin. *Corruption and Reform: Lessons from America's Economic History.* Chicago: University of Chicago Press, 2006.

Goodrich, Thomas. *Bloody Dawn: The Story of the Lawrence Massacre.* Kent, OH: Kent State University Press, 1991.

———. *War to the Knife: Bleeding Kansas, 1854–1861.* Lincoln: University of Nebraska Press, 1988.

Gottfried, Bradley M. *Brigades of Gettysburg; The Union and Confederate Brigades at the Battle of Gettysburg.* New York: Da Capo Press, 2002.

Graves, Frank P. *The Burial Customs of the Ancient Greeks.* Brooklyn, NY: Columbia College, 1891.

Heckethorn, Charles W. *The Secret Societies of All Ages and Countries.* Vol. 1. London: G. Redway, 1897.

Henderson, Lillian. *Roster of the Confederate Soldiers of Georgia, 1861–1865.* 6 vols. Hapeville, GA: Longino and Porter, 1959–64.

Hess, Earl J. *Pickett's Charge—The Last Attack at Gettysburg.* Chapel Hill: University of North Carolina Press, 2001.

Horigan, Michael. *Elmira: Death Camp of the North.* Mechanicsburg, PA: Stackpole, 2002.

Jacob, Margaret C. *Living the Enlightenment: Freemasonry and Politics in Eighteenth-Century Europe.* New York: Oxford University Press, 1991.

Jewell, Horace. *History of Methodism in Arkansas.* Little Rock, AR: Press Printing Company, 1892.

Jones, Robert Alun. *Confederate Corsair: The Life of Lt. Charles W. "Savez" Read.* Mechanicsburg, PA: Stackpole, 2000.

Kaufman, Jason A. *For the Common Good? American Civil Life and the Golden Age of Fraternity.* New York: Oxford University Press, 2002.

Ladd, David, and Audrey Ladd, eds. *The Bachelder Papers: Gettysburg in Their Own Words.* Vols. 1–3. Dayton, OH: Morningside, 1994.

Lanman, Charles. *The Red Book of Michigan: Civil, Military, and Biographical History.* Detroit: E. B. Smith, 1871.

Leslie, Edward E. *The Devil Knows How to Ride: The True Story of William Clarke Quantrill and His Confederate Raiders.* New York: Da Capo Press, 1998.

Lester, Ralph P. *Look to the East! A Ritual of the First Three Degrees of Freemasonry.* Whitefish, MT: Kessinger Publishing, 2004.

Lipson, Dorothy A. *Freemasonry in Federalist Connecticut.* Princeton, NJ: Princeton University Press, 1977.

Mackey, Robert R. *The Uncivil War: Irregular Warfare in the Upper South, 1861–1865.* Norman: University of Oklahoma Press, 2004.

McPherson, James M. *Battle Cry of Freedom: The Civil War Era.* New York: Oxford University Press, 1988.

———. *The Negro's Civil War: How American Blacks Felt and Acted during the War for the Union.* New York: Vintage Books, 1991.

Melish, William B. *History of the Imperial Council Ancient Arabic Order Nobles of the Mystic Shrine, 1872–1921.* 2nd ed. Cincinnati, OH: Abingdon Press, 1921.

Miers, Earl Schenk, and Richard A. Brown. *Gettysburg.* New Brunswick, NJ: Rutgers University Press, 1948.

Mills, Charles. *The History of the Crusades for Recovery and Possession of the Holy Lands.* Philadelphia: Lea and Blanchard, 1844.

Mitchell, William Ansel. *Linn County, Kansas—A History.* Kansas City, MO: Campbell-Gates, 1928.

Monaghan, Jay. *Civil War on the Western Border, 1854–65.* Boston: Little, Brown, 1955.

Moore, Frank. *The Civil War in Song and Story, 1860–1865*. New York: P. F. Collier, 1899.

———. *The Rebellion Record: A Diary of American Events*. New York: G. P. Putnam, 1863.

Morgan, William. *Illustrations of Masonry by One of the Fraternity*. Batavia, NY: David C. Miller, 1827.

Motts, Wayne E. *Trust in God and Fear Nothing: Gen. Lewis A. Armistead, CSA*. Gettysburg, PA: Farnsworth House, 1994.

Neely, Jeremy. *The Border between Them: Violence and Reconciliation on the Kansas-Missouri Line*. Columbia: University of Missouri Press, 2007.

Nesbitt, Mark. *35 Days to Gettysburg: The Campaign Diaries of Two American Enemies*. Harrisburg, PA: Stackpole Books, 1992.

Nofi, Albert A., and David G. Martin. *The Gettysburg Campaign, June–July 1863*. 3rd ed. Conshohocken, PA: Combined Publishing, 1997.

Palmer, John C. *The Morgan Affair and Anti-Masonry*, Whitefish, MT: R. A. Kessinger, 2006.

Palmer, Michael A. *Lee Moves North: Robert E. Lee on the Offensive*. New York: John Wiley and Sons, 1998.

Pfanz, Henry W. *Gettysburg: The First Day*. Chapel Hill: University of North Carolina Press, 2001.

———. *Gettysburg: The Second Day*. Chapel Hill: University of North Carolina Press, 1987.

———. *Gettysburg: Culp's Hill and Cemetery Hill*. Chapel Hill: University of North Carolina Press, 1993.

Poe, Clarence H., and Betsy Seymour, eds. *True Tales of the South at War: How Soldiers Fought and Families Lived, 1861–1865*. New York: Courier Dover Publications, 1995.

Prichard, Sarah J. *The Town and City of Waterbury, Connecticut*. Vol. 3. New Haven, CT: Price and Lee, 1896.

Ratner, Lorman. *Anti Masonry: The Crusade and the Party*. Englewood Cliffs, NJ: Prentice-Hall, 1969.

Roberts, John M. *The Mythology of the Secret Societies*. New York: Charles Scribner's Sons, 1972.

Rogers, Horatio. *Record of the Rhode Island Excursion to Gettysburg, October 11-16, 1886: With the Dedicatory Services of the Battlefield Memorials of the Second Rhode Island Volunteers, and Batteries A and B, First R.I. Light Artillery*, Providence: E. L. Freeman and Son, State Printers, 1887.

Rollins, Richard, ed. *Pickett's Charge: Eyewitness Accounts of the Battle of Gettysburg*. Mechanicsburg, PA: Stackpole, 2005.

Rolph, Daniel N. *My Brother's Keeper: Union and Confederate Soldiers' Acts of Mercy during the Civil War*. Mechanicsburg, PA: Stackpole, 2002.

Rosen, Robert N. *The Jewish Confederates*. Columbia: University of South Carolina Press, 2000.

Rosier, William Henry, and Fred Lamar Pearson Jr., eds. *Grand Lodge of Georgia, 1786–1980*. Macon, GA: Masonic Home Print Shop, 1983.

Ross, Peter. *A Standard History of Freemasonry in New York*. New York: Lewis Publishing, 1899.

Russell, William Howard. *My Diary North and South*. London: Bradbury and Evans, 1863.

Scharf, John Thomas. *History of the Confederate States Navy from Its Organization to the Surrender of Its Last Vessel*. 2nd ed. Albany, NY: J. McDonough, 1894.

Schildt, John. *Eyewitness to Gettysburg*. Shippensburg, PA: Burd Street Press, 1997.

Schmidt, Alvin J., and Nicholas Babchuk. *Fraternal Organizations*. Westport, CT: Greenwood Press, 1980.

Scott, William Walter. *Annals of Caldwell County (North Carolina)*. Lenoir, NC: News-Topic Print, 1930.

Sears, Stephen W. *Gettysburg*. New York: Mariner, 2004.

Shaffer, Donald R. *After the Glory: The Struggle of Black Civil War Veterans*. Lawrence: University Press of Kansas, 2004.

Shaw, David W. *Sea Wolf of the Confederacy: The Daring Civil War Raids of Naval Lt. Charles W. Read*. Dobbs Ferry, NY: Sheridan House, 2005.

Sheldon, George. *When the Smoke Cleared at Gettysburg: The Tragic Aftermath of the Bloodiest Battle of the Civil War*. Nashville: Cumberland House, 2003.

Siepel, Kevin H. *Rebel: The Life and Times of John Singleton Mosby*. New York: St. Martin's Press, 1983.

Sifakis, Stewart. *Compendium of the Confederate Armies: South Carolina and Georgia*. New York: Facts on File, 1995.

Speer, Emory. *Lincoln, Grant, and Other Biographical Addresses*. New York: Neale Publishing, 1909.

Speer, Lonnie R. *Portals to Hell: The Military Prisons of the Civil War*. Mechanicsburg, PA: Stackpole, 1997.

Stanley, Peter. "Military Culture and Military Protest: The Bengal Europeans and the 'White Mutiny' of 1859." In *Rebellion, Repression, Reinvention: Mutiny in Comparative Perspective*, edited by Jane Hathaway and Geoffrey Parker. Westport, CT: Praeger, 2001.

Starr, Stephen Z. *Jennison's Jayhawkers: A Civil War Cavalry Regiment and Its Commander*. Baton Rouge: Louisiana State University Press, 1973.

Stewart, George R. *Pickett's Charge: A Microhistory of the Final Attack at Gettysburg, July 3, 1863*. Boston: Houghton Mifflin, 1959.

Stiles, T. J. *Jesse James, the Last Rebel of the Civil War*. New York: Alfred A. Knopf, 2002.

Stine, J. H. *History of the Army of the Potomac*. 2nd ed. Washington, DC: Gibson Bros., 1893.

Stone, DeWitt B., Jr., ed. *Wandering to Glory: Confederate Veterans Remember Evans' Brigade*. Columbia: University of South Carolina Press, 2002.

Taylor, Frank Hamilton. *Philadelphia in the Civil War, 1861–1865*. Philadelphia: The City, 1913.

Truesdale, John. *The Blue Coats, and How They Lived, Fought, and Died for the Union*. Philadelphia: Jones Bros., 1867.

Tucker, Glenn. *High Tide at Gettysburg*. Old Saybrook, CT: Konecky and Konecky, 1993.

Tuttle, Charles. *An Illustrated History of the State of Wisconsin*. Boston: B. B. Russell, 1875.

Tyler, Lyon G., ed. *Encyclopedia of Virginia Biography*. Vols. 1–5. New York: Lewis Historical Publishing, 1915.

Utley, A. J. *The Master Mason's Guide: Containing All the Monitorial Instruction in Blue Lodge Masonry*. St. John's, MI: Hilton and Smith, 1865.

Washington, Booker T. *The Story of the Negro: The Rise of the Race from Slavery*. Vol. 2. New York: Doubleday, 1909.

Welcher, Frank J. *The Union Army, 1861–1865: Organization and Operations*. Vol. 1. Bloomington: Indiana University Press, 1989.

Wert, Jeffrey D. *Gettysburg: Day Three*. New York: Simon and Schuster, 2001.

Wheeler, Richard. *Gettysburg, 1863*. New York: Penguin Putnam, 1999.

Wiley, Bell I. *The Life of Johnny Reb*. Baton Rouge: Louisiana State University Press, 1999.

Williams, Louis L., and Alphonse Cerza, eds. *The Regius Poem*. Bloomington, IL: Masonic Book Club, 1975.

Williams, Robert Hamilton. *With the Border Ruffians: Memories of the Far West, 1852–1868*. Lincoln: University of Nebraska Press, 1982.

Young, James Bowman. *The Battle of Gettysburg*. New York: Harpers, 1913.

Electronic Sources

Gallaher, Dewitt C. "Diary of DeWitt Clinton Gallaher," March 1, 1865 (notes). *The Valley of the Shadow: Two Communities in the American Civil War*. University of Virginia, Spring 1998. At http://jefferson.village.virginia.edu/vshadow2/.

Goellnitz, Jenny. *Stonewall's Surgeon: A Biographical Website Devoted to Dr. Hunter Holmes McGuire, M.D.* At http://www.huntermcguire.goellnitz.org/.

Scholarly Articles

Anderson, James W. "A Confederate Prisoner at Camp Chase—Letters and a Diary of Private James W. Anderson." Edited by George C. Osborn. *Ohio State Archeological and Historical Society Quarterly* 59 (1950): 38–57.

Aptheker, Herbert. "The Negro in the Union Navy." *Journal of Negro History* 32, no. 2 (1947): 169–200.

Barr, Alwyn. "Confederate Artillery in the Trans-Mississippi." *Military Affairs* 27, no. 2 (1963): 77–83.

Bastian, David F. "Opening of the Mississippi during the Civil War." *New Aspects of Naval History: Selected Papers from the Fifth Naval History Symposium* (1985): 129–36.

Block, W. T. "A Towering East Texas Pioneer: A Biographical Sketch of Colonel Albert Miller Lea." *East Texas Historical Journal* 32, no. 2 (1993): 23–33.

Bright, Robert A. "Pickett's Charge." *Southern Historical Society Papers* 31 (1904): 228–36.

Brown, Gary D. "Prisoner of War Parole: Ancient Concept, Modern Utility." *Military Law Review* 156 (June 1998): 200–223.

Bush, David R. "Doing Time: How Confederate POWs Weathered Captivity." *Archaeology* 52 (July–August 1999): 46–50.

Connolly, James A. "Letter to Wife—Before Atlanta, July 31, 1864," from the Diary of Major James Austin Connolly. *Illinois State Historical Society* 35 (1899): 215–438.

Davis, Harry E. "Alpha Lodge No. 116, New Jersey." *Journal of Negro History* 20, no. 2 (1935): 180–89.

"Did General Armistead Fight on the Federal Side at First Manassas or Confess When Dying at Gettysburg That He Had Been Engaged in an 'Unholy Cause'?" *Southern Historical Society Papers* 10 (August–September 1882): 424–28.

Dobak, William A., ed. "Civil War on the Kansas-Missouri Border: The Narrative of Former Slave Andrew Williams." *Kansas History* 6 (Winter 1983/84): 237.

Gallman, J. Matthew. "Gettysburg's Gettysburg: What the Battle Did to the Borough." In *The Gettysburg Nobody Knows,* edited by Gabor Boritt, 144–74. New York: Oxford University Press, 1997.

Gist, Noel P. "Secret Societies: A Cultural Study of Fraternalism in the United States." *University of Missouri Studies Quarterly* 15, no. 4 (1940): 1–184.

Glatthaar, Joseph T. "The Common Soldier's Gettysburg Campaign." In *The Gettysburg Nobody Knows,* edited by Gabor Boritt, 3–30. New York: Oxford University Press, 1997.

Gramm, Kent. "The Chances of War: Lee, Longstreet, Sickles, and the First Minnesota Volunteers." In *The Gettysburg Nobody Knows,* edited by Gabor Boritt, 75–100. New York: Oxford University Press, 1997.

Green, J. U. "Prison Life and Escape of Col. Green." *Confederate Veteran* 7, no. 2 (1899): 57.

Gunn, Joshua. "The Two Rhetorics of Freemasonry; or, On the Function and Necessity of Masonic Secrecy." *Heredom* 15 (2007): 1–34.

Hage, Anne A. "The Battle of Gettysburg as Seen by Minnesota Soldiers." *Minnesota History* 32 (July 1963): 245–57.

Hatley, Paul B. "Army General Order Number 11: Final Valid Option or Wanton Act of Brutality? The Missouri Question in the American Civil War." *Journal of the West* 33 (1994): 77–87.

Hoole, William Stanley, ed. "A Southerner's Viewpoint of the Kansas Situation, 1856–1857; The Letters of Lieut. Col. A. J. Hoole, C.S.A." *Kansas Historical Quarterly* 3, no. 1 (1934): 43–68.

Krick, Robert K. "Armistead and Garnett: The Parallel Lives of Two Virginia Soldiers." In *The Third Day at Gettysburg and Beyond,* edited by Gary W. Gallagher, 93–131. Chapel Hill: University of North Carolina Press, 1994.

Langsdorf, Edgar. "Jim Lane and the Frontier Guard." *Kansas Historical Quarterly* 9 (February 1940): 13–25.

Martin, Rawley, and John H. Smith. "Accounts of Colonel Rawley Martin and Captain John Holmes Smith." *Southern Historical Society Papers* 32 (1904): 183–95.

Miller, Robert E. "War within Walls: Camp Chase and the Search for Administrative Reform." *Ohio State Archeological and Historical Society Quarterly* 96 (Winter–Spring 1987): 33–56.

Osborne, George C., ed. "A Confederate Prisoner at Camp Chase—Letters and a Diary of Private James W. Anderson." *Ohio State Archeological and Historical Society Quarterly* 59 (December 1950): 45–57.

Palmer, Edward N. "Negro Secret Societies." *Social Forces* 23, no. 2 (1944): 207–12.

Reardon, Carol. "'I Think the Union Army Had Something to Do with It': The Pickett's Charge Nobody Knows." In *The Gettysburg Nobody Knows,* edited by Gabor S. Boritt, 122–43. New York: Oxford University Press, 1997.

———. "Pickett's Charge: The Convergence of History and Myth in the Southern Past." In *The Third Day at Gettysburg and Beyond,* edited by Gary W. Gallagher, 56–92. Chapel Hill: University of North Carolina Press, 1994.

Skocpol, Theda, et al. "How Americans Became Civic." In *Civic Engagement in American Democracy,* by Theda Skocpol and Morris P. Fiorina, 27–80. Washington, DC: Brookings Institution Press, 1999.

Tatsch, Jacob H. "An American Masonic Crisis—The Morgan Incident of 1826 and Its Aftermath." *Ars Quatuor Coronatorum* 34 (1921): 196–209.

Torrey, Charles C. "Concerning Hiram ('Huram-abi'), the Phoenician Craftsman." *Journal of Biblical Literature* 31, no. 4 (1912): 151–56.

Trotter, Joe W. "African American Fraternal Organizations in American History: An Introduction." *Social Science History* 28, no. 3 (2004): 355–66.

Unrau, William E., ed. "In Pursuit of Quantrill: An Enlisted Man's Response." *Kansas Historical Quarterly* 39 (Autumn 1973): 379–91.

Upton, William H. "Prince Hall's Letter Book." *Ars Quatuor Coronatorum* 13 (1900): 54–61.

Williams, Burton J. "Quantrill's Raid on Lawrence: A Question of Complicity." *Kansas Historical Quarterly* 34 (Summer 1968): 143–49.

Worts, F. R. "The Apron and Its Symbolism." *Ars Quatuor Coronatorum* 74 (1961): 133–37.

Archival Material

Bessel, Paul M. "Letter to Wayne E. Motts, December 21, 1994" with enclosed manuscript of Donald M. Robey, Past Grand Master of Virginia. Wayne E. Motts Collection, Gettysburg, PA.

Burcham, Jeffrey G. "Letter to Most Worshipful Donald M. Robey, July 24, 1993." Wayne E. Motts Collection, Gettysburg, PA.

Grand Lodge of Pennsylvania. *Membership Records.* The Masonic Library and Museum of Pennsylvania, Philadelphia, PA.

History of Union Lodge No. 7, Junction City, Kansas, 1857–1976. Junction City, KS: Privately published, undated, Union Lodge No. 7, Junction City, Kansas.

Miller, Alexander R. Diary, 1861–1864. 1 vol. [typed copy]. Location: H:3. Louisiana and Lower Mississippi Valley Collections, LSU Libraries, Baton Rouge, LA.

Records of Atlanta Lodge No. 59. Grand Lodge of Georgia (Disk No. 222 for 1892, 1893).

"Remarks of the Master, St. John's Lodge No. 47, January 10, 1863." St. James Lodge No. 47 (Baton Rouge, LA) Records, Mss. 2860. Louisiana and Lower Mississippi Valley Collections, LSU Libraries, Baton Rouge, LA.

Walker, John Grimes. Family Papers. Wichita State University Library, Wichita, Kansas.

Newspapers and Periodicals

Abbott, John S. C. "Heroic Deeds of Heroic Men. XVI.—The Capture, Imprisonment, and Escape." *Harper's New Monthly Magazine* 34, no. 200 (1867).

"The Blue and the Gray." *Confederate Veteran* 1, no. 3 (1893).

Bradshaw, Jim. "Chrétien Point Remembers Plantation Days, Civil War." *Lafayette* (LA) *Daily Advertiser* (History of Acadiana), 30 September 1997.

Carter, James T. "Flag of the Fifty-Third Va. Regiment." *Confederate Veteran* 10 (June 1902): 263.

Cunningham, S. A. "A Model U.C.V. Camp." *Confederate Veteran* 7 (April 1899): 167.

Easley, D. B. "With Armistead When He Was Killed." *Confederate Veteran* 20 (September 1912): 379.

Green, J. U. "Prison Life and Escape of Col. Green." *Confederate Veteran* 7 (February 1899): 57.

Harding, Milton. "Where General Armistead Fell." *Confederate Veteran* 19 (August 1911): 371.

Hartwig, D. Scott. "It Struck Horror to Us All." *The Gettysburg Magazine* 4 (1 January 1999): 89–100.

Holland, Thomas C. "What Did We Fight For?" *Confederate Veteran* 31 (November 1923): 422–23.

———. "With Armistead at Gettysburg." *Confederate Veteran* 29 (February 1921): 62.

Irwin, Samuel R. "Unusual Funeral Recalled in St. Francisville." *The Advocate* (Baton Rouge) 18 June 2006.

Lewis, H. F. "General Armistead at Gettysburg." *Confederate Veteran* 27 (November 1920): 406.

McGuire, W. P. "An Incident of Masonic Power." *Confederate Veteran* 30 (October 1922): 396.

Mason, John E. "A Masonic Incident as Told by Sir Knight John Edwin Mason." *Knight Templar* 21, no. 3 (1975): 24.

Mason, J[ohn] Stevens. "Retaliation by Col. John S. Mosby." *Confederate Veteran* 14 (February 1906): 68.

"Masonic Burial By an Enemy." *Confederate Veteran* 14 (September 1906).

Reeves, Jay. "Masons in South Struggling with Racial Separation." *Decatur* (Alabama) *Daily News,* 22 October 2006.

Scarborough, J. A. "Joe Cothern's Capture of a Cannon." *Confederate Veteran* 12 (January 1904): 29.

Turney, J. B. "The First Tennessee At Gettysburg." *Confederate Veteran* 8 (December 1900): 535–37.

"Yankee Grave Dixie Decorates." *Times-Picayune* (New Orleans), 24 October 1937.

Government Documents

[McAfee, J. B.]. *Official Military History of the Kansas Regiments during the War for the Suppression of the Great Rebellion.* Leavenworth, KS: W. S. Burke, 1870.

Military Operations of the Civil War: A Guide-Index to the Official Records of the Union and Confederate Armies, 1861–1865. Washington, DC: National Archives and Records Service. General Services Administration, U.S. Government Printing Office, 1968.

Official Roster of Soldiers of the State of Ohio in the War of the Rebellion. 12 vols. Akron, OH: Werner Company, 1886–95.

Supreme Court of Pennsylvania. "Testimony of Charles H. Banes," *Reed et al. v. The Gettysburg Battle-Field Memorial Association et al.,* Middle District, No. 30. May Term, 1891.

United States Bureau of the Census. *The Eighth Census [1860].* Washington, DC: U.S. Government Printing Office, 1864.

United States Congress. *Henry Harrison Bingham: Memorial Addresses Delivered in the House of Representatives and the Senate of the United States.* Washington, DC: U.S. Government Printing Office, 1913.

———. *Journal of the Executive Proceedings of the Senate of the United States of America.* Vol. 15 (February 13, 1866 to July 28, 1866). Washington, DC: U.S. Government Printing Office, 1837–.

United States Naval History Division. *Civil War Naval Chronology, 1861–1865.* Washington, DC: U.S. Government Printing Office, 1971.

———. *Dictionary of American Naval Fighting Ships.* Washington, DC: U.S. Government Printing Office, 1959–.

United States Naval War Records Office. *Official Records of the Union and Confederate Navies in the War of the Rebellion, Vols.* Series I, vols. 1–27; Series II, Vols. 1–3. Washington, DC: U.S. – Office, 1894–1922.

United States Sanitary Commission. *Sanitary Memoirs of the War of the Rebellion.* New York: Hurd and Houghton, 1867.

United States War Dept. *The War of the Rebellion. A Compilation of the Official Records of the Union and Confederate Armies.* 128 vols. Washington, DC: U.S. Government Printing Office, 1882–1900.

Masonic and Fraternal

Adams, John Quincy. *Letters on the Masonic Institution.* Boston: T. R. Marvin, 1847.

Allyn, Avery. *A Ritual of Freemasonry Illustrated by Numerous Engravings, to Which Is Added a Key to the Phi Beta Kappa, The Orange, and Odd Fellows Societies with Notes and Remarks.* New York: William Gowans, 1853.

Ashe, Jonathan. *The Masonic Manual; or, Lectures on Freemasonry, Containing the Instructions, Document, and Discipline of the Masonic Economy.* New York: J. W. Leonard, American Masonic Agency, 1855.

Canaday, David, and Barbara Canaday. *Georgia Freemasons, 1861–1865.* Georgia Lodge of Research, 2001.

Canaday, David L. "John B. Gordon: Senator—Governor—Patriot." *Transactions of the Georgia Lodge of Research.* Vol. XI (January 31, 1997), 1–3.

Coil, Henry W. *Coil's Masonic Encyclopedia*. New York: Macoy Publishing, 1961.

The Constitutions of the Free-Masons. Containing the History, Charges, Regulations, &c. of that most Ancient and Right Worshipful Fraternity. For the Use of the Lodges. London, 1723.

Crawford, George W. *Prince Hall and His Followers; Being a Monograph on the Legitimacy of Negro Masonry.* New York: Crisis, 1914.

de Hoyos, Arturo, and S. Brent Morris. *Freemasonry in Context: History, Ritual, Controversy.* Lexington, MA: Lexington Books, 2004.

Denslow, Ray Vaughn. *Civil War and Masonry in Missouri.* Masonic Service Association of Missouri, 1930.

Denslow, William R., and Harry S. Truman, Missouri Lodge of Research. *10,000 Famous Freemasons.* Vols. 1–4 (Richmond, VA: Macoy Publishing and Masonic Supply Co., 1957–61).

Edwards, Lewis, and W. J. Hughan, eds. *Anderson's Constitutions of 1738.* Bloomington, IL: Masonic Book Club, 1978.

Gould, Robert Freke. *Military Lodges: The Apron and the Sword of Freemasonry under Arms.* Aldershot, England: Gale and Polden, 1899.

Grand Lodge of Pennsylvania. *F&A.M. Memorial Volume, Franklin Bi-Centenary Celebration.* Lancaster, PA: New Era Printing Co., 1906.

———. *Minutes of the Right Worshipful Grand Lodge of the Most Ancient and Honorable Fraternity of Free and Accepted Masons of Pennsylvania (1859–1864).* Vol. 10. N.p., 1906.

Grand Lodge of Virginia. *Free Masonry and the War: Report of the Committee under the Resolutions of 1862, Grand Lodge of Virginia.* Richmond: C. H. Wynne, Printer, 1865.

Hardie, James. *The New Free-Mason's Monitor; or, Masonic Guide for the Direction of Members of That Ancient and Honourable Fraternity.* New York: George Long, 1818.

Hyneman, Leon. *World's Masonic Register.* Philadelphia: J. B. Lippincott, 1860.

Jewell, Jacob. *Heroic Deeds of Noble Master Masons during the Civil War from 1861 to 1865 in the U.S.A.* Pueblo, CO: Privately published, 1916.

Judson, L. Carroll. *The Masonic Advocate.* 2nd ed. Philadelphia, 1859.

McDonald, Thomas C. *Freemasonry and Its Progress in Atlanta and Fulton County, Georgia: With Brief History of the Grand Lodge F. & A.M. of Georgia, 1786–1925,* N.p., 1925.

Macoy, Robert. *General History, Cyclopedia, and Dictionary of Freemasonry.* New York: Masonic Publishing Co., 1870.

Mackey, Albert G. *An Encyclopedia of Freemasonry and Its Kindred Sciences.* Vols. 1–2. New York: Masonic History Co., 1919.

———. "Freemasonry in the Civil War." *The Builder* (December 1922): 370.

———. "Freemasonry in the War—A Series of Sketches." *The Key-Stone* 2, no. 4 (1866): 178–81.

———. *The Mystic Tie; or, Facts and Opinions Illustrative of the Character and Tendency of Freemasonry.* 10th ed. New York: Masonic Publishing and Manufacturing Co., 1867.

———. *The Principles of Masonic Law.* New York: J. W. Leonard, 1856.

Masonic Review. Vol. 23, no. 4 (1860).

———. Vol. 26, no. 6 (1862).

———. Vol. 27, no. 4 (1862).

———. Vol. 28, no. 5 (1863).

———. Vol. 28, no. 9 (1863).

———. Vol. 30, no. 1 (1865).

———. Vol. 30, no. 2 (1865).

———. Vol. 30, no. 3 (1865).

———. Vol. 30, no. 7 (1865).

Melish, William B. *History of the Imperial Council Ancient Arabic Order Nobles of the Mystic Shrine, 1872–1921.* 2nd ed. Cincinnati, OH: Abingdon Press, 1921.

Moore, Charles W. *The Freemason's Monthly Magazine.* Vol. 18. Boston: Hugh Tuttle, 1859.

———. *The Freemason's Monthly Magazine.* Vol. 21. Boston: Hugh Tuttle, 1862.

———. *The Freemason's Monthly Magazine.* Vol. 22. Boston: Hugh Tuttle, 1863.

Moore, James, and Cary L. Clarke. *Masonic Constitutions; or, Illustrations of Masonry; Compiled by the Direction of the Grand Lodge of Kentucky.* Lexington, KY: Worsley and Smith, 1818.

Morris, Rob. "Honors to the Faithful Who Upheld the Banners of Masonry during the Season of Political Anti-Masonry, 1826 to 1836 in Western New York." *Voice of Masonry* 2, no. 6 (1864): 241–43.

Morris, Robert. *The Lights and Shadows of Freemasonry: Consisting of Masonic Tales, Songs, and Sketches, Never before Published.* Louisville, KY: J. F. Brennan, 1852.

———. *Tales of Masonic Life.* Louisville, KY: Morris and Monsarrat, 1860.

Morris, S. Brent. *The Complete Idiot's Guide to Freemasonry.* New York: Alpha Books, 2006.

Newton, Joseph F. "Albert Pike's Masonic Library: A Civil War Incident." *Master Mason* 2, no. 5 (1925): 410–11.

Pollard, Ralph J. *Freemasonry in Maine, 1762–1945.* Portland: Grand Lodge of Maine, n.d.

Pratt, Foster, ed. *The Michigan Freemason.* Vol. 6. Kalamazoo, MI, 1875.

Proceedings, Grand Lodge of Georgia. Macon: S. Rose and Co., Printers, 1857.

———. Macon: S. Rose and Co., Printers, 1859.

Proceedings, Grand Lodge of Illinois. Springfield, n.p., 1865.

Proceedings, Grand Lodge of Indiana. Indianapolis: Elder and Harkness, 1860.

Proceedings, Grand Lodge of Louisiana, February 14, 1859. New Orleans: Bulletin Book and Job Office, 1859.

Proceedings, Grand Lodge of Massachusetts, March 10–December 27, 1858. Boston: Hugh H. Tuttle, 1859.

Proceedings, Grand Lodge of Virginia. Richmond: Grand Lodge of Virginia, 1861.

Proceedings of the Supreme Council of the Sovereign Grand Inspectors General of the Thirty-Third and Last Degree, Ancient Accepted Scottish Rite for the Northern Masonic Jurisdiction of the United States of America. Binghamton, NY: Binghamton Republican Printers, 1899.

Proceedings of the United States Anti-Masonic Convention, September 11, 1830. Philadelphia: J.P. Trimble, 1830.

Ridgely, James L. *The Odd-Fellows' Pocket Companion: A Correct Guide in All Matters Relating to Odd-Fellowship.* Cincinnati: R. W. Carroll, 1867.

Roberts, Allen E. *House Undivided: The Story of Freemasonry and the Civil War.* 2nd ed. Richmond, VA: Macoy Publishing and Masonic Supply Co., 1990.

———. *Masonry under Two Flags.* Washington, DC: Masonic Service Association, 1968.

Rosier, William Henry, and Fred L. Pearson Jr. *Grand Lodge of Georgia, 1786–1980.* Macon, GA: Educational and Historical Commission, Grand Lodge of Georgia, 1983.

Ross, Peter. *A Standard History of Freemasonry in New York.* New York: Lewis Publishing, 1899.

Ross, Theodore A. *Odd Fellowship, Its History and Manual.* New York: M. H. Hazen, 1888.

Stevenson, David. *The First Freemasons, Scotland's Early Lodges and Their Members.* Aberdeen: Aberdeen University Press, 1988.

———. *The Origins of Freemasonry: Scotland's Century, 1590 to 1710.* Cambridge: Cambridge University Press, 1988.

Transactions of the Grand Royal Arch Chapter of Michigan. N.p., 1907.

Transactions of the Supreme Council of the 33d Degree for the Southern Jurisdiction. October 1895.

Voorhis, Harold V. *Negro Masonry in the United States.* Whitefish, MT: Kessinger Publications, 1995.

Vrooman, John B., and Allen E. Roberts. *Sword and Trowel; The Story of Traveling and Military Lodges.* Fulton, MO: Ovid Bell Press, 1964.

Ward, Henry Dana. *The Anti-Masonic Review, and Monthly Magazine.* Vol. 1, no. 8. New York: Vanderpool and Cole, 1828.

Index

acacia, 137, 193

Adams, John G. B., 115

Adams, John Quincy, 159–60, 166

African-American Masonry, 7, 152–57

African Lodge No. 1 (UD), 154

African Lodge No. 459, 154

aid, fraternal. *See* obligations, fraternal; prisoners, Masonic; property, protection of; relief

Albatross, 134

Alexandria-Washington Lodge No. 22, 10–11

Allen, Clement "J.C.," 83–84

Allyn, Avery, 39–40

amputation, 118

Anderson, Mrs. Meriweather, 61

Anderson, Robert, 49

Angerona Lodge No. 168, 177n11

Anti-Masonic Party, 38

anti-Masonic sentiment, 37–39, 52–53, 159–60, 161, 162–63; reversal of, 115–16, 150, 159, 164

aprons, 44–45, 61, 65, 114, 127, 130, 132, 193–94

Archer, 91

Armistead, George, 9

Armistead, Lewis A., 6; death, 8–9, 16, 23–26; injury, 18–21; Masonic activities, 10–11; Masonic appeals by, 19–23, 26–30; military career, 9–10; personal attributes, 11–12; and Pickett's Charge, 12–17

Armistead, Walker K., 9

Atlanta Lodge No. 59, 49

aude, vide, tace, 201

Bachelder, John B., 23, 27

badges of office. *See* jewels

Banes, Charles, 22–23, 27–29

Barker, Thomas E., 120–21

Baron de Kalb, 124

Barr, Hugh, 93–94

Bartlett, Asa W., 82–83

Battle of the Wilderness, 83

Bayou City, 1

Beam, John E., 129–30

Beauregard, P. G. T., 49

Beck, John S., 147

Bendix, John E., 67–68

Bengal mutiny, 161

Benson, Andrew M., 105–6

Benton, Thomas Hart, Jr., 64

Berry, John S., 68

Best, William L., 85

Bingham, Henry H., 8, 24–25, 26–27, 29

Bliss, George N., 90–91

Blue Lodge, 47, 48, 54, 140, 160, 193–94, 195, 200

Boggs, Samuel S., 113–14
Book of Constitutions (Anderson), 193
Borland, Matthew, 87–88
Bosang, James N., 120
Bossieux, Virginius, 109, 110, 111
Boyd, Belle, 104
Bright, Robert A., 14–15
Brinton, Daniel Garrison, 26
Brown, John C., 23–24, 27
Brown, Joseph Emerson, 78–79
Bull Run. *See* Manassas, battles of
burial of the enemy, 1–2, 46, 113, 133–39
burial rights, 128–30
burial services, 130–33
Butler, Benjamin F., 68, 73–74
Bynum, George W., 85

cable tow, 194
Caleb Cushing, 91–93
Campbell, James B., 69–70
Camp Bragg Lodge, 143
Canton Lodge No. 60, 177n14
Carter, James T., 16–17
Casco, 92
census (1860), 3, 50–52
certificate. *See* diploma
Chamberlain, Joshua, 49
Champion's Hill, battle of, 67
Chancellorsville, battle of, 66, 82–83
Charity Lodge No. 190, 171n46
charter, 57, 71–72, 112, 142
Chartiers Lodge No. 297, 170n43
Chase, Jackson H., 68–69
Cherokee Lodge No. 66, 174n5
Chesapeake, 92–93
Chickamauga, battle of, 93–96
chivalry, 2, 77
civilians, 7, 57, 64–65, 101, 140, 145
Claiborne, John H., 104–5
Clark, Charles M., 145–46
clemency, 73–74
Columbian Lodge, 123
communications, 194
compasses, 38, 44–45, 124, 141, 195
Confederate Veteran, 89, 94

Connolly, James Austin, 133
Conoho Lodge No. 131, 71–72
Constitutions of the Freemasons, 31, 161–62
Cook, James, 85
Cooper, Alonzo, 101–2
Copley, John M., 114–15
Corinth, battle of, 66
cowan, 195
Craft Lodges, 194
Cromwell, Oliver, 33
Cross, Edward E., 84
Culpepper, Simon F., 83–84
Cummings, Ariel Ivers, 135–36
Cummings, Charles, 138–39
Curtis, Newton M., 85
Custer, George A., 88

Daggett, Rufus, 107
Dana, Charles, 67
David, Phineas Sterns, 147–48
Davis, Joseph J., 117
degrees (of Masonry), 47, 195–98, 202
demit, 196
deputy, 196
Dimmick, Robert A., 93–94
diploma, 45–46, 136, 196–97
dispensation, 142, 197
Dockery Lodge, 143
Doubleday, Abner, 171n45
Dove, John, 54
Downsville Lodge No. 464, 140
Dubey, Edward A., 93
Duganne, Augustine, 135
Duguid, Edward M., 103–4
Dumenil, Lynn, 35–36, 39
Durgin, John M., 82–83
Durkee, Joseph H., 83

Eagle Lodge No. 431, 177n14
Easley, Drewry B., 18–20, 27, 29
Elmira Prison Camp, The (Holmes), 159
Elwell, Andrew A., 72
emblems. *See* jewelry
Emporia Lodge No. 12, 83
Euclid Lodge No. 45, 90

Excelsior Lodge No. 195, 69
experimentum crucis, 75–76

Farinholt, Benjamin L., 17, 29
Feliciana Lodge No. 31, 134
Finley, George W., 16
Floyd, John, 99
foraging, 74–76, 149
Forest City, 92
Forrest, Nathan Bedford, 65
Fort Gregg, battle of, 89
Fort Pillow, battle of, 83
Foy, Thomas, 136–37
Frank Leslie's Illustrated Newspaper, 88
Franklin, Benjamin, 159, 166
Franklin Lodge, 136
fraternal obligations. *See* obligations, fraternal
fraternal organizations, 2, 35–37, 39–43, 58,
    97, 152
fraternization, 4, 94, 106, 150–52, 165
Fredericksburg, battle of, 81
Fredericksburg Lodge No. 4, 67–68
Freemasonry: American (*See* Freemasonry in
    the U.S.); burial rights, 128–33; degrees
    of, 47, 195–96, 197, 198, 202; hierarchy
    of, 43, 46–48; initiation rituals, 39–41;
    joining, 3, 46–47; oaths (*See* oaths); ob-
    ligations of (*See* obligations, fraternal);
    officers, 43–44, 70, 199, 202; origins,
    31–35; physical requirements, 118; poli-
    tics and, 165–66; proof of membership,
    58–59, 201; rank in, 46, 146; religious as-
    pects, 130; rights of, 128; Southern (*See*
    Freemasonry in the Confederacy); vir-
    tues of, 201
Freemasonry and American Culture, 1880–1930
    (Dumenil), 35–36
Freemasonry in Maine, 1762–1945 (Pollard),
    157
Freemasonry in the Confederacy, 52–53, 56–
    57, 142–43, 155–56
Freemasonry in the U.S.: anti-Masonry move-
    ment, 37–39; character of, 2–4, 35–39,
    47–48, 50; demographics of, 3, 50–53;
    military membership, 49, 141; organiza-

tion of, 50; origins, 33; race and, 153–57;
    secession and, 53–57, 165
Freemason's Monthly, 71
Fremantle, Arthur, 12
Fuger, Frederick, 20–22, 27, 29
funerals, 128–33
furniture, 195, 197

Gallaher, Dewitt, 100–101
Gate City Lodge No. 2, 174n5
Gettysburg, battle of, 3, 6, 8, 12, 59. *See also*
    Pickett's Charge
Gettysburg Campaign, June–July 1863, The
    (Nofi), 21, 24
Gist, Noel P., 35, 199, 201
Goodloe, Albert, 100
Gordon, John B., 49
Graber, Henry W., 89–90
Grand Lodge of England, 154, 201
Grand Lodges, 44, 197–98; authority of, 43,
    50, 112; funeral rites prescription, 130;
    limitations of, 58, 60; military lodges and,
    142–45; Prince Hall lodges and, 157; se-
    cession response, 54–57, 165
Gray, William H. W., 155
grips, 40–42, 201
guerilla warfare, 86–89
Gunn, Joshua, 41

Hall, Prince, 154
Hamilton, Charles M., 81
Hancock, William H., 154
Hancock, Winfield Scott, 8, 10, 12, 24–25,
    27, 29
handclasps, 40–42, 201
Harding, Milton, 17–18, 29
Hargis, Samuel H., 118
Harmony Lodge No. 6, 1
Harmony Lodge No. 9, 137
Harriet Lane, 1
Harris, Charles, 83
Hart, John E., 134–35
Heckethorn, Charles W., 35
Heg, Hans C., 127
Hemming, Samuel, 33

Hermann, Isaac "Ike," 119–20
Heroic Deeds of Noble Master Masons During the Civil War (Jewell), 5–6
Hinds, William, 71–72
Hinley, J. L., 114
Hiram, 33, 193, 202
Hiram Lodge No. 21, 66
History of the Philadelphia Brigade (Banes), 22–23
Holbrook, Charles L., 123
Holland, Thomas C., 15, 17
Hollands, Charles, 81
Holmes, Clay W., 159
Hoover's Gap, battle of, 151
Hosmer, James K., 150
House Undivided (Roberts), 5, 6

Illustrations of Masonry (Morgan), 19–20, 23
Illustrations of Masonry by One of the Fraternity (Preston), 130, 198–99
Independent Order of Odd Fellows. *See* Odd Fellows
initiation rituals, 39–41
Ives, Samuel S., 100
Ivy Lodge No. 397, 116

Jackson Lodge No. 17, 112
Jacob, Margaret, 32–33
Jewell, Jacob, 5–6, 81
jewelry, 45, 79–81, 94, 105, 118, 123, 137, 141; prisoner-made, 120–22
jewels, 45, 64, 70–72, 146, 198
Jones, Joseph, 112
Julia A. English Lodge, 143
J. W. C., 118–19
J. W. T., 94–96

King, Finlay M., 63, 77
King Solomon's Lodge No. 11, 137
Knights Templar, 33, 47, 106

labor, 198
lambskin. *See* aprons
Lane, Everett, 123

Larew, Isaac H., 118
Leake, William W., 134–35
lectures, 198
Lee, Henry C., 91
Lester, Ralph, 41
Lewis, Winslow, 55
Lincoln, Abraham, 104
Linsley, Solomon F., 102–4
lodges, 198; black, 7, 153–57; clandestine, 142, 154, 157; communications, 194; first American, 33; hierarchy of, 43–44; prisoner aid, 115–17; protection of, 67–74; requirements for, 142; traveling (*See* lodges, military); withdrawal from, 196. *See also* Grand Lodges
lodges, military, 7, 57–58, 126, 142–45, 157–58, 164; Prince Hall Masonry and, 154, 155–57
lodges, military, by regiment: 1st Arkansas Infantry, 143; 1st New York Engineer Regiment, 126, 141–42; 10th New York Volunteers, 148–49; 12th Indiana Infantry, 141; 19th Arkansas Infantry, 143; 38th Arkansas Infantry, 143; 39th Illinois Infantry, 145–46, 147; 39th Massachusetts Infantry, 123, 146–48; 43rd Massachusetts Volunteers, 146; 46th Indiana Infantry, 146; 54th Massachusetts Infantry, 155; 102d Illinois Infantry, 141; Dockery's Brigade, 143
Lodge UD, 142
Look to the East (Lester), 41
Ludwig, Charles H., 148–49

Mackey, Albert G., 33–34, 62–63, 128–29, 194, 198, 200–201, 202
Magruder, John B., 1
Malvern Hill, battle of, 12
Manassas, battles of, 59, 79, 93
Martin, Rawley W., 17
Masonic creed, 62
Masonic Prison Association, 117
Masonic Review, 46, 55, 88, 118
May, William H., 45

McCartin (Corporal), 110–11

McClellan Army Lodge No. 6, 123

McDaniel, John R., 55

McDermott, Anthony W., 22, 29

McElroy, John, 113

McGuire, Hunter H., 100–101

McKinley, William, 65–66

McRae Lodge, 143

membership, 3, 46–47; benefits of, 128;
    physical requirements, 118; proof of,
    58–59, 201; right of, 128

Mercer Lodge No. 50, 49

Merryman, James H., 92–93

Metropolitan Lodge, 135

military lodges. See lodges, military

Miller, Anson C., 59

Miller, Horace H., 64

Miners Lodge No. 273, 177n20

minutes, 198

Mitchie, Henry C., 16

monitors, 198–99

Monroe Commandery No. 6, 80

Montjoy, Richard P., 89

Moore, Charles, 71–72

Moore, Cornelius, 118

Moore, Jonathan B., 140

Moorefield Lodge No. 29, 182n40

Morgan, William, 19–20, 23, 37–38, 162–63

Morgan, William A., 81–82

Mosby, John S., 86, 88–89, 124

Moss, William A., 91

Mosscrop, Thomas D., 93–94

Munro, D. D., 119

Mystic Lodge No. 131, 69

Natchez Lodge No. 1, 140

National Zouave Lodge (UD), 148–49

ne varietur, 45, 196

Nofi, Albert, 21, 24

oaths, 31, 41, 152, 159–63, 165, 199; con-
    flicting, 38, 161, 165

obligations, fraternal, 2, 41, 58–59, 76–77,
    117, 139, 149–50, 160, 162–65, 199;

failure of, 77, 85; limitations on, 58, 74;
    towards prisoners, 87–89; towards the
    enemy, 89–93, 97; towards wounded,
    79–86, 93–96. See also burial of the
    enemy; prisoners, Masonic; property,
    protection of

Odd Fellows, 36–37, 39–40, 42, 50, 52, 58,
    99, 101–2

Oden, John, 85

officers (of the lodge), 43–44, 70, 199, 202

Orr Lodge No. 104, 178n33

Osborne, Clem, 101

Pacific Lodge No. 233, 174n2

Palmer, Innis N., 72–73

Paul, Isaac D., 133

Perry, James B., 84

Phillips, Henry M., 54–55

Pickett's Charge, 12–17

Pike, Albert, 64

pins. See jewelry

Pollard, Ralph J., 157

Preston, William, 130, 198–99

Prince Hall Affiliation (PHA) Masonry,
    154–57, 190n34

prison conditions, 107–12, 122

prisoner exchange, 102

prisoners, Masonic, 60, 65, 98–101, 118–20,
    124; allowed to escape, 87, 111, 141; co-
    hesion of, 112–13, 164; freed, 88–89; fu-
    neral attendance, 104, 135; jewelry-mak-
    ing, 120–21; lodges' assistance of, 115–17;
    Masonic Prison Association, 117; prefer-
    ential treatment, 102, 104–7, 113–15,
    121–22, 151

prisoners, non-Masonic, 117, 121

property, protection of: Lodge, 64, 67–73,
    149; personal, 59, 61, 64–67, 74–77,
    85, 89

Putnam Army Lodge (UD) No. 8, 146–48

Ralston, Bob, 78–79

Randolph, John, 95–96

Ransom, John L., 108–12

Rawlins, John A., 67
Raynor, William H., 79–80
Read, Charles W., 92
recognition, 200
recognition signals, 40–42. *See also* signs
Redman, Jarret C., 149–50
Rees, Richard R., 11
Reese, John M., 107
regalia, 44–46, 64, 65, 68, 70–71, 77, 125, 127
Regius Poem, 31
relief, 37, 65–66, 80, 120, 128, 148, 162. *See also* obligations, fraternal; prisoners, Masonic; property, protection of
Revolutionary War, 144
Rhodes, Elisha Hunt, 137–38, 164
Rice, James Q., 137–38
Roberts, Allen E., 5, 6
Rockwell, Hosea A., 116
Royal Arch Masonry, 47, 54, 140, 194, 196, 200, 202

sacred law, 142, 197
Sayer, Antony, 193
Scottish Rite, 47, 48, 64, 200
secession, 53–57, 165
Secret Societies (Gist), 35, 199, 201
Secret Societies of All Ages and Countries (Heckethorn), 35
segregation, 155–57
Sharp, Thomas J., 133
Sherman, William T., 74, 86–87
Shiloh, battle of, 80
signs, 19–22, 40–42, 58–59, 75–76, 78–79, 82–83, 119, 138, 161–63, 200–201
Sisson, Henry T., 150–51
Smith, Abel, Jr., 176n8
Smith, Calvin, 57
Smithville Lodge, 57
South Boston Lodge No. 91, 18
South Mountain, battle of, 85
Sprague, Homer, 99
square and compasses, 38, 44–45, 124, 141, 195
St. James Lodge No. 47, 67

St. John's Lodge No. 2, 129–30
St. John's Lodge No. 3, 125, 154
St. John's Lodge No. 55, 153–54
St. Tammany Lodge No. 5, 68–70, 149
Stanton, Edwin M., 104
Stevenson, David, 32
Stine, J. H., 15
Stones River, battle of, 81, 127
Strafford Lodge No. 29, 83
Strong, George A., 80–81
Symington, W. Stuart, 14

Taylor, James E., 88
Temple Lodge No. 14, 68
Temple of Solomon, 202
Thompson, Joseph B., 89
Tinkham, Samuel A., 66
Todd, George Rodgers Clarke, 83
tokens, 42, 58, 200–201. *See also* signs
traveling lodges. *See* lodges, military
Tucker, Glenn, 28–29
Turner, M. G., 89

UD (under dispensation), 142, 201
Union Lodge No. 7, 11
Union Lodge No. 31, 135
Union Lodge No. 95, 116–17
Union Lodge No. 121, 171n43
United Lodge No. 8, 49

visit, right of, 128, 201

Wainwright, Jonathan Mayhew II, 1–2, 133
warrant. *See* charter
Wasden, Joseph, 136–37
Wash, William A., 115–16
Washburn, Henry W., 135
Washington Lodge, 135
Watkins, Guy H., 66
Webb, Alexander, 15, 20
West Point, battle of, 85
White, George M., 102–4
White, Samuel F., 134–35
"widow's son," 21, 22–23, 26–29, 85, 193, 202

Wildemore, Jacob, 28–29
William McKinley Lodge, 177n14
Williams, Erasmus, 17
Williams, John, 153–54
Williams, L. J., 140–41
Winchester Hiram Lodge No. 21, 10
Woodbury, Augustus, 136–37

words, 40–42, 59, 119, 162
working tools, 142, 202

York Rite, 47, 48, 202

Zeredatha Lodge No. 80, 81
Zerubbabel Lodge No. 15, 141